LEAVING MUNDANIA

Inside the Transformative World of Live Action Role-Playing Games

LIZZIE STARK

CHICAGO REVIEW PRESS

Published by Chicago Review Press, Incorporated
814 North Franklin Street
Chicago, Illinois 60610
ISBN 978-1-56976-605-7

Library of Congress Cataloging-in-Publication Data
Stark, Lizzie.
  Leaving mundania : inside the transformative world of live action
role-playing games / Lizzie Stark.
    p. cm.
  Includes bibliographical references.
  Summary: "The story of adults who put on a costume, develop a persona,
and interact with other characters for hours or days as part of a LARP, or
Live Action Role-Playing game. A look at the hobby from its history in the
pageantry of Tudor England to its use as a training tool for the US mili-
tary"—Provided by publisher.
  ISBN 978-1-56976-605-7 (pbk.)
  1. Fantasy games. 2. Role playing. 3. Shared virtual environments—
Social aspects. I. Title.

  GV1469.6.S63 2012
  793.93--dc23

                                    2011041606

Cover design: Rebecca Lown
Cover photograph by Kyle Ober; bus image © Alloy Photography/Veer
Interior design: Sarah Olson

Printed in the United States of America
5 4 3 2 1

For the larpers. And George.

Contents

All the world's a stage,
And all the men and women merely players:
They have their exits and their entrances;
And one man in his time plays many parts.

—Shakespeare, *As You Like It*

Prologue

I n real life, they drive your trucks and make your copies. They teach your children, and repair your computers, and when you have a heart attack, they're first on the scene. They fight your wars and stock your stores and build your roads. They research new vaccines and obscure old deities. They care for your mentally ill. They train your FBI agents and catch child molesters. They are students, EMTs, lawyers, detectives, computer gurus, security guards, professional sideshow freaks, filmmakers, chefs, insurance administrators, scientists, and businessmen.

On the weekends, they are elves, magicians, cowgirls, vampires, zombies, arcane priests, samurai, druids, Jedis, zeppelin pilots, and chain-mailed warriors of unreasonable strength. They save the world. A lot. They are larpers, and they are misunderstood.

A larp, or a live action role-playing game, is similar to a theatrical play performed with no audience and no script.* One or more directors, called game masters, or GMs, organize everyone, select the form of the performance, and decide whether the setting resembles, for example, *Lord of the Rings*, *Hamlet*, or *Buffy the Vampire Slayer*. Game masters have many jobs. They create plot obstacles for the player characters, challenges for the players to solve during the game. They also collect props and set the scene either by describing it verbally or by dressing the space—a church fellowship hall, a Boy Scout camp, a hotel room—to look like part of the game. Sometimes the game masters write out the characters and cast them. Other times the players write their own characters. The outcome of every larp remains in question, as the characters improvise all their lines and use their wiles to solve the plots laid out for them. In all things, the game master is the final authority, the god of this little world, capable of deciding who wins the cowboy shootout in the climactic scene, if there is any dispute, and whether that found trinket is magical or merely pretty.

Just as there are many types of movies and novels, there are many styles of larp. Some larps resemble page-turning genre fiction and offer players an escapist adventure, while other larps seem more akin to literary fiction, helping players explore particular emotions, such as jealousy or love. The setting of a larp is only limited by one's imagination. There are medieval fantasy larps, Wild West larps, vampire larps, cyberpunk and steampunk larps, and larps that take place in particular historical periods. Some games involve fantastical elements such as magic or vampires, while other games are firmly rooted in the rules of reality. A game may last a few hours, a weekend, or, in rare cases, longer. One-shot games are intended to be run once,

---

* In the United States, larp is often written LARP, since it is an acronym denoting live action role-playing. The word is adaptable—one can larp, play in a larp, go larping, be a larper. Like the acronyms scuba, laser, and radar before it, many think it's time for larp to lose the caps and enter language as a regular, lowercase word, a move that I hope will destigmatize the hobby, making it seem less like unrelatable jargon. The Nordic countries, which have a long-established discourse on larp aesthetics, have already de-capitalized it.

as a stand-alone experience, while campaign games run for years, decades even, spread over monthly or yearly events. Although larps are commonly called "games," there is no winning or losing in the traditional senses; there is only having fun or not having fun, truly immersing oneself into a character and developing that character, or not. The performers themselves are the only audience, each player the ultimate judge of his or her own experience.

Essentially, larp is make-believe on steroids for adults. Computer games, with all their realistic scenery, are nothing compared to a larp. Sure, a computer character can wear cool armor and swoop through the detailed landscape of the game world, but in a larp, players actually stalk down their enemies in the woods, moving silently, muffling the jingling of their coin pouches.

There is no single sanctioning body of larpers, no tally of how many people participate in this hobby, but there are hundreds of larp groups across the United States, with memberships ranging from a few people up to hundreds. In addition, dozens of gaming conventions across the country feature larps as part of the fun each year. The twice-yearly conventions run by the New Jersey group Double Exposure, for example, draw hundreds of larpers. The hobby has a global following, with numerous groups in Europe and Australia. The convention Knutepunkt, which means "nodal point" or "knot-point" in Norwegian, rotates around Scandinavian countries each year, changing its name according to the host language. Knutepunkt treats larp as an art form and is less a convention than a conference offering panels on the nature of larp itself. Each year it publishes a book of scholarly essays on the hobby.

If the idea of adult make-believe—grownups in elf ears, dressed in bodices and Renaissance skirts, or clad in black trench coats and sunglasses indoors—seems frivolous to you, you are not alone. Larp has a bad rap, conjuring pictures of jobless misanthropes living in their parents' basements. In fact, larp is so geeky a hobby that other geeks—comic book lovers, reenactors, trekkies, and Dungeons & Dragons enthusiasts—often pooh-pooh it as a lower form of nerdery. Despite the stereotype, I found many larpers to be employed, clever, and, yes, cool. It takes a certain self-assurance to put on a costume outside of

Halloween or a theatrical production and to play a swashbuckler or a mad scientist. And in a world full of digitized interactions, I found it remarkable that so many people were willing to make time—once a month, in some cases—to see one another and further the narrative.

Larp is far more than a game. It's a multimedia entertainment, an über-hobby, one that can encompass other forms of play. Many larps offer players games-within-games, from games of chance, such as poker, to contests of strength and balance performed with padded weapons. Players often show off other skills and hobbies during a larp. A singer might perform during a game set in a nightclub, a chef might play a cook and dole out real food to genuine compliments, and those skilled with needle and thread create fabulous costumes for themselves and others. Some players get into the technical aspects of larp—reading rules and crunching numbers to come up with the most favorable skill combinations—while others blow off steam by killing monsters. There are players who love to solve game master–created puzzles or get into the heads of their characters. Others want to soak up an otherworldly atmosphere.

The saying "Entertainment is what you pay for, but fun you make yourself," seems particularly relevant to larp. In order to make the game world more realistic, larpers are constantly on the prowl for cheap, everyday objects that might be transformed into props. The most obvious example is the transformation of PVC pipe and foam into a boffer, a homemade padded weapon used for combat in some games. One larp I attended built a primitive sprinkler system out of pipe at a Boy Scout camp to make it "rain" indoors on a band of characters. Sometimes, it's the thrift shop that provides costuming inspiration or tchotchkes that might help set a historical scene just so. Few game masters earn money from organizing events; rather, they do it for the joy of giving pleasure to others.

The drive to larp, to simulate reality for one's own edification and amusement, has ancient roots and modern applications. The Tudors of England enjoyed lavish, outdoor multimedia entertainments, for example, while the King Arthur–obsessed Victorians held medieval jousts with sometimes-disastrous results. Nowadays, many institutions use larp-like activities for educational purposes. Medical schools enlist fake patients to help train their doctors, law schools run mock trials, and most impressively, the US Army builds fake towns, shoots mock explosives made of foam, and costumes its own soldiers with stomach-churning wounds in the service of pre-deployment training.

Larp can also teach less concrete skills. As a social interaction, it gives players plausible deniability through the ego-saving excuse, "It wasn't me; it was my character," an excuse that helps people take social chances. For example, some players told me that larp made them more comfortable approaching new people or speaking in front of groups. Because there is something of the player in every character, larp can also serve as a tool of self-reflection. Some players, intentionally and unintentionally, re-create and work through real-life conflicts in larp.

Most of all, larp joins its players into a tightly knit community through shared experience—after all, many bands of larpers have faced "death" together. This community has its own lingo, its own sacred space—the terrain of the game—and its own ritual in the form of the game itself. Thanks to its ethereal, time-bound existence, larp is strictly a "you had to be there" sort of hobby. The game can't be relived, and the anecdotes gamers tell each other afterward sound like inside jokes to anyone who wasn't there. The shared experience of the game creates a strong community linked by two layers of social bonds. Each character has in-game relationships with other characters—their lords, subjects, friends, or enemies—as well as out-of-game relationships with the same group of people. Ask any long-time larper why he or she has been attending the same game for four, eight, or twelve years, and inevitably you'll hear, "What really keeps me coming back is the people."

I have always had a soft spot in my heart for geek culture, because at core, geeks care deeply about something, and I think that's incredibly cool. Maybe it goes back to my adolescence, which I spent engrossed in fantasy novels and serial mysteries. In middle school, my clique of friends dubbed itself the "Multiplying Fractions Anonymous Group" during a relevant unit in our honors math class, sort of like Alcoholics Anonymous but, obviously, for those addicted to math. In high school, we were not the girls sneaking a drink on Friday nights and making out with boys. We were the theater nerds who got up early for a cappella choir practice.

I first learned about larp years later from a good friend, Sarah Miles, who had found her roommates on Craigslist. During Sarah's and my weekly *Xena* marathons, she'd talk about these roommates, larpers, and describe with relish the strange implements found in their house—the foam swords and shields, the costuming—and the odd half-performance, half–rules-bound way they had of working out plot points. We both kind of wanted to try it out, a desire fulfilled during the writing of this book. I have never been a gamer. In fact, I strongly dislike competitive games, especially strategy games—I find something pitiless and rage-provoking about the idea of a winner and loser. However, subcultures and performance have long fascinated me, first as a young fiction writer and then as a journalist. The idea of the larpers, with their self-made costumes, collaboratively writing—well, living—the stories of their characters fascinated me. I wanted to know more about this hobby and its participants, and I began researching.

While my first few games didn't fully convince me of larp's charms, over the three years I spent researching and writing this book, the community won me over. Admittedly, I did drink the Kool-Aid (although we called it "wine" and pretended to be drunk afterward), but despite my intoxication with the deeply engaged, quirky species of human, homo pretendus, I hope my account of its oddities, both good and bad, may be trusted.

The Expert and the Noob

I am still not sure how I ended up in a fake black corset and glittery red hat listening to a woman in a leather vest tell me about her lost pup—by which she meant her son—who vanished during a chase in a parallel universe.

I'm pretty sure that somehow, Molly Mandlin is responsible.

Before I knocked on Molly Mandlin's door on a fateful day earlier in 2008, I had been to one gaming convention, where I'd seen grown men in lab coats and period reproductions of Revolutionary War uniforms. I'd seen grown women in Old West harlot outfits, in medieval corsets, and in plaid shirts with fake rifles à la Annie Oakley. But I'd felt a sort of vague confusion about the whole process, tinged, perhaps, with contempt that adults could spend their free time on something so frivolous as dress-up.

Meeting Molly at her apartment changed all that. She wasn't the first larper I'd met, although she was, perhaps, the most passionate. She lived in Brooklyn with Rob, her boyfriend of five years, and their apartment was crammed with gamers' treasures—old copies of games such as Heroes and Dungeons & Dragons and piles of fanzines for various role-playing games. A box filled with mystery novels sat in front of a bookcase, the books on those shelves obscured by Rob's collection of Nerf guns.

Molly invited me into their small living room, and I sat on the couch while she pulled up her rolling desk chair. The armchair next to us had been rendered functionless by a pile of carefully arranged stuffed animals, including two linen rag dolls maybe two and a half feet tall that sat on the lap of a large bear. The dolls' faces were blank except for noses made from a gathered knot of fabric. One wore a purple outfit, the other a blue one—not doll clothing but real children's clothing. Both dolls had on real black wigs topped by headbands attached to bunny ears. Within five minutes of my arrival, Molly was introducing me to the dolls, who represent the twins Kayleel and Thea (short for Athena), the children of Andromache, the futuristic character that Molly had dreamed up as part of a game. We jumped into the first of many conversations about her characters.

Andromache was an assassin trained by the government of a technologically advanced world in which ancient Greek culture had become the prevalent world culture. In what I learned was typical gamer fashion, Molly had plenty to say about her character.

After she shared the basics of Andromache's story with me, Molly pulled a clear plastic suitcase out from under the desk in the den and unzipped it, revealing many tiny costumes, each one in its own plastic bag. She unzipped one labeled "Halloween costume" and showed me a gauzy tutu and some cat ears on a headband. The twins, I learned, were ballerina cats this year for Halloween. Each twin had her own lunchbox, outfits, and toys.

I don't know what I expected, but certainly not props of this specificity, displayed with what was unmistakably pride mingled with self-consciousness. Molly knew that not everyone would understand her gaming life, but she pursued it anyway because it was her passion. I might not understand why yet, but I could respect that. Toward the end of our five-hour interview, Molly showed me the baby book she had made for the twins during the time that Andromache was pregnant. It had little handprints and footprints in it, rubber stamped with ink, and handwritten notes from Andromache to her children.

"I know I'm a little too into this stuff," she said.

Molly plays Andromache in a larp called the Avatar System, a game that has two or three sessions each year, primarily during the gaming conventions run by Double Exposure, which also created the game. In between events, characters interact with one another using online forums, and many players post fiction or narration relating to their characters. The Avatar System is set in a fictional world called the Nexus, which exists between all possible realities. For this reason, players can create whatever characters they can imagine—there are vampire slayers, space pirates, sentient computer programs, popes from cartoon worlds, and medieval kings.

Molly began playing Avatar after her then-boyfriend brought her to a Double Exposure convention, and soon she was hooked. After they broke up, Molly says, the community reached out to keep her involved in the game. One player, Dave Stern, even drove into Manhattan from New Jersey to pick her up for conventions.

Over the next few months and several visits to her apartment, I try to unravel exactly what a bright, if unconventional, woman like Molly gets out of larp.

At heart, Molly is a storyteller. She doesn't simply use the various characters she plays in games to tell stories. Like many other larpers, she turns every aspect of her life into a story. She tells me about her fibromyalgia, a chronic condition characterized by body pain, how it went undiagnosed for many years: the terrible dry mouth, fatigue, and bone pain that make small things like leaving the house to go shopping very difficult. She tells me about Jason, her former fiancé whom she met over the Internet and then discarded after he bilked her out of $15,000, hocking her platinum engagement ring to defray the debt. She tells me about teaching in the South Bronx before her fibro became so bad that she had to stop working, about the children's books she hopes to write and illustrate. Her paintings, some abstract, some representational, all representing no small measure of talent, are strewn across the apartment. She tells me the story of her father, a surplus buyer who purchases large quantities of odd things from auctions and surplus sales, how in her childhood he once bought so many flats of rubber bands that she and her brother jumped on them like a trampoline when they visited the warehouse. She tells me about the giant wheels of Camembert that her father bought and the small ice cream fridge that housed them, how she and her brother ate Camembert sandwiches at school for many months.

I learn the surprisingly innovative backstories of the strong female characters Molly has dreamed up. I hear about Polly Rogers, an Aztec pirate queen whose mother married a conquistador and then abandoned her. Molly never played Polly because she developed the character so much in her mind that she felt there was nothing left to discover in-game, nowhere for the character to grow. Molly's second Avatar character, Echo, is a cyberpunk kid with a rare disease that her super-smart parents cured by inventing nano-robots. And it is these nano-robots that give Echo superpowers. When I ask, Molly agrees that Echo's family is an idealized version of her own; Molly's parents are divorced, but Echo's parents stayed together until a powerful corporation abducted them. Echo's parents were able to cure their daughter of a debilitating illness, but Molly's parents, through no fault of their own, could not do the same, and for a long time, chalked Molly's fatigue up to weakness of character.

Echo and Polly Rogers aside, Andromache is the center of Molly's fantasy life, a life that Molly puts a great deal of energy into developing, posting as Andromache regularly on the Avatar System's in-character online forum. She shows me the Barbie doll she made over to look like Andromache and a comic book cover with a woman in leather on it, one that Molly says resembles Andromache.

Andromache does not look like Molly. Although they are around the same age, in their early thirties, Andromache is tall and Amazonian, with brown, Mediterranean skin, large breasts, an anatomically impossible waist, and long, cascading blue-black hair. Molly is pale and wears her straight brown hair pulled into a small bun or ponytail. She says that her generously proportioned figure represents one of the many side effects of fibromyalgia—she feels too crummy to exercise.

When she gets a new cane, she shows that to me, too, and says she always used a hand-me-down cane and finally decided to get one for herself. The cane is made of anodized aluminum and is colored electric turquoise. Its laser-etched floral pattern glints silver in the sunlight.

As the big summer gaming convention DEXCON approaches, we begin to talk about me. I need help. I've never done this before. My imagination is rusty from a year of graduate work, so I will need to rev it back to life. If I'm going to write about larp and discover its draw, then I need to try it, both to get inside the community and to decipher the seemingly endless amount of jargon—IC, OOG, GM, meta-gaming, munchkin, min-maxer. At least, that's what I tell myself, that I'm doing this because it's part of the job.

My fascination with larp is a little hard to explain. As a child I loved the Arthurian legends, medieval fantasy novels, and adventure films, solitary activities that are made into communal ones through the interactive storytelling of larp. Maybe larp speaks to my failed theater aspirations in high school, where I was a perennial chorus member and never the lead actress I wanted to be. Maybe larp fascinates me because I stubbornly like things that are weird, DIY, or on the fringes of the cultural landscape—experimental literature, soap making, fermented pickles, obscure Japanese film. Perhaps my larp fetish derives from jealousy that there are others in this world who can join a community without making a sardonic joke of themselves.

Rob and Molly advise me over several visits. Rob is a couple years older than Molly, in his mid-thirties, a tall black man with a quiet, unassuming demeanor and a subtle, sarcastic sense of humor so dry that it sometimes passes over my head. He installs computer software, and he had met Molly at Avatar, which he has been playing for upward of ten years. He based his character, Zane, on *The Prisoner*, a 1960s TV show starring Patrick McGoohan. Talking to me about Zane made Rob nervous because he had plots in motion that wouldn't come to fruition for years, and he worried that my book would come out before he was able to spring his various traps.

A cadre of larp veterans in addition to Rob and Molly offered me suggestions on what sort of character to create. I was to choose a genre that spoke to me, that I knew backward and forward, for my first character, to give in to the secret fantasies I harbored about myself while huddled under the sheets with a book as a child. My feminist sensibility recoiled at my first thought—a princess—so I had to delve deeper.

I had my character's name before I had anything else: Verva Malone. It inexplicably popped into my head and stuck. The whole point of larp is to play pretend, to be someone I usually didn't get to be, so a journalist was out. I opted for the next best thing: a private eye. I intended to report as I larped, and clearly a private eye would have an in-character reason to carry a notebook.

The more I imagined Verva as a private eye, the more it made sense. The first books I ever liked on my own came from the Nancy Drew series, which I read so voraciously that my mother rationed books while we were on family vacation. I'd loved detectives my whole life, from Sherlock Holmes to film noir to the pulpy paperbacks I read guiltily while in a graduate program for literary fiction.

Molly scoured the Internet for private eye outfits to use as models, and together we came up with a costume concept. She lent me a beige clutch handbag and the four inch purple heels she could no longer wear but loved. Rob talked to me about Verva, where she was from (California), and how she arrived in the Nexus (mysterious explosion).

The week before the convention, I scoured costume shops in New York for long strands of fake pearls, a toy pistol, and gloves. I burned hours on eBay searching for the perfect cloche hat but had to settle for a cheap flapper rendition bought at a costume store. I even read a Raymond Chandler novel to get myself in the proper mindset.

Finally, Wednesday, July 16 arrived and DEXCON 11 began with great fanfare at the East Brunswick Hilton in New Jersey. Molly sat between Rob and me at a round table in one of the hotel's ballrooms. Perhaps two hundred of the one-thousand-plus convention goers who would arrive over the course of the weekend sat around tables covered by white tablecloths with their chairs pushed back, sated from the all-you-could-eat buffet. Not everyone was a larper, per se, but all these people were gamers, and the crowd definitely had a self-selected look. There were reedy young men with ponytails, rotund women poured into their jeans, men representing the so-called fatbeard contingency, spindly young women of the Goth persuasion, middle-aged bald bikers in leather jackets and military hats, and many people of average build in black shirts with kicky slogans like "Joss Whedon is my master now." As a diehard fan of *Buffy the Vampire Slayer*, I related to that sentiment.

Over the course of the five-day convention, these people would collectively play a jillion rounds of Dungeons & Dragons and other role-playing games, war games with hand-painted miniatures, collectible card games such as Magic: The Gathering, badminton, trivia games, Monopoly, Risk, and more. Over twenty different larps would also run. Vincent Salzillo, president of Double Exposure, the company that ran the conventions and the Avatar System, even put together a puzzle with one clue on each convention-goer's badge.

Vinny Salzillo had dark brown hair, a Burt Reynolds moustache, and an impressively diverse collection of gamer humor T-shirts bearing such slogans as "+20 Shirt of Smiting" and "Everything I know, I learned from gaming." At conventions, he was famous for wearing bright patterned lounge pants and walking around the convention floor without shoes. He'd grown up in the Bronx, where he attended the Bronx High School of Science, a magnet school where he created and ran his very first games for his fellow students. He'd been a fixture on the sci-fi fandom and gaming convention circuit since the early 1980s, and over time he became known both for writing games and for running theme parties at various conventions. He fondly remembers running thirteen parties over three days at the Disclave convention in 1990, including a Teenage Mutant Ninja Turtle party that featured pizza bagels and a party inspired by the book *The Hitchhiker's Guide to the Galaxy* that featured the Pan-Galactic Gargle Blaster, which Vinny concocted for the occasion out of dry ice, grain alcohol, blue food coloring, and lemon extract. In 1992, at age twenty-six, he'd run his first DEXCON, keeping up the tradition of theme parties with SUGARFEST, a sweet-themed shindig, and a chocolate fondue party. In 1995 he introduced the Avatar System at

Double Exposure's first DREAMATION convention, which ran that January.

As I found a seat in the banquet room for my first day at DEXCON, I read the phrase "Are you ready for some football?" scrolling across a scrim at one end of the room in large letters. The tiny script "then you're in the wrong place" followed. Eventually, the lights dimmed, and a short homemade film that poked gentle fun at gamers played.

The crowd clapped and cheered at the end of the film, and as the lights were turned up, a group of men walked slowly and reverently through the sea of tables, each holding the edge of a white piece of cloth that draped between them but did not touch the floor. When they reached the front of the room, they attached one side of the fabric to an inverted U of PVC pipe and hoisted the banner high. Various multisided dice were outlined with electrical tape on the banner. Later that evening, many audience members would use similarly shaped bits of plastic to play Dungeons & Dragons, or D&D, as it was commonly abbreviated.

Molly turned to me. "You know how some people talk about having a flag?" she said. "Well that's our freak flag. And we actually like to fly it."

As men finished raising the flag, the audience burst into applause, and several people shouted "Do-ba! Do-ba!" (pronounced "dough-bah")—some inside joke from the Avatar System that had not yet been explained to me. Molly wouldn't tell me what it meant. Evidently, I'd have to hear the origin myth from Michael Smith, an affable high school physics teacher who played a character named Michael Lovious Smith in the Avatar System. And he only told the Doba story once per convention.

Onstage, Vinny officially welcomed everyone to the con and introduced key members of his staff to his audience. He introduced us to the spunky Avonelle Wing, who had a mass of red waves flowing to below her shoulders, and to Kate Beaman-Martinez, who smiled a lot and had a cloud of dark brown hair to match Avonelle's. They were more than Vinny's nexts-in-command; the three of them loved one another and lived together in a polyamorous relationship that others sometimes called "the Triad." Recently, the three of them had become mutually engaged, despite the fact that the law wouldn't recognize their three-prong union.

Vinny took turns calling various other staff members to the stage, where they each had a chance to say a few words. Finally, Molly and Rob came up to the microphone. This would be Molly's first convention on senior staff; she was in charge of Con Suite, the convention space where anyone could come for chips, soda, or Gatorade. Molly took the mic and spent a few minutes telling everyone how excited she was to be helping out. "But seriously, you all are my family," she concluded, echoing the sentiment of many other staff members.

"Do-*ba* do-*ba*," the audience shouted back.

The following evening, Molly began her transformation. She put on black pants and a green tank top with an empire waist; it looked like silk but was made of something cheaper. She slung a black sheet across her, toga-style, and dabbed makeup on the exposed skin of her neck, shoulders, and arms to make her appear more tanned and Mediterranean and less pale and Caucasian. She bundled her brown hair under a wig that was black and curly. Long, shining earrings of linked metal jingled around her ears.

In less time than it took Molly to put on her earrings, I nervously slithered into my costume. Verva Malone was from a 1920s world, because I liked the that era's style so much that I sported a bob haircut with bangs during my hours in "mundania," as larpers occasionally termed real life. I exchanged my sensible reporting clothes for a white collared shirt that had a flimsy black corset-looking thing sewn to it. A large quantity of costume pearls was slung about my neck. I fit my sweaty palms into black lace gloves and perched a red monstrosity with glitter, a bow, and feathers atop my head. I slapped on black eye shadow and red lipstick and slipped my feet into the too-big purple stilettos.

Molly wore her costume effortlessly. I appeared conspicuously uncomfortable, like a teen in her first bikini.

As Molly and I left the hotel room, I began to dread what was about to happen. I would not be taking a vacation from myself or working out any personal issues or experiencing catharsis. I looked like a freak; surely, the people downstairs would send mocking glances my way, stares that told me how much I didn't belong. I had once visited a convicted murderer at Rikers Island while working on a story, but somehow this was scarier; I was about to embarrass myself.

I nearly turned around in the hallway, but Molly pushed me on. We pressed the button for the elevator and waited.

"Will other people be in costume down there?" I said.

"Maybe," Molly said.

Great, I thought. We'll be even more obvious. In the mirror beside the elevators, the ridiculous feathers on my hat were actually quaking.

Downstairs, people who were largely not in costume milled around the convention floor, a square room on the second floor of the hotel. Tables outlined the perimeter of the room, spread with genre fiction, comic books, and material advertising various larps. Conference rooms branched off the main area, each one home to a different sort of game—painted miniature war gaming, video gaming, board games, and tabletop role-playing games, also called RPGs. Tabletop RPGs were one of larp's forebears, and the most famous game of the genre is Dungeons & Dragons. Often called paper-and-pencil role-playing games, they tell a story using a complex set of rules, dice, and a lot of imagination.

As Molly and I stepped onto the floor we ran into Rob's mother, surrounded by a gaggle of her children and their friends. My shoulders tensed. One of the children gestured to me and told me I looked "hot." With my esteem temporarily bolstered by that twelve-year-old girl, who I was sure had eminently adult taste in fashion, I left Molly to her conversation and went in search of the other Avatars.

Unlike other larps at DEXCON, the Avatar System did not occur at a particular place and time. Vinny had originally conceived of it as a downtime activity between other games at the convention. Players roamed the halls in costume or lack thereof; if you wore your Avatar button and had your character card in your pocket, then you were "in-game." By default, most of the weekend's Avatar action would take place in the Con Suite, so I headed there first.

I found Vinny's fiancée, Avonelle, whom everyone called Avie, in the Con Suite. As the senior game master for the Avatar System, when plot needed to happen, Avie would direct it, describing the scenery to the Avatars and playing any supporting roles—townspeople, baby dragons, deities of the Nexus—that the plot required. Otherwise, players were on their own.

I pinned the neon pink button Avie gave me to my blouse, which let other players know that I was a newbie or noob, a zero-level character who couldn't be harmed . . . for the moment. A visible button signified "that you're open to role-play," Avie told me. It sounded vaguely dirty. As soon as my character joined a house, an in-game faction of like-minded players, I would replace the pink button with a white one rimmed in black that bore the insignia of my house in its center.

I spotted the Avatars by their strange dress and house buttons, walked up to them, and took a deep breath. "What's going on over here?" I said, in a very un-hard-boiled way.

One of the women had frizzy copper-red hair belied by its gray roots. She wore a tight leather vest that displayed her décolletage. Earlier in the day I had seen her sporting a pink pin, so I knew she was new. Since then, she had chosen a house—now she wore a button with a yellow cup on it, the symbol of House Galahad, the coterie of the noble and often tortured hero.

Across the table, another woman wore a backcombed blonde wig with bangs and a black streak at one temple, a high-necked shirt, a vest, and a long green skirt. She carried the hooded skeleton of a small rat. The rat was supposed to carry a scythe, made of a stick attached to some aluminum foil, but the scythe kept falling apart, and she couldn't keep the rat upright on the table. I understood that she played Susan, from Terry Pratchett's *Discworld* books, the granddaughter of death. The rat in her arms was the Death of Rats, another character from the series. Verva, of course, had never seen any of these people before and was confused about where she was.

Two men in street clothing also sat at the table with their buttons on. One was rather rotund, and from talking to Molly I knew he played a sentient tree that had recently been turned into a human. The other, very slender, man wore a limp white T-shirt and round glasses. He told me that I didn't have physical form and that I wouldn't until I chose a house. To illustrate his point, he moved his staff toward my head and told me that it went right through my body as if I were air.

Then he put his fist on top of his head and said, "You see a tall man with a staff in swirling brown robes."

"What?" I said.

He returned his fist to his head. "You see a tall man with a staff in swirling brown robes."

"What?" I said.

He explained that that was what I saw when I examined him, despite the street clothes he wore. As I soon learned, putting a fist atop one's head signified an out-of-character remark, as did crossing index and middle fingers and holding a hand aloft as if taking an oath. Many Avatar characters also covered their buttons to go out-of-character, or OOC. Out-of-game, or OOG, was the preferred term for this in other games.

"What's your name?" he said, back in-game.

"Verva," I said.

"God bless you," he said, as if I had sneezed. He laughed. Verva glared. Evidently she didn't appreciate jokes about her name.

With that brief introduction out of the way, the table turned its attention to the frizzy-haired woman, who talked about her fright and wanted to know where her pup was. By asking questions about her world we established that she was a werewolf who had popped into the Nexus during some sort of chase.

I was next on the agenda. It was like a game of twenty questions. Did I suck blood? No. Did I make giant machines? No. Did I come from a world that had magicians? Yes, but they were charlatans, I think. Was I a princess? Definitely not. I was a detective, for chrissakes. Everyone breathed a sigh of relief. The melancholy elven princess character in need of rescuing was a well-known trope in the larp world, and most players found her tiresome. Was my world called Earth? I thought it probably was. Did I remember how I got here? Well, I was investigating a crime, and the last thing I remember was an explosion. They, the others, the villains, had gotten me. Oh, everyone nodded, *they*. Who were they?

Lucky for me, I didn't have to explain too much. Many Avatars new to the Nexus suffer "Nexal amnesia," a condition that is both plot point and character device. Noobs could selectively remember their origins, which allowed new players, or old players with new characters, to take some time to develop a backstory.

After a half hour or so, I was ready for the action to start. Weren't we supposed to go on some sort of adventure? Everyone remained seated, exchanging small talk in the personas of their characters. It was like a cocktail party where I wasn't allowed to talk about the articles I'd read or the movies I'd seen because, of course, Verva hadn't read or seen anything from the twenty-first century. Over the course of the next hour, I began to realize that these kinds of conversations helped develop character. As the Avatars talked with one another, they swapped stories about their past or about past adventures inside the Nexus. It took me some time to realize that these tales must be partially improvised. When someone asked me whether I had tommy guns in my world, I was flummoxed. Did I want to come from a world with gangsters or not? I hadn't considered Verva in these terms before.

Over the course of the evening, I discovered that Verva liked logic and hard facts, eschewed emotion, did not believe in God, had a drinking problem, and lit (fake) cigarettes in her cigarette holder to keep her hands busy when she was out of her element.

At DEXCON, Friday night is always black tie night. Years earlier, one of the convention staffers had proposed the event because she wanted a chance to re-wear old bridesmaid dresses, and many of the women of the convention quickly jumped behind her. A tradition was born. Kate and Avie had lots of costumes that they seldom got a chance to wear because they were busy running the convention. Kate, Avie, and Vinny held larp and the Avatar System close to their hearts—they had met and fallen in love with one another through the game. So when Kate and Avie declared a night for dress up, the women of the Avatar System and the convention staff, along with a few of its men, complied. One guy also had "dress like a gamer" night, which ran coincidentally with formal night, and the bulk of the convention members participated, most of them unwittingly.

The council meeting, the only formally scheduled Avatar event, also took place on Friday, so whether players incorporated black tie into costuming or dressed up in their full costumes was a matter of judgment. The council, the governing body of the Nexus, had fifteen members, each one a house representative. Once a year the characters elected a new head of council, a source of great politicking.

The previous year Andromache had been the council head, but some allegedly shady backroom deals fixed the vote at the previous convention in January in favor of Hyran Starseeker, a Han Solo–esque rogue.

All fifteen house representatives crammed around a long conference table in one of the smaller rooms off the main convention floor. One of the house reps, a real-life chaplain, wore the long white robes of a holy man and a homemade cardboard pope hat with three cartoon bombs on it—his character, Pope Frig'emall, was a cartoon character who worshipped chaos and venerated bombs. He represented House Lugosi, house of vampires and other baddies. There was also the king of House Avalon, the house of questers, in a blue velvet pirate coat, and Molly as Andromache, representing House Delphi, the enlightened ones. Because Hyran was the head of the council, his player, Bill, sat at one end of the long table, a stuffed otter in a pirate costume standing on the table to his left. By decree of the GMs, Bill was the only player allowed to represent both of his characters, Hyran the rogue and Cutthroat the celestial otter, simultaneously. Cutthroat was a crack shot, a brutally effective pickpocket, and a total slut for chocolate chip cookies. Cutthroat and Hyran belonged to House Lightfoot, the thugs and thieves of the Nexus.

Perhaps two dozen lower-level players lounged around the table, leaning against walls, sitting on the ground, or skulking into the curtained windows that ran along one side of the room.

As players slipped in and out of character, Avie raised one hand like a schoolteacher and yelled above the clamor for everyone to stop. We had some new players here, she said, so would everyone please describe him- or herself.

Many people, particularly those in costume, said, "What you see is what you get," or something with the gist of "What you see is what you get, but I'm taller and thinner."

With the formalities dispensed, the council immediately began arguing about Cody, an Avatar played by Kate of Triad fame, who had disappeared at the last convention after terrorists exploded a sort of mystical dirty bomb in the Nexus. Everyone had been driven quite mad by exposure to the substance that the explosion dispersed. Avie reminded everyone that outside of the council chambers where we sat, we'd have to role-play the effects of this madness.

The council decided that the first order of business was to try to reduce the effects of the dirty bomb across the game world. After a lengthy bureaucratic discussion, they decided to try the Doba song, which produced magical effects in the Nexus. The room began to sing "Do-ba, do-ba do, do-ba do—" to the tune of "Kumbaya," and after we finished, Avie told us that we could feel the dust's effect reducing, and the mental links that some characters shared snapping back into place. With everyone temporarily sane, except for Pope Frig'emall, who was normally insane and bomb-crazed, the real and very tedious arguing about how to find Cody began.

The house reps and other experienced players argued the way family argues at the Thanksgiving table, spanning the divide between friendly and deadly serious. At times, the brawl had an element of fun to it, an element of "of course *you* would say that," but at other times, genuine rancor seemed to come through. In the weeks leading up to the convention, I'd interviewed a large number of Avatar players, and I'd discovered a high concentration of people with complicated family relationships—dead siblings or sick relatives or estranged parents. For example, there was Robert Nolan, a man in his mid-thirties who had been nicknamed Buddha for his affability and corpulence. His mother abandoned him when he was six months old, leaving his grandparents to raise him in New Jersey, while his father worked in Virginia. Robert saw his father only a few weeks each year, until his dad died of a heart attack when Robert was only fourteen. In some ways, it makes sense that Buddha shaves his eyebrows and head before conventions and dons a custom-made metal head plate with wires protruding from it as he plays Yuri, an emotionally distant Soviet general from a parallel universe. Avie escaped an abusive childhood and moved to New York City in her late teens, arriving with all her worldly possessions in a backpack and all her worldly wealth—$16.75—in her pocket. A single tragedy can't define someone's life, but the amount of familial turmoil concentrated in this game, and the close relationships these players formed with each other over years, struck me. Avie found love, in the form of Vinny and Kate, while Buddha found friendship and community.

While the council bickered, a few younger players advised me on which house to pick. I was leaning toward House Fleming, the faction of spies, which Vinny had named for Ian Fleming, author of the 007 books, or toward House Lillith, the house of strong women, traditionally a bastion of girlfriends who had been brought to larp against their wills and currently headed by an ex-army man who played a succubus with admirable commitment to the feminine role.

Hyran yelled for silence from everyone not on the council, and the young avatars grumbled because it was boring to listen to the council argue about who should go where to save Cody. Eventually, someone had the bright idea that the lower-level characters might be able to band together and go on a separate journey that might help Cody. We left the council arguing and departed with Avie and Kate as our GMs, who would run a new scene for us.

This was exciting to me. Instead of sitting around making small talk, Avie and Kate were going to take us on a journey where something would undoubtedly happen. Fifteen or so of us, plus Avie and Kate, still dressed in their ball gowns, meandered down to the second floor of the hotel.

On our trip down, several of the more experienced characters told us that if we all believed enough, when we stepped left we would be in a place to help Cody. Apparently, in the Nexus, a person's force of will makes them who they are, and pure belief has the power to alter reality.

We sat in a balcony area that overlooked the hotel's lobby. One side of the balcony led to the parking garage through a glassed hallway.

Avie asked if everyone wanted to "step left," and we all closed our eyes, stepped left, and were transported to a marble chamber that contained two mysterious doors. We decided to open one of the doors, and Kate dragged a chair behind the real-life door that led into the glassed hallway and stood on it, explaining that when we opened the door we saw a large, burly man. In a cockney accent, he told us we couldn't go through and then whipped out his cell phone to call the man behind the other door, played by Avie, who stood behind us. As they talked, we took advantage of their distraction and rushed through the hallway doors, trading on the large men's slowness.

The scene unfurled from there, with Avie and Kate guiding us, describing what we saw, and playing the characters we came across— also termed the NPCs, or nonplayer characters. The players yelled out what they wanted to do, asked questions of the cyborg we met on top of a dais, for example, and announced that they were fiddling with various bits of our imaginary scenery. As the cyborg, played by Kate, called someone on her cell phone, the real-life doors behind her, which led into the hotel's parking garage, opened, and two young men walked through. The cry went up, "Normal people! Normal people! Let 'em through!" Someone also yelled "Car!" as if we were children playing outdoors on the street.

The vampires, gangsters, samurai, maidens, cartoons, sentient trees turned human, and animated floating sparks parted as sleekly as Superman's hair and hugged the walls on either side of the hallway. Two men walked through the gauntlet, glancing from side to side and picking up their pace, as the yelling continued, "Normal people! Normal people!"

I was smoking a fake cigarette out of a holder, wearing an old ball gown of my mother's, and could not, by any stretch of the imagination, consider myself "normal" in this context.

As they exited the hallway, it was "game on!" and in our minds the throne room clicked into place.

The rest of the scene was a blur. We jumped down the hole and found ourselves in a study in sixteenth-century Venice. Some more norms walked through the hallway. "Normal people!" "Car!"

"We're not normal!" they called to us. "We're here for the Volkswagen convention." Oh yeah? I thought. Liking cars seemed the epitome of normal to me at that moment.

We walked across a rainbow leading out of the window of the study to a tree house in the mist. I couldn't tell the significance of this. Soon, we began to sing the Doba song again, fifteen of us in a hotel hallway, and the magic of the song returned us from wherever we'd been. As we began to regroup to return to the council meeting upstairs, some more people walked through the hallway, and I too took up the call, "Normal people!"

Growing Up Gamer

Once upon a time, there was a tall, broad man named Dave Stern, who loved his two boys, Gene and Renny, very much. Each night, Dave would tuck his boys into their bunk beds, sit in their darkened room, and tell them a bedtime story. He rarely read the stories out of a book; rather, he spun tales that his sons were part of. Gene, who was around five, became Garth the Strong, a fighter in armor that gleamed, while Renny, who was three years older, became the great wizard Ralphard. Garth and Ralphard went on many adventures together. They battled orcs and goblins, sought treasure, and saved a princess. Dave described the surroundings in which Ralphard and Garth found themselves and allowed them to describe back to him what they were doing. Mythology, medieval fantasy, and fairy tales inspired Dave. Garth and Ralphard had *Lord of the Rings* moments, when they fought alongside the Riders of Rohan, and Hansel and Gretel moments, although unlike the titular children, the two boys had a chance to attack the evil witch with swords. Sometimes the boys helped Hercules, who starred in their favorite show, defeat Ares's most evil monster.

Dave Stern was a practiced storyteller who routinely GMed Dungeons & Dragons for his friends, and he used his storytelling ability to teach his sons morals and problem-solving skills. Gene and Renny vividly remember the time that Ralphard and Garth encountered a man holding a scroll in the middle of the road. The man declared that with this scroll, he'd control Garth and Ralphard's hometown. As was their custom, Ralphard and Garth attacked the man, destroying him and his scroll. When they returned home, they saw it had been pillaged and burnt. Evidently, the scroll had contained the man's master plans for taking over the village, and if Garth and Ralphard had talked to the man, instead of killing him, they might have been able to acquire the scroll and prevent this destruction. The lesson that unthinking violence is not the solution to all problems stuck with both of them.

As Renny and Gene grew older, the bedtime stories became bedtime adventures. Dave would arrive in their bedroom with papers, dice, and figurines and would run them through short scenarios. The boys knew what to do with each of these items, since they'd watched their father play Dungeons & Dragons with his friends. The papers, emblazoned with a form, served as their character sheets and contained lists of numerical attributes called statistics, which had been randomly generated with dice and controlled what a character was able to do. Their special skills and equipment were also written down on the sheet, along with any items they found during adventures. The various dice were used in conjunction with the character sheet to determine whether their characters overcame a challenge, such as climbing a cliff or swinging a sword at a monster. The inch-high figurines were used during combat to visualize logistics, with a tiny Garth and Ralphard standing against one or more tiny monsters.

These latter-day bedtime games were not quite as complex as full-blown Dungeons & Dragons but were a step up from the bedtime stories, and they taught the boys the basics of how to role-play. Of course, their father said, if they wanted to play the real Dungeons &

Dragons, they would have to read the rule book. Both boys couldn't wait to play D&D, thanks to their bedtime games and because they idolized their father as the greatest man alive. They wanted to be like him. Since Renny was older, he was able to read the rule books for himself first. Soon, Dave and Renny began to play together at various sci-fi and gaming conventions.

Conventions were a fixture of life in the Stern household. They frequented many conventions in the tri-state area, but chief among these was Lunacon, a large annual New York convention celebrating the science fiction genre. Lunacon had many attractions, including panels with authors and artists on them, an art gallery, a room for watching anime, and a large dealers' room where conventioneers could purchase costuming, books, toys, and many other items. On the fringes of the convention there was a small area for playing games: role-playing games, board games, and card games, which Dave and his wife, a card and board gaming enthusiast, ran. As the joke went, Renny started attending Lunacon as a toddler, while Gene attended his first convention in utero.

Aside from Lunacon, the family attended the yearly series of gaming conventions run in their home state of New Jersey by Double Exposure, as well as several other local conventions. Most of these conventions had one thing in common: RPGA games. The RPGA, the Role-Playing Gamers Association, is a group backed by the publisher of the Dungeons & Dragons books, and it allowed players to take their characters from game to game at numerous conventions. The RPGA track offered a couple four-hour slots, with breaks during each day of a convention. During each slot, several short adventures, called modules or mods, would run, and players could pick among them. Only the official rules, as written in the Dungeons & Dragons rule books, were allowed. "Homebrew" rules, rules that a GM might bend, say, when he was running a game at home, were not permitted. To Renny's delight, most of the players were adults, and as a kid, he thought it was cool to play this grown-up pretend. At conventions, Renny and his father often adventured on the RPGA track in all three slots, gaming for up to twelve hours. It was their alternative to playing catch in the backyard.

When Gene became old enough to understand the rules, around age ten, he joined Dave and Renny, and they all played D&D together at conventions while their mother was off board gaming. At one point, the three created and played a distinguished family of elves, called the Silverhairs, which served as an in-game proxy for their familial relationship.

As the boys grew older, gaming became an incentive. In the evenings, Dave would ask his sons whether they wanted to play later, and when they inevitably said yes, he'd say, "Finish your homework and we'll see what happens." If they were done early enough, they'd get a game before bed.

When Gene was in middle school and Renny in high school, they embarked on an era of exploration via the local hobby shop in Sayreville, New Jersey. Every Wednesday, they went to the shop and tried out different games, set in a whole variety of worlds—fantasy worlds, space worlds, dystopian future worlds. The games they tried also had different types of rules systems, systems that relied on different types of dice rolls and different sets of statistics. Not only did they find a favorite—a game set in the gothic Wild West called Deadlands—they also made friends, and Dave sometimes ran games for his sons and their buddies at the shop.

Gene and Renny spent a great deal of time observing how their father worked as a GM and learning from him. Dave could keep the rules in his head, and he thought well in the heat of the moment. If players decided to depart from the plot he'd planned, he never railroaded them back on course but created something wonderful and interesting on the spur of the moment. Whether he was in-game or at a party, Dave told stories that people wanted to listen to—he had a quick wit and a confidence in himself that shone through when he was in the GM seat. At poker, he mastered the slow game, staying quietly in the background, watching his opponents until the last minute, when he often took the hand. He worked as an administrator for a paper company, but he captivated that hobby shop all by himself. He was definitely the cool dad.

In 1998 a puffy-haired, chubby Renny entered high school. He didn't have many friends. One day in the cafeteria, a goofy-looking kid with a ponytail, shaved sideburns, and a spindly adolescent beard walked up and introduced himself to Renny. His name was Francis Martinez, and he'd noticed Renny building a deck for the collectible card game Magic: The Gathering. Soon Renny was asking Francis, whom everyone called Frank, if he'd ever played Dungeons & Dragons. They spent lunchtime the rest of that week rolling up a character for Frank, and after school he played Dungeons & Dragons in a campaign with Renny and a couple of his friends, including Jason Michaeli, who also frequented the hobby shop and who would become a regular with them on the gaming circuit.

Frank didn't have a father in his life, since his parents had had a falling out when he was an infant. A rotating cast of uncles lived with him and his mother, some on a permanent basis and some temporarily. Dave ended up filling the dad-shaped hole in Frank's life. They first met during a Deadlands game Dave ran at the hobby shop, a perfect four-hour adventure about a runaway train, but soon their relationship deepened. Frank and Renny rode the same bus home from school and became inseparable, with Frank spending many afternoons at the Stern household. He began to look up to Dave and talked to him about girl trouble, schoolwork, and issues at home. Dave's advice, Frank says, was matter-of-fact wisdom delivered from a sage or yogi. He trusted Dave's word absolutely. Dave handled problems coolly and logically, Frank noticed, unlike his own family, which seemed quick to make decisions and fly off the handle. From Frank's perspective, Dave also radiated happiness. He talked to Frank about how much he enjoyed being a father and the pleasure he took in gaming, how if he had these two things, his sons and his freedom to game, he didn't need much more. Frank began to model his own way of thinking on Dave, and Dave treated him as a son.

Dave took Frank to conventions along with his sons. Money was tight around Frank's house—his family scraped together money to pay for his convention tickets, with a little left over for a souvenir. If Frank couldn't afford admission to a convention, Dave would pay for it. If the family went out to eat, Frank came, too, and Dave paid. Dave made a steady, if modest, salary, and he managed his money well enough to afford these outings.

One year at Lunacon, Gene, Frank, and Dave were cruising the dealers' room when they found a man making belts. He'd cut a strip of leather to order right there, punch holes in it, and attach the buckle of your choice. Gene and Frank really wanted belts. Gene had his eye on a tan one stamped with dragons, while Frank wanted a plain, sturdy black one but couldn't afford the twenty-odd dollars it cost. Dave bought a belt for Gene and then turned to Frank and said, "I'm buying you that belt." Frank followed Dave down the hall, saying, "Thank you, thank you, thank you." That kind of thing never happened to Frank, people buying him things just to be nice. For Frank, it was a big deal. He wore the belt for six or seven years until it stretched out. He still uses it to bind up his larping equipment.

Dave may have been a wonderful father, but he wasn't a great husband. After Renny graduated from high school, he and the boys' mother divorced. In the boys' eyes, their father had been the understanding, fun parent, while their mother had been the disciplinarian, the one to make sure they got to appointments on time and did their homework. Gene and Renny had a closer relationship with their father, and the young Gene blamed his mother, unjustly, he says, for the divorce. He and Renny elected to live with their father and rarely saw their mother for years afterward.

The Stern men were not yet larpers, although they'd been around larp for some time at Lunacon and the Double Exposure conventions. Gene first tried the Avatar System when he was ten. At that age, he says, he didn't understand the rules and probably cheated a lot. His game play consisted of getting Nexus Credits from his family, who earned them playing other convention games, and then spending those credits at the in-game bazaar on fabulous magic items. Years later, at age fourteen, Gene returned to the game as Vegeta, a character from the anime cartoon *Dragon Ball Z*, a sort of bratty teenage boy who thought he was the best at everything. Gene says the character reflected who he was at the time—a jerky teenager in and out of game. He developed an in-game rivalry with George Pereira, a man in his mid-thirties who played the head of House Ares, the war-like house, and the two quickly became friends out-of-game. The Avatar System also reinforced Gene's relationship with Jason Michaeli, who frequented the hobby shop and went to high school with Renny. Jason, a tall, thin man with long blond hair and an encyclopedic knowledge of the rules of any game, played a character named Cappy Zoom, and forever after his nickname has been Cappy. Soon Frank joined the Avatar System, and after much persuasion, Renny joined as well. Even Dave Stern dipped in his toe. And they were hooked.

Cappy persuaded Gene, George, and the rest of the hobby shop crew to try out a new space-cowboy larp called Svaha. The group decided to enter the game together as the crew of a spaceship called the *Tiger Shark*. Cappy played the captain, with Dave Stern as first mate, Renny as the pilot, Gene as the doctor, and George as the security officer. Frank joined as the ship's "cook," in reality, an undercover melee combat expert. Other friends from school, the hobby shop, and the Avatar System joined the crew, for a couple sessions or longer. Over time, the positions got rejiggered as some characters died or were retired from the game, but the players—Renny, Cappy, Gene, Dave, Frank, George, and a few others—remained the same.

The crew of the *Tiger Shark* stood in awe of their GMs' efforts. They spun stories and plot points out on Post-It notes that covered entire walls in their hotel rooms.

Playing a larp in a group was a different experience from the ad-hoc way the *Tiger Shark* crew had been playing the Avatar System. At the end of each session, instead of talking about what each of their characters had done, they talked about the goals of the ship as a whole. The after-game discussion was far more interesting because everyone was invested in whether a source had been successfully worked for information, for example. They weren't a gang, but they had a gang mentality. And so, when Svaha ended after a few years, the crew of the *Tiger Shark* felt devastated. The depth of their love for Svaha inspired them and made the crew of the *Tiger Shark* want to give that experience, that love of the game, to their friends. They decided to run their own larp, a game based on their favorite tabletop, the gothic Wild West of Deadlands. The crew of the *Tiger Shark* transformed itself into a gaming organization they dubbed FishDevil as Renny and Frank were graduating high school.

Dave served as the group's front man, ensuring that FishDevil had space to run at the Double Exposure conventions and good time slots, but left the details in the hands of his boys. Renny provided the group's creative direction and served as head GM. Frank ran character creation for the first couple of years, because he wasn't yet confident as a storyteller, while Cappy, a power gamer known for his mastery of rules systems, served as their walking rule book and could play NPCs (nonplayer characters) or point out system imbalances in a pinch. Gene and several other members of the GM team helped adapt the tabletop Deadlands rules into a larp system, replacing the dice with card pulls. Other friends filled in as support GMs and NPCs.

Their first game was choppy but went well enough to run a second time. George joined the GM team, and Deadlands slowly earned a small following.

Two years into FishDevil's existence, disaster struck. Dave Stern had never been very good at taking care of himself; he hated going to the doctor, so when he got sick, he simply soldiered through. In late 2005, Dave was hospitalized with renal failure, a shot liver, and lungs that were filling with fluid. A few years before, he'd been hospitalized with a staph infection in his spine, which was still affecting him, and on top of everything, he had diabetes. The boys had been living with their father since the divorce, but since the seventeen-year-old Gene was still a minor, he went to live with his mother, while Renny, who was twenty at the time, continued living at their father's place. Dave was in and out of the hospital—but mostly in—for several months, the worst months of Gene's and Renny's lives. Dave's illness thrust Renny into adulthood. Suddenly, he had to cook all his meals and pay the bills and do the laundry all the time and all by himself. It wasn't that he hadn't done these things before, but something about the routine, knowing that he was the ultimate responsible party in the house, wore on him. He spent days and nights at the hospital, eating hospital food, sitting in the hospital parking lot, and talking to his father's doctors. Gene felt heartsick about his father's illness.

Dave's illness also devastated Frank, who joined Gene and Renny at the hospital frequently during those months. On January 31, 2006, Dave called Frank into his hospital room alone. Dave had been a big, strong guy, tall and rotund, with a bushy moustache, glasses, and eyes that had a smile behind them. Now he was weak. His lungs were filled with fluid, and he constantly coughed up clear mucus. His chest rumbled every time he breathed, and he was hooked up to machines by his wrists, which were bruised from the many IVs he had endured. Dave looked at Frank, and in that look, Frank felt Dave's strength and sincerity. In a weak voice he said, "If anything happens to me, take care of my boys and make sure they're OK." The next day, he died.

Gene, Renny, and Frank don't remember much of the days that followed. A funeral was held, and perhaps a hundred people attended, people who had known Dave from work or cons. Molly Mandlin was present and stood up twice to talk about Dave. She felt oddly like she was mourning doubly that day, for Dave as a person and for his Avatar character, whom she would never meet again. Dave had always been kind to Molly. Although he lived a short distance from Double Exposure's conventions in New Jersey, he often drove into Manhattan to pick her up so she could attend. It had made her feel that the community wanted her. For Dave, such trips were a way of paying forward the kindness of others—before he'd had a car, others gave him rides to conventions.

The community that Dave helped foster held after his death. After the funeral, Frank's family helped Gene and Renny out with groceries for a bit. Vinny renamed Double Exposure's annual poker tournament in honor of Dave. And one day, in a Dunkin' Donuts, FishDevil decided that although they'd lost their heart, they would continue running games because that's what Dave would have wanted.

The next few years were difficult. Renny and Gene briefly moved in together, and it didn't go well, in part because a bad run of disappointments plagued Renny. He hadn't taken college very seriously before his father's death, and afterward he didn't have the money to continue, so he dropped out. He bounced from job to job, unable to make rent sometimes. Gene, in contrast, found steady work out of high school working for Lowe's pushing carts and stocking the shelves. Their employment situations seemed to reverse their roles; the responsible Gene began to seem more like the older brother. According to Frank, this tension contributed to the drag-out fights the two had. As in any living situation, both Gene and Renny had issues they felt stubborn about, and that didn't help, either. At the same time Renny and Frank's girlfriend didn't get along, so for a while the two men weren't on speaking terms. As Gene's and Frank's relationships with Renny weakened, the bond between the two of them grew stronger, with Frank serving as a surrogate older brother to Gene. Renny felt angry about being displaced for a time.

Eventually, the tense situation resolved itself. Renny started living with his girlfriend, and later, the two of them moved to Albany. Gene moved in with George and Cappy, as well as Cappy's on-and-off girlfriend, also a gamer. As for Frank, he and his girlfriend broke up. The physical distance eased the tension between all three parties, who reconciled. Frank even gained a dad—at age twenty-one, he contacted his biological father, and the two have since built a relationship together.

Despite the upheaval, FishDevil continued to run games, although some of the GM team faded and new friends stepped up to take their place. Gene, Renny, Frank, Cappy, and George remained the constants in the equation, although at times each of them has grown tired of the responsibilities of running larps twice a year at conventions. They'd expanded their line of larps to include two other games, a dystopian future game called Concrete Jungle and a pan-Asian game called Legend of the Five Rings in addition to Deadlands.

In 2009, the FishDevil clan rolled up a rambunctious band of Celts and started attending a long-running outdoor larp called Knight Realms, a game that used boffers—foam weapons—to settle combat instead of dice or cards. The following year, they also began playing a new zombie apocalypse boffer larp called Dystopia Rising.

Renny, Gene, and Frank still go to conventions together, run games, and crack wise. Renny has their father's humor and charisma, his ability to improvise a scene when the players run wild, and his knack for creating strange and wonderful plots. He is still figuring out who he is and where he is going, but Albany, where he lives with his girlfriend, seems to be a good place for that. Gene has inherited Dave's ability at poker, his charisma, and his ability to think deeply about things from different angles. Three or four nights a week, people gather at his house for tabletop campaigns, grabbing dice by the fistfuls from an ice bucket filled to the brim. Frank still carries within him Dave's calm view of the world, and he's followed Dave's advice, finishing college. He's a Renaissance man now, a pottery hobbyist and Revolutionary War reenactor who hunts, fishes, and knows how to put up drywall. At conventions Renny and Gene still run into people who remember what they were like as babies, people they don't remember meeting but who knew their parents. Gene, Renny, and Frank are still brothers, and FishDevil lives, for what the game master brings together, let no man put asunder.

Queen Elizabeth, Larper

T he desire to pretend is ancient and pervasive. The Romans held
mock naval battles and hosted costumed theme parties; the medieval British held a "Feast of Fools" in which master-servant relationships were playfully reversed; and Italians from the sixteenth to the
eighteenth centuries had a tradition of commedia dell'arte, in which
troupes of actors engaged in improvisational comedy.[1] Larp's modern
incarnation emerged in the 1970s and 1980s, although it has a whole
bevy of contemporary siblings from Halloween and Mardi Gras dress
up, to improv comedy, to the artistic happenings of the beatnik age.
And while contemporary culture often thinks of adult dress-up and
make-believe as activities meant for dorks, dweebs, nerds, and geeks,
that wasn't always so. The pageantry of sixteenth-century Europe is
one of larp's closest ancient analogues and was an activity reserved
for the highest echelons of society: the rich, titled, and famous.

One morning in 1510, for example, King Henry VIII put on a costume—a short hooded coat and some hose—and accessorized with a bow and arrows and his sword and buckler. Along with a group of his men, dressed in similar outfits, he snuck into Queen Katherine's bedchamber, surprising and startling her. Having astonished the queen, the band did a dance and left.[2] Two weeks later, on February 3, Shrove Tuesday, Henry left his dinner and returned with the Earl of Essex, both of them dressed as Turks, accompanied by two pairs of nobles dressed as Russians and Prussians and torchbearers who blackened their faces to look like Moors.[3] After dinner, he and his men changed into blue and crimson and donned visors to dance with a group of ladies who had covered their skin with fine black cloth. Costuming was common practice for the young Henry and his men, who once surprised Cardinal Wolsey at a banquet by dressing up like shepherds.

Henry VIII's love of costuming was part of the courtly entertainment tradition of the masque, in which a group of costumed dancers would show up unexpectedly in court, their appearance sometimes explained by a brief theatrical skit. After dancing with one another in their costumes, the performers then chose partners from among the court and danced again before leaving.

Henry particularly loved Robin Hood, according to historian Cornelia Baehrens. During a May 1515 shooting trip, "Robin Hood and his merry men" met Henry and his retinue, led them to their forest hideout, and served the nearly two hundred people a banquet of venison and wine. On the way home, the group met women dressed up as Lady May and Lady Flora—personifications of wild nature—who sat in a carriage drawn by costumed horses, each of which had a singing child sitting atop it.

If Henry VIII was not quite a larper, he was close to it, proof that people—even kings—have long wanted to live the mythic and heroic lives that escape a mundane human's grasp. And while larp itself is a modern creation, derived from a peculiar Prussian war game of the nineteenth century (more on this later), its spiritual heritage lies, perhaps, in Renaissance Europe in the fabulous pageants, disguisings, and outdoor entertainments thrown by and for Europe's monarchs.

Elizabeth I, Henry VIII's daughter, presided over some of England's most opulent examples of the outdoor entertainment. During her reign, Elizabeth and her court made a series of journeys across England, known as progresses. Having a mobile court allowed her to maintain her visibility among the common folk and to keep the scheming nobility—many of its members capable of raising a standing army—on its toes.

The cost of putting up the queen and her hundreds-large retinue was daunting for many of the nobility, but not as daunting as the rich gifts they were expected to present, including entertainments. In 1575, Robert Dudley, the Earl of Leicester, threw Queen Elizabeth an entertainment so ostentatious that it would put the most vulgar modern-day displays of wealth to shame. He reportedly paid about £1,000 per day for board and entertainment during Queen Elizabeth's visit, and she stayed for at least seventeen days.[4] It's hard to measure what the cost of £17,000 would mean in present-day terms, but an estimate would be something on the order of £3.2 million, or roughly $4.5 million.[5] For comparative purposes, in Elizabethan times, a soldier earned about five pennies a day, a pound of beef cost about three pennies, and theater tickets cost between one and three pennies.[6] For the same amount of money that the good earl probably spent on Elizabeth's entertainment, he could have fielded an army of nearly 1,000 soldiers for an entire year, purchased 566,000 pounds of beef, or gone to the theater between 566,000 and 1.7 million times.

When Queen Elizabeth arrived at the castle on the evening of July 9, Dudley stopped his castle clock to illustrate that the queen's greatness transcended the boundaries of time.[7] A sibyl, a mythic prophetess, clad in white silk, met Her Majesty at the gate and recited a poem written for the occasion by the queen's chaplain, predicting that her reign would be full of virtue, peace, and the love of the people. Passing along farther, she met an excessively tall porter, Hercules, also dressed in silk. At first he berated her for making so much noise with her retinue, but then he recognized her and humbly knelt to beg her pardon. He cued a band of trumpeters eight feet tall, probably papier-mâché figures with real trumpeters inside or behind them.[8] Beyond the trumpeters, the queen passed by the Kenilworth castle lake, where the Arthurian Lady of the Lake, accompanied by two nymphs—all in silk, of course—appeared to glide over the water to her, conveyed by a moveable island lit by torches.[9] When Elizabeth finally made it into the castle, she was greeted by decorative posts left as gifts by seven mythic gods. A small boy explained the significance of the gifts in poetry composed for the occasion.

Then the entertainments really got serious, with fireworks, hunting, bear baiting, acrobats, fake jousts, and plays, with figures from folklore and myth periodically popping out of the shrubbery to praise the queen. On July 10, for example, the queen encountered a folkloric Savage Man on her way back from hunting. The Savage Man was played by poet George Gascoigne, who was responsible for much of the verse recited during the entertainment. He arrived "with an oken plant pluct up by the roots in hiz hande, him self forgrone all in moss and Ivy," according to a letter about the event that the merchant-adventurer Robert Laneham wrote.[10] The Savage Man was talking to Echo, the figure from Greek mythology, about the events at the castle since the queen had come to visit. Eventually, the figures recognized the queen's presence, knelt, and humbly praised her.

It got even larpier. The following Monday, as the queen returned again from hunting, she encountered the sea-god Triton as she passed over the pool that lined one side of the castle. He swam up to her in a merman costume and explained, in verse composed for the occasion, of course, that the Lady of the Lake had been imprisoned in the lake by Sir Bruce, who was trying to rape her in order to avenge his cousin Merlin, whom the Lady of the Lake encased in rock in punishment for his inordinate lust. According to Triton:

> Yea, oracle and prophecy,
> say sure she cannot stand,
>
> Except a worthier maid than she
> her cause do take in hand.
>
> Lo, here therefore a worthy work
> most fit for you alone;

> Her to defend and set at large
> (but you, O Queen) can none:
>
> And gods decree and *Neptune* sues
> this grant, O peerless Prince
>
> Your presence only shall suffice
> her enemies to convince.[11]

Luckily for the Lady of the Lake, the queen was a "worthier maid," whose presence scared off Sir Bruce. The lady glided over the water on her moveable island to thank the queen again. As the queen walked farther over the bridge, the mythical musician Arion appeared out of a twenty-four-foot-long mechanical dolphin with a six-piece band hidden inside it, a boat made up so that its oars appeared to be its fins. The Greek god Proteus sang to Elizabeth to thank her for saving the Lady of the Lake. While George Gascoigne and Laneham thought the scene was delightful, another report says that the man playing Arion was hoarse and tore off his disguise to tell the queen that he wasn't Arion but "honest Harry Goldingham," here to welcome Her Majesty to Kenilworth.[12]

In royal pageantry, as in a larp, not everything goes according to plan. Gascoigne writes that the scene was supposed to be introduced by a naval battle between Sir Bruce and the Lady of the Lake's forces that never came to fruition. Likewise, Gascoigne wrote a play about a nymph and had the actors all ready to perform. A Savage Man was supposed to introduce the play in the forest by pleading with the queen to help remove his blindness. The play never went off, most likely because it rained for several days and the opportunity never arose.[13]

Sixteen years later, in 1591, the Earl of Hertford at Elvetham put on a similar entertainment for Elizabeth, albeit a shorter one, during which mythical figures also met her at the gate. The entertainment featured a crescent-shaped artificial lake, dug for the occasion, complete with a "Ship Isle," a fort, and a "Snail Mount"—whatever that is—from which mythical ocean gods offered her gifts and which served as the backdrop for a battle between the sea gods and wood gods.[14]

Such Tudor pageants are similar to larp in terms of structure and presentation. The action isn't presented for an audience locked behind the fourth wall; it's dispersed, presented dynamically, with costumed actors appearing in the woods, on a pond, behind castle walls, and so on. The queen is in the midst of the action, and she is involved in the outcomes of the various plots. It is her presence that banishes Sir Bruce and frees the Lady of the Lake. As in a larp, planned spontaneity governs the event. Not every plot point actually occurs—it rains, and so Gascoigne's play is canceled. The actors, essentially NPCs, have to predict where the queen will be and wait there in order to surprise her with their speeches. As the modern scholar David Bergeron puts it, Elizabeth was often an "active participant in the outcome of the dramatic presentation. She is an 'unscheduled actor' in the sense that no part is explicitly written for her; on the other hand, it is intended that she will be an 'actor' in the whole dramatic scene."[15]

The sentiment behind the Tudor pageants is also comparable to larp. The pageants of Elizabeth I and the disguisings of Henry VIII look backward toward a mythical past, including the past of King Arthur and Robin Hood that so many larpers seek out today. Furthermore, this mythical past does not exist in a vacuum; larpers sometimes use scenarios to represent, re-create, or work out real-life issues. The organizers of Elizabeth's entertainments had real-world goals—first, of course, to honor and flatter the queen by elevating her to mythical status. Elizabeth's courtiers also used the pageants to advance political and personal causes by way of allegory. During the 1578 *Lady of May* put on by the Earl of Leicester, who also threw the Kenilworth entertainment, a woman with two suitors—a shepherd and a forester—surprised Elizabeth in the woods and asked for help in choosing between them. Sir Philip Sydney had written the scene to advance Leicester's agenda with the queen during a moment when Leicester was in ill favor. Leicester had once been considered a possible husband to the virgin queen, and Sydney wrote the forester to resemble him. In selecting the shepherd as the woman's fiancé during the scene, Elizabeth made a political statement. In 1624, King James I canceled the performance of the entertainment *Neptune's Triumph* because he disagreed with the coded message it was sending about policy toward Spain.[16]

The Tudors were far from the only figures to stage the mythological past in spectacular fashion. The Victorian era brought a craze for everything medieval, from fake Gothic ruins put up on the property of nobility, to the Gothic novel, to jousting tournaments. The jousting tournament had been a staple of British royal entertainments from the Middle Ages on through the Tudors—Henry VIII was a notorious fan of and participant in tournaments, and Queen Elizabeth presided over a tilt nearly every year of her reign.

In the early 1800s, driven by his love of medieval lore and literature, and at the height of the Gothic revival, Archibald Montgomery, the Earl of Eglinton decided to host a tournament. The tournament took its inspiration from Sir Walter Scott's novel *Ivanhoe* (1819). Scott had also written a romance, *Kenilworth*, based on the earlier entertainment thrown for Queen Elizabeth.

The tilt at Eglinton Castle was years in the making. At the end of 1838, Lord Eglinton had assembled a roll of 150 young men who wished to compete—the same number of knights who swore to honor the rules of Arthur's Round Table—and they met to discuss the terms of the fight. They eventually settled on a tournament in the style of the sixteenth century—a civilized joust rather than the brutal melees of earlier centuries. More than half of the knights resigned in protest on the spot.

In the coming months, driven by the heat of the Gothic revival, the press got word of the upcoming tournament and published sensational gossip about the knights, their custom-made armor, and the arrangements being made. In an era that lauded privacy, Lord Eglinton became a tabloid celebrity. As historian Ian Anstruther put it, the tournament "had made him a national figure, and within the limits of those days when important people still had privacy, everything he said and did was published in the press."[17]

The tournament itself was a disaster. Lord Eglinton had been prepared for about four thousand people to make the journey to his Scottish estate to see the tilts, but the rural area was overrun with one hundred thousand spectators. No food, drink, or lodging could be had in the small town for any price. A freak torrential downpour clouded the spectators' views of the tournament, and the biblical amount of

mud on Lord Eglinton's property ruined the lovely medieval costumes that many women wore to the event, ensuring that the Eglinton Tournament would go down in history as an infamous failure.

Why did Lord Eglinton go to the extravagant expense of holding such a tourney? According to Anstruther, his romantic tempera-
ment was to blame: "One of the deepest yearnings of all people with
romantic temperaments in the 19th century was the urge to experience every emotion personally; and the great ambition of every
Gothic revivalist was to taste the drama of medieval life in as many
ways as possible—in hawking, archery, in a Merry Xmas in the Baron's Hall with a yule log, malmsey wine and a boar's head; and also,
naturally enough if given the opportunity, in wearing armour and
taking part in a tournament."[18]

The yearning to experience personal emotion is one of the hallmarks of the larp movement today. Many larpers want to experience emotions—the loss of a friend, the thrill of battle, the pain of
betrayal—that they would never have occasion to feel in everyday life.

If the spiritual heritage of larp as performance is somewhat ancient,
its formal, gaming roots are unapologetically modern. It is difficult to
trace the precise lineage of larp, and there is no single "mother larp"
that started the craze; instead, it rose up like some grassroots political campaign, with people in different areas of the United States and
elsewhere spontaneously deciding to hit their friends with padded
sticks in backyards. The first blade of grass poking its way to the surface nearly forty years before the rest of its kin is Atzor, an early larp
mentioned in the March 3, 1941, issue of *Life*. University of Nebraska
student Frederick Lee Pelton created the idea for this foreign world
in 1934.[19] Originally, the planet Atzor had two countries, but by the
time the *Life* article was written, seven years later, it had ten, "each
governed by a Lincoln, Neb. boy or girl with a good imagination
and willingness to activate Frederick Pelton's dream." The monarch
or monarchs of each land designed their own stamps for mail and
issued their own currencies. The article's accompanying photos show
the players dressed up as nobility circa World War I, with women in
flowing gowns and sashes and men in military uniforms or coats and
breeches, wearing medals hung on ribbons. The pictures also include

the method for resolving war: naval battles were decided with small models, and night naval battles, the caption notes, are staged in a "blacked-out basement" with the opponents "actually firing ships." Tactical troop movements took place with opponents hammering pins into a topographical map and an umpire measuring the distance between the pin and the intended target to determine whether it had hit. The *Life* article concludes that, to the players, "Atzor is incomparably more real, more absorbing than Lincoln, Neb. Their parents sometimes wonder how it will end," a sentiment that could describe many modern-day larps and larpers.

Atzor is an early example of larp, though it is not described in those terms, demonstrating that the idea of creating one's own world for imaginative play is not a new one. The renaissance of larp was still decades away.

Modern larp came out of a propitious cultural moment in the 1970s and early 1980s, decades marked by the rise of genre fiction, sci-fi and comic book conventions, the beginning of cult fandom in the form of the Trekkers, and by the watershed moment when *Star Wars* was released in 1977, events that enflamed the imaginations of Americans, offering heroic alternate worlds for fans to imagine themselves into.

The era also saw the invention of the tabletop game Dungeons & Dragons, which allowed players to enter and affect an imaginary world themselves. According to performance studies researcher Daniel Mackay, Dungeons & Dragons arose indirectly from a game that the nineteenth-century Prussian military required its officers to play. Mackay reports that in 1811, Herr von Reiswitz and his son, who was a Prussian military officer, modified the rules to a game called War Chess and in doing so re-envisioned it as a strategy game, which they intended to help train Prussian officers. The new game, called *Kriegsspiel*, involved a miniature landscape populated by counters that stood in for different sorts of troops. An impartial umpire decided which side won each encounter by following a set of rules. Dice rolls simulated the unpredictable elements that attend any real-world event. The game was quickly adopted by the military and proved a success—the British attributed the prowess of Prussian soldiers during the Franco-Prussian War to it and developed their own tactical game to train officers, which is still in use today.[20]

Kriegsspiel, which is German for "war game," eventually evolved into a leisure activity enjoyed by the late Victorians. In 1913 the writer H. G. Wells transformed concepts from *Kriegsspiel* into a war game meant for amateurs called Little Wars, which featured tiny figurines instead of the abstract counters in *Kriegsspiel*.[21]

For the next five decades, war gaming garnered a small but dedicated group of enthusiasts, and while rules didn't radically depart from Wells's Little Wars, they became ever more complicated in order to simulate battlefield conditions with increasing accuracy.

In 1968, the next big development arrived in the form of Dave Wesley, a war gamer on the Minneapolis-St. Paul scene, who was fed up with the way that war games would often degenerate into arguments about the rules. According to game designer Lawrence Schick, Wesley "became interested in the theory behind simulation games and undertook his own course of study into games and game theory" and investigated "multiplayer games, where different players have different abilities and goals, and nonzero-sum games, where players can get ahead without cutting each other down."[22] In the course of his research, he read *Strategos: The American Game of War* by Charles Adiel and Lewis Totten, a war game from the 1880s that recommended a disinterested referee who could settle disputes and control information.

Wesley synthesized his research into a war gaming session with Napoleonic miniatures that featured the fictional town of Braunstein, which was caught between two armies. Different players represented factions in the town and advance elements of the two armies, each with their own separate abilities and goals. The players quickly became embroiled in intrigue, and the game ended chaotically, with Wesley believing that Braunstein had been a failure. His players disagreed and begged him to run another session.

Wesley ran more Braunsteins, and eventually his players started refereeing their own versions. In particular, a gamer named Dave Arneson began to run Braunsteins, but by 1971 he was ready to try something new. He incorporated his love of *Lord of the Rings* into his gaming by running players in a medieval fantasy setting, each one controlling a single character instead of a battalion. Arneson had been corresponding with a game fan named Gary Gygax, an insurance underwriter in his mid-thirties who had written a series of medieval war-gaming rules called Chainmail. They collaborated, play-testing the rules and setting, and in 1974 they published Dungeons & Dragons, the world's first role-playing game. Over the next five years, it went through several versions and spawned a host of imitators. [23]

Dungeons & Dragons, now published by Wizards of the Coast, is based around statistics generated with dice. Players use dice to generate a list of numbers that provide numerical values for different character attributes. For example, a character with an intelligence of 6 is dumb, a character with an intelligence of 14 is smart, and a character with an intelligence of 20 is a genius. Some larps use the same technique to generate character statistics, occasionally substituting cards for dice, while others give players a set number of points to allocate among different statistics or use another technique. A referee runs the game, which may take place over the course of a single session or in multiple sessions that can run years—a "campaign." The referee, or game master (GM), has different names depending upon which tabletop role-playing game a group is playing. In Dungeons & Dragons, the GM is called a Dungeon Master or DM; in Chaosium's Call of Cthulhu, the GM is called the Keeper; and in several games, most notably in White Wolf's Vampire: The Masquerade, the GM is called a Storyteller or ST. During a game session, the GM describes a setting to the group of characters: "You wake up in a muggy, poorly lit dungeon. There is a door at one end of the room." The players, in turn, describe their actions to the GM, for example, "I walk over to the door and try to open it." If the door is locked, game mechanics happen. If a thief wants to pick the lock, he rolls a specific set of dice to generate a random number and then adds that number to the relevant stat on his card. That number is checked against the numerical difficulty of the lock, which is assigned by the GM, either in advance or on the spot. If the thief's number is larger, the attempt to pick the lock succeeds. In a fight between a character and a monster, the mechanic is more difficult. First, players and monsters roll dice to determine the order in which they may take their turns, an action called "rolling initiative." During each turn, a character or monster who wants to attack rolls a twenty-sided die to determine whether he or she hits the target and then rolls a collection of one or more dice to determine how much damage that hit does. For example, in Dungeons & Dragons, if I am a warrior with a basic long sword who has hit a monster, I roll an eight-sided die, also known as a d8, and add it to my strength modifier to determine how many points of damage I do. If I were wielding a mace instead, I would roll a six-sided die, or a d6. In a video game, the computer does all of this random number generation and checks the numbers against one another.

The basic idea behind D&D, that character stats plus a random element can determine an end result, is central not just to the mass of role-playing games that came out after Dungeons & Dragons but to the way larp functions. Larps typically simplify the mechanic, but different larps do this in different ways. Some of them replace dice with easier-to-hold cards and use card pulls from a small stacked deck, while some use rock-paper-scissors instead. Some larps say that in order for my character to hit your character I have to hit you with a beanbag or touch you with the foam-padded weapon I'm carrying. Some larps do away with the random element entirely by allowing different sets of stats to be directly compared to one another. For example, if my character wants to pin another character to the ground, instead of pulling cards or rolling dice and adding them to our strength stat, we might simply compare our strength stats. If mine is higher, I succeed, and if my opponent's stat is higher, my attempt fails. The way such issues get resolved depends on the type of rules system used and the game.

Dungeons & Dragons was not the only role-play-based subculture that reared its head in the 1970s. A few years earlier, in 1966, a group of friends gathered in Berkeley, California, to have a party. The invitation to this gathering announced that it was a tournament and ordered "all knights to defend in single combat the title of 'fairest' for their ladies."[24] Everyone enjoyed the event so much that they decided to get together again, and the Society for Creative Anachronism was born. News of the SCA spread by word of mouth and through science-fiction fandom. In 2010, the group had more than 31,000 paying members on five continents, though it's likely that more people participate in the many SCA events held each year.

The SCA is dedicated to the reenactment of the medieval world as it never was. Participants take on a persona situated in history, for example, a fifteenth-century British peasant or a thirteenth-century Chinese monk, and costume that character. Unlike in larp, in the SCA there is a premium on historical accuracy, on doing and wearing things in the same way that they were done in a particular medieval era. On a metalevel, however, the community doesn't precisely replicate medieval life, since the SCA doesn't hew to a particular medieval time and place—characters from different medieval places and times mingle. While actual medieval societies were full of lots of peasants and a few rich and noble gentles, SCA personas tend to be nobles rather than commoners. The SCA has many guilds and other groups dedicated to specific facets of medieval culture, such as dancing, calligraphy, heraldry, brewing, and music, all done in the old way. SCA members fight with rattan (wooden) weapons, and participants can gain status within the community by excelling on the battlefield, earning titles such as lord, prince, and even king. The "known world" of the SCA is divided into kingdoms, each with a king and queen, and from there into principalities, baronies, shires, cantons, and so on.

While the SCA and larp both involve taking on a persona, the two groups have very different aims. In the SCA, staying in character is only minimally required, while in a larp taking on a character, playing that character, developing that character's story, and leveling up one's character is the ultimate aim. Leveling up entails attaining enough experience points, which are doled out for successful adventuring, to increase one's statistics, number of skills, or skill proficiencies. The real point of the SCA is to find community while learning about and practicing past ways of living. The SCA has different sizes of event, from grand festivals such as the yearly Pennsic War, a multi-week camping trip that draws tens of thousands of participants and features combat and culture, to smaller local events, a medieval dancing class, for example, with as few as five to ten participants. At the end of an SCA event, a member may have defended a title on the battlefield, milled around in a pretty costume, or learned how to create an illuminated manuscript or brew beer at home. Ideally, her real-life knowledge has been improved, taught, or at least practiced. In contrast, at the end of a larp, ideally, my character has developed further—maybe that character's long-lost mother has returned to town for an emotional scene, maybe someone taught that character how to throw fire-balls and there is a new skill on my character card, or maybe I've simply hung out in a costume and had a good time with my friends. Members of the SCA, or SCAdians (pronounced "SKAY-dee-ens"), as they're sometimes called, can win honor and titles inside the organization by demonstrating excellence or persistence in a real medieval skill, sort of the way that Boy or Girl Scouts earn badges. In a larp, a lord character might bestow a title on another character, not because that player is good at fighting but because it's politically expedient or because on some quest that character picked up a mystical sword of awesomeness that could be useful to the lord. In short, while the SCA is geared toward doing real-life things in the old-world way while in unusual outfits, larp is geared toward building an imaginary life, also in unusual outfits. The SCA is bound by history and medieval code, but larps are bound only by the rules of the game and the imagination of their players.

The 1970s gave birth to an early larp called Dagorhir, an ongoing medieval fantasy game founded in Maryland in 1977 by Brian Wiese. Toward the end of high school, Wiese developed an obsession with everything medieval. He spent hours with his parents' old books, poring over illustrations of medieval battles and of ancient Romans and Celts. He devoured the *Lord of the Rings* series and checked out numerous books on the medieval era from the library. He saw every medieval movie he could, including *The Lion in Winter* (1968) with Katharine Hepburn and *Robin and Marian* (1976) with Sean Connery and Audrey Hepburn.

After his freshman year at Montgomery Community College in Maryland, Wiese acted in a play called *Hagar's Children* that proved so successful that a New York producer decided to bring it and its cast to the Big Apple for a spring run of shows. Wiese went with the production, living with one of his fellow cast members in a tiny apartment on the Lower East Side, next to a burned-out building they raided for scrap wood to burn in their fireplace. That spring in 1977, Wiese and his roommate spent their evenings drinking beer, smoking pot, and reading favorite passages out of *Lord of the Rings* by candlelight. They talked about the books' epic battles and began to discuss how they might re-create similar fights. Brian decided to make the dream a reality—he'd have a pseudo–*Lord of the Rings* battle in the woods with some of his backpacker buddies, combining hunting orcs, acting, and capture the flag. From there, the idea snowballed.

Brian dubbed his venture the Hobbit War and invited friends. When he returned to DC from New York, he met up with the interested parties, and they devised appropriate weaponry through experimentation. They sandwiched tree branches between couch cushion foam and secured it with glue and duct tape. They took children's fiberglass bows and modified real wooden arrows by cutting off the metal tips and wrapping a cylinder of duct tape around them, about a half-inch in diameter, and then attached chunks of foam to that base with duct tape. The result was arrows tipped by foam and duct tape as big as a light bulb. Being hit with one felt like being pegged with a tennis ball.

The first battle took place in October 1977 on a farm in Montgomery County, Maryland, that belonged to the parents of one of the boys who came to fight. It ended up sort of like a high school keg party; people who weren't friends with Wiese showed up—about twenty-five boys and girls from the local high school in all, mostly ones who knew Wiese or his girlfriend's younger sister from school. They divided the players into two armies, a red army and a blue army. Wiese and his friends had made extra weapons for people to fight with, but there weren't enough for everyone. They'd invited people to bring their own combat-safe weapons to the battle, with the advice to test all weapons on themselves. The ad-hoc weapons included a foam-wrapped pool cue and a foam-wrapped fiberglass bicycle flagpole. One guy rolled up with a baseball bat wrapped in T-shirts and was sent packing. They came, they fought, they had fun.

The following March, Brian decided to have another battle and recruit more people. After this one, he realized that local high school kids looking for a keg party weren't the kind of people he wanted, so he advertised on a local commercial-free radio station, the kind of station that ran want ads for bassists and rock singers. His ad simply said that he was looking for actors and warriors to participate in a Hobbit War and included his phone number. Wiese also advertised at gaming shops and at a Tolkien festival. Forty people showed up for the third battle in June 1978, including some people Wiese is still friends with.

By the spring of 1979, Wiese had dubbed the group Dagorhir. The rules had evolved considerably. Weapons were checked for safety, costumes became a requirement, and people selected "battle names" like Grimbold, Haldor, and Turgon, names mostly derived from J. R. R. Tolkien's Elvish dictionary. Players tried to weed out twentieth-century lingo while on the field of battle to help create a more medieval atmosphere. The organization bought a dedicated answering machine to handle all its incoming calls and to announce upcoming battles so that Wiese wouldn't have to call fifty people to tell them about each new event. Soon two armies faced each other on the field of battle about once a month, and a hundred people were showing up for the battles, which were organized around units. A group of friends formed a unit, and two team captains selected units for their teams in secrecy, so no one would know who was chosen last, and the battle commenced. The hobby truly exploded once *PM Magazine*, a documentary TV show on a local DC station, did a segment on the game. When *PM Magazine* became syndicated across the United States, letters to Brian Wiese poured in, although he was afraid to answer any of them for fear that he might be held liable for injuries in other states that occurred while using Dagorhir rules. Wiese couldn't inspect weapons in Seattle or Minnesota, after all, and although the head was forbidden as a target in-game, accidents still happened. In the early days of Dagorhir, when weapons were cruder, black eyes and bloody lips weren't unusual, and more than one person ended up in the emergency room for stitches. The Dagorhir crew had quickly realized that shield backs needed foam on them, so a player didn't brain himself, and that unpadded sword pommels could graze someone's head accidentally and make it bleed.

While Dagorhir isn't quite larp—the emphasis is on the sport of fighting and tactics rather than on advancement of one's character—it does represent an important point in the origins of larp, notable for its early use of boffers and for its marginal emphasis on role-playing, costuming, and alter egos. While the idea of Dagorhir spread across the country, thanks to *PM Magazine*, role-play–hungry citizens were left to work out their own rules for pretend, which may have contributed to the diverse regional character of the US larp scene.

From there, the history of larp becomes so disparate that to trace every lineage and chronicle the many smaller local scenes would fill any number of books. However, there are a few games that impacted the national scene as a whole. The New England Role Playing Organization, NERO, was founded out of a gaming shop in Arlington, Massachusetts, in the late 1980s. NERO combined boffer fighting and adventure with the puzzles of D&D and influenced the larp scene because it was franchised. According to the NERO website, the game currently has nearly fifty chapters across the country, and players may take their characters with them if they travel to a new area to play. It is the granddaddy of most of the medieval boffer-style larps in the New Jersey area, although it now faces stiff competition from its small-scale progeny, games such as LAIRE and Knight Realms, the latter a game I attended for two years.

A parallel sort of larp, sometimes called theater-style larp or parlor larp, evolved in Boston in the 1980s, at science fiction fandom conventions and through two university societies, the Harvard Society for Interactive Literature (SIL), founded in 1982, and the MIT Assassins' Guild, organized in 1983, both of which ran live action games at conventions and on campus. In boffer games, as in Dungeons & Dragons, combat is a central activity; encounters or plots often end in violence. SIL and the Assassins' Guild focused instead on games that were based on puzzle solving and politicking, games that sometimes allowed violence but did not necessarily place it at the center of the story.

Finally, gaming company White Wolf's World of Darkness games have impacted the US larp market. Its flagship game, Vampire: The Masquerade, released in 1991, was a popular pen-and-paper tabletop role-playing game, and soon after White Wolf introduced the Mind's Eye Theatre system, which allowed Vampire: The Masquerade to go from tabletop to live action. That system replaced dice rolls with weighted games of rock-paper-scissors as a method of resolving disputes between characters. The rules spawned scores of chapters of live action Vampire: The Masquerade across the country, some sharing a core world mythology.

Larp continues to evolve. There are e-mail listservs focused around the development of larp as an art, geared toward figuring out the underlying aesthetic principles behind how larp works and ought to work. An organization spun off of the Society for Interactive Literature called the Live Action Role Playing Association, or LARPA, runs a series of conventions called Intercons dedicated to theatrical-style larp. New games are starting as long-time larpers put their own ideas into action; for example, a zombie apocalypse boffer larp called Dystopia Rising has sprung up in the Connecticut-New Jersey area. In Europe, the northern countries hold a gaming convention each year that examines avant-garde larp. And if Queen Elizabeth II or the president of the United States hasn't freed the Lady of the Lake from bondage, well, there's still time yet.

The King of Make-Believe

James C. Kimball has serious hair, a thick, straight light-brown mane that falls to the middle of his back. It's the hair a shampoo commercial wishes it had, it's hair that says, "I am not your ordinary man," that screams "vive la différence," hair that seems vaguely 1980s when paired with his typical tidy uniform of a button-down tucked into jeans, worn with a blazer and swashbuckler boots. It's serious hair but hair that doesn't take itself too seriously. It's hair that his friends and players mention when they impersonate him, ribbing he takes in good spirit. It's hair that he himself jokes about, shaking it when it's mentioned or mocking the fact, for example, that his hair gel happens to contain pheromones to "up his game." It's Antonio Banderas hair, Brad Pitt in *Interview with the Vampire* hair, Fabio hair. Most of all, it's hair from another era.

James keeps his hair immaculate, gelling the top bit to keep it out of his face or gathering it into a low ponytail. Despite the new-fangled hair products he uses, this hair is hair from some unspecified time and place in the past, hair that doesn't make precise sense unless James is wearing one of his many medieval costumes. When I first met James, he was leaning out of a clapboard shack at a Boy Scout campground in a national park. He wore a pirate coat in blue and silver with large cuffs and big shiny buttons on it, and his long hair streamed behind him. The hair and the medieval coat went together, giving him the air of a serious knight, transforming him, as one of his players put it, into "a sexy pirate."

When I visit James's apartment, inside a large old house in a small Pennsylvania town, I discover that his hair isn't his only anachronism. The interior of his apartment resembles the restricted section of the Hogwarts library. In his study, a large stained glass window, rippled with age, sits above his desk, which is a glossy wooden table with curved legs, lion-claw footed. Though James would have preferred a wood-burning fireplace he settled for a gas one. It runs along one side of the room, covered by a wrought-iron screen. The rest of the room is strewn with antiques or things that simply appear antique. A stand containing a beige globe with charmingly inaccurate outlines of the continents opens up to reveal a cache of liquor bottles. A small table holds a variety of leather-bound books, some of them real antiques—such as the 1750 edition of a German Bible, part of his stash of old Bibles—and some of them *New York Times* bestsellers, such as *Air Frame* by Michael Crichton, that have been rebound in leather, purchased from a website that specializes in decorative leather books.

James had invited me to his apartment to get the scoop on Knight Realms' origins. After I'd gotten the surprisingly scenic house tour, we sat down in his office to talk about the game and about James. For starters, he hasn't always had that hair. Before he owned and operated Knight Realms, he was a self-described nerd. Like many larpers, his first exposure to the world of gaming was through the tabletop game Dungeons & Dragons, which his older brother would run for the eight-year-old James and his friends. His father, like many parents of the era, thought the game had ties to Satanism and hid James's first box set edition of Dungeons & Dragons to prevent him from playing, to no avail. James remained a daydreaming, gaming nerd, who in un-nerdy fashion did poorly in school. As a teen, he played D&D and painted models for it, enjoyed early video games, and dreamt of being a police officer—he even went to police academy camp one summer when he was about sixteen, before discovering that his thick glasses meant that if he entered the force, he'd have to have a desk job. Years later, he would undergo eye surgery to correct his vision. In high school he began growing out his hair, and at the tender age of fourteen the movie *Robin Hood: Prince of Thieves* changed his life. At the theater, James saw a series of makeshift posters advertising something called NERO. On the posters and at the theater's ticket booth there were little tri-folded black and white pamphlets advertising the game. James picked one up and ended up going to some events, once by himself and once with his older friend Rob Bean, a man who'd joined his gaming group after meeting a mutual friend at one of Double Exposure's gaming conventions.

At their local NERO chapter, James played a roguish jack-of-all-trades while Rob played a sorcerer, and they quickly became close friends. A few years after they joined NERO, it became a new game called LAIRE, which, like its predecessor, used boffers to resolve combat. After playing LAIRE for a couple years, Rob and James helped a friend create an offshoot of LAIRE called FX. Soon, the pair began to think about starting their own game. At first it was a joke between the two of them, but over the next year or two, James, who was in his late teens, Rob, who was in his mid-twenties, and a couple of their friends began to write and test the rules for their new game. They collected costuming, masks, and props. James spent his paycheck from managing a bookstore to help purchase everything they'd need. They differentiated their game from both LAIRE and FX by offering a wide variety of classes—almost forty—for players to choose from. A character class is essentially a profession, or perhaps, more accurately, a character's identity, representing a character's natural type of skills and abilities. At the time, medieval larps in the area offered a much smaller variety of classes, on the order of five, professions that almost always included warrior, rogue, healer, and mage (magic-user). James is particularly proud of the wide range of so-called "support classes" that his team wrote. Support classes are classes of character that don't have fighting as their primary skill but have skills that benefit other players, for example, healers, alchemists, bards, priests, and scholars. The Knight Realms team also distinguished their game from others at the time by including a full pantheon of good, evil, and neutral deities. Many contemporary role-playing games, both tabletop and live action, did not allow in-game religion, since evangelical groups of the time accused role-playing gamers of recruiting children for Satanic cults through witchcraft. Although now it's not unusual to find in-game religions in a larp, at the time, Knight Realms' setup was rare.

As for James, he tells me that he is religious, that he's convinced that there's a God or that at a minimum, he must have saved a busload of nuns in a former life, since he's one lucky son-of-a-gun. In addition to running a successful game, he says, he's got a smart, beautiful, and rich girlfriend, Misha, a lawyer to whom he's been affianced for more than a decade. He can't tell me how lucky he is, he says, shaking his head and smiling. After all, he had the chance to buy land, the pipe dream of anyone who runs a longtime larp.

The wide range of classes and the availability of in-game religion distinguished Knight Realms in its early days, but not all of James and Rob's innovations were so successful. The director of a larp often plays the king of town, the uppermost noble, in a move that sometimes feels like a director making him- or herself a literal fiefdom. Rob and James didn't want to do this; they wanted the in-game social structure to be composed entirely of players, creating, essentially, an in-game meritocracy. Like most utopian dreams, this one worked better in theory than in practice. In a medieval game, nobility has a key role in communicating plot to players and in helping create solutions to plot. At a minimum, nobles serve an important role in crowd control. They can herd players toward plot points, either directly ("I need you to go take care of the goblins I've heard about on the edge of town.") or indirectly ("The baron tells me a strange old house has appeared in the woods."). As high-ranking characters, nobles can serve as the origin point for a plot ("Oh no! The baron's been kidnapped! We have to find him.") and as the solution to plot points, with the power to corral troops to fight an invading army or to launch a diplomatic mission. The problem with player nobility is that even the most dedicated player periodically misses events, and if there is no baron, duke, or lord in town, the storytellers have a problem. To compensate, Rob and James began to play certain key members of the nobility as a safeguard. Over time, a compromise between the two extremes—a player-driven nobility and a staff-driven nobility—evolved. Travance, the barony where Knight Realms takes place, has four lands (Alisandria, Drega'Mire, Kaladonia, and Pendarvin), each one headed by a lord, who in turn are ruled by the baron. In addition, the Count of Winterdark, who rules a different territory but has stewardship over the land surrounding Travance, is often in town and has his own separate court with named knights, a parallel court that can create political conflict with the barony. James plays the count while various players step in and out of the four lord and baron roles. In order for a player to become a lord, he or she must go through in-game and out-of-game channels. In game, a player has to maneuver his or her character into a position to inherit the title, usually by becoming a knight of one of the four lands. Out-of-game, the player must prove to James that he or she is reliable and is going to show up to most events. In general, this means that many of the nobility are also members of the Knight Realms staff, although holding a staff position is not necessary to gain an in-game title.

During the early years of Knight Realms, James and Rob tweaked the rules repeatedly based on feedback from their players. Over time, they created new races and pared down the list of character classes. Presently, new players can choose from thirty-four professions, from acrobat to witch hunter, and twenty-four races, from barbarian to sylph. Early on, James dealt mostly with storylines while Rob, the social butterfly, dealt with logistics and was the public face of the game, persuading camp owners to let a group of fifty-plus adults behave in silly fashion on their property. If parents had doubts about letting their kids attend the game, Rob would set up a face-to-face meeting to explain what the game was about and allay concerns. So when Rob tragically and suddenly died two years into the life of

Knight Realms, many players felt devastated. They channeled their grief into keeping Rob's baby, Knight Realms, alive.

James's bedroom is visible from his study through a large doorway. It holds a four-poster bed with a dark red bedspread on it and a dark brown wingback chair. Sconces on either side of the bed hold battery-powered pillar candles, and a circular light fixture of what looks like thick, grayish metal hangs from the ceiling, with fake pillar candles concealing the light bulbs. The flat-screen in his bedroom is permanently tuned to Fox News. While we talk, he at his desk, I in a heavy chair across from him, we laugh about his conservatism. He says that although he's a small business owner, people expect someone with his hair to be some sort of liberal hippie.

James's apartment is conservative, solemn, and theatrical. He's even painted the wainscoting and the trim around the doors dark brown to resemble old, varnished wood. The only items that truly break the medieval aura are the gigantic flat-screen in the bedroom, the desktop computer in the study, and the modern conveniences that fill his kitchen, like his fancy coffee machine, which turns out single-serving cups of coffee that James goops up with flavored cream. The apartment is as out-of-time as his hair—both are hewing toward a certain aesthetic, one that does not represent any one place or time but suggests a sort of fantastic, vague, hyperreal past in which people read leather-bound books and stood, heroically brooding, over their vintage mantelpieces.

Clearly, for James, the appearance of something has the ability to create a certain mood, a belief that has made Knight Realms the premiere larp in the tri-state area. Many players say that the game's stagecraft and its ability to make the game feel real keep them coming back. James is as careful about Knight Realms' setting as he is about his apartment decor. The game has a collection of spare costuming for the NPCs, or nonplayer characters. NPCs can be anything from attacking monsters to random commoners who have recently escaped slavery to traveling masseuses. Essentially the purpose of an NPC is to engage the players by fighting them or through role-play that confronts players with information or puzzles or adds to the atmosphere of the game, making the world seem more real. Unlike player characters, NPCs aren't trying to figure things out. In a video game, they'd be the monsters a player kills, the local barkeep who passes on a crucial rumor, and the princess who gets saved in the endgame. More impressively, the Knight Realms' NPCs aren't just costumed, they're armed with expensive cast foam-latex weapons that look uncannily real compared to homemade duct-taped boffers. In-game areas such as the Dragon's Claw Inn, the monastery, and the count's manor are dressed with props such as fur pelts, plastic ivy and grapes, bleached animal skulls, fake candles, leather-bound books, black and red bedsheets, paintings, and tchotchkes such as small wooden chests to help players suspend their disbelief and feel in-scene. Many players decorate their personal cabins with similar props, and every month a contest is run to determine whose decorations are the best.

In addition to being a boffer-style game, Knight Realms is also a campaign larp, meaning that the plot continues from one session to another, running continuously since 1997. Some players have been embodying the same characters for all that time. The game meets roughly once a month over a weekend, lasting from Friday evening through Sunday afternoon, nights included, and takes place at one of several Boy and Girl Scout camps that James has scoped out in New Jersey and Pennsylvania. Knight Realms' setting is medieval fantasy, the universe of *Lord of the Rings* or King Arthur as reimagined by James. The game is set in Travance Proper, a frontier town named for the barony that contains it, on the edge of the sprawling nation of Kormyre, a town separated from the rest of the country by a mysterious magical rift. Travance sits close to a deeply evil inverted tower of unknown depth that attracts beasts, evil geniuses, and vampire overlords like James's hair attracts compliments.

As a campaign larp, each monthly event builds on the last, representing the next installment in Travance's history. In between events, time passes at the same rate that it passes in the real world, so characters visit the town of Travance once per month, during a "Baronial Feast"—the in-game reason to gather. The year in Travance is the current year minus eight hundred. So if it's 2010 in the real world, it's 1210 in Travance.

After thirteen years of running the game, the staff has its method of operation down. Generally, the same things happen every weekend. Players show up on Friday. Those who arrive early help decorate common spaces with the usual props. People claim bunks and decorate their own cabins. Around 5:00 PM, Logistics opens. The Logistics cabin is where anything that must happen out-of-game happens throughout the weekend. It houses the costumes and makeup that the NPCs will use to transform themselves into monsters, and on Friday evening, it's where check-in is held. Players line up, pay James the base rate of forty-five dollars for the weekend or fifty-five dollars if they want an extra point of build, which allows them to advance their characters slightly faster. In return, players receive a character card, a sheet of thick fake parchment that lists everything a player needs to know about his or her character. The Knight Realms character sheet shows how much gold a character has in the bank, the special skills a character can perform, such as prayers, defenses, and special attacks, and a series of statistics including health points, career points, and available build. Health points represent how tough a character is and how much damage he or she can take before death. Knight Realms has several different kinds of career points, but roughly, they are a measure of mental energy and dictate how many spells or prayers a character can cast before becoming exhausted. Build is Knight Realms' way of keeping track of levels. A character that has spent ten build points is level 1, while a character who has spent five hundred build points is level 50. Build is the raw stuff of character creation, and players can decide how to spend it. Build may be invested into learning new skills or may be used to raise a character's health or career points. The reverse of the character sheet contains a schedule. Every twelve hours during the game, career points refresh. If a character is down to one magic point at 5:59 AM on Saturday morning, at 6:00 AM, he's back to having his maximum. Players are expected to keep track of their health and career points and to record any "buffs"—spells that bolster a character's skills or stats—that another player might cast on them. In addition to receiving character cards at check-in, each player also selects a mandatory four-hour NPC shift, during which time they will report to Logistics in nondescript clothing and get sent out as monsters, wandering merchants, or any other character that might entertain the rest of the player characters, or PCs.

Around 9:00 or 10:00 PM on Friday, James gathers everyone at the central building with a kitchen that doubles, in-game, as the Dragon's Claw Inn. He makes a few safety announcements about bears and dehydration, and calls lay-on, which officially starts the game. Anyone who is not in costume leaves to change. For ten minutes, the inn area, always an oblong room studded with tables and benches, is full of people in corsets, armor, and body paint walking with purpose or meandering deliberately, greeting one another and imparting any burning information they've discovered between events through the use of the "inn wall," an online bulletin board that is in-game, or through personal messages—in-game letters sent via the Knight Realms website. Soon thereafter, the weekend plot begins, introduced by a set of NPCs on the first shift. In addition to lay-on, there are three other fixed events during the weekend. On Saturday afternoon, there's a bazaar in the inn called Market Faire, where players may sell real food and crafts; Saturday evening, someone cooks a three-course hot meal for everyone in the game called Feast; and usually a giant battle that will involve the whole town, dubbed "main mod," the biggest module of the weekend, occurs on Saturday night. Sunday, around noon, James calls the clean-up hold, and everyone cleans up and goes home, perhaps stopping at a local diner on the way to kvetch about the weekend's events.

The framework is simple, but what happens between lay-on and the clean-up hold is action-packed and complex. Running a larp every month is a little like directing a stage production: the framework is the same from production to production, but you don't know any of the scene runtimes or how the play will end. The preparation for such an event can take months.

The planning begins when a player or group of players come up with a weekend plot idea and send it to Knight Realms' staff of Storytellers. Perhaps Travance's sworn enemy, the vampire Pesmerga, is loose again and bent on revenge; perhaps the dark elves have surfaced from the Underdark to attack the town for some purpose; perhaps some wandering scholar of dubious origins has arrived with dread rumors of a powerful undead sorcerer enslaving nearby towns. Ten to fifteen experienced GMs sit on the storytelling committee, and they read through the plot ideas and comment on them digitally, through the Knight Realms website. Plots that involve the end of the world are generally deep-sixed, since in any main plot characters must have the chance to fail or succeed, and if characters fail and the world ends, well, that's a problem for the game. After some back-and-forth between the authors and the committee, the plot is approved and scheduled. Some of the storytellers write up stats for the main weekend monsters, while whoever is running the plot casts any important NPCs—usually including the arch-villain for the weekend—and assembles necessary props.

The weekend's main plot is split into a number of smaller encounters called modules or "mods." On Friday night, generally speaking, whoever is running the weekend plot introduces it by sending one or more NPCs into town for several small introductory encounters. Players often spend Saturday trying to track down mystical objects. Perhaps the town must collect components for a ritual to banish that pesky undead sorcerer, or maybe some powerful arch-demon needs a set of magic gems to establish his evil reign, and the town wants to find them first. The plot reaches a crescendo on Saturday night around 10:00 PM, with main mod, a giant, spectacular battle in the woods or in an open field against the weekend's chief enemy, typically one or more powerful NPCs, played by the same people throughout the weekend, and a rotating cast of henchman, portrayed by other players during their mandatory NPC shift. Perhaps Pesmerga is raising an undead army to attack the town; perhaps the enslaved fairies must be freed by battling their captors; perhaps the town must hold off hordes of necromancers while performing a ritual to ensure that one of the Gods of Light is able to regain her full strength. Main mod is set up so that everyone in town—usually some one hundred people—can participate in the brawl, which often rages for an hour or more. Saturday night, there is a *denouement,* and by Sunday, the main weekend plot is generally complete.

This main plot is designed so that any character in town, regardless of level, can participate if they so choose. It is far from the only plot offered. Open-ended plots continue across many events at a slow burn: a daimyo from the East Asian–inspired Khitan is in town for several moons and his intentions are unclear; a pesky group of Lond- wynians is trashing a local forest and the druids are up in arms about it; the node that enables the town healers to do their work is being overloaded with energy. These plots build gradually, offering one or two modules per weekend, and may eventually end up as a weekend plot. These plots often target a group of players, but anyone can join. For example, the other Khitanians in town will be interested in find- ing out more about the daimyo, as will the lord of the land where the daimyo has docked his ship. Members of the storytelling team orga- nize and run some of the open-ended plots, and players who want to take a stab at storytelling without running a whole weekend also propose and run shorter mods, sometimes only once but sometimes across several events.

Invite-only modules run each weekend as well. Thieves and rack- eteers meet up with the Fence to do jobs for the Rogues' Guild or to eliminate non-guild members who are horning in on Travance's terri- tory with non-guild-sanctioned stealing, but in order to participate in this plot, a character has to be a member of the Rogues' Guild. Team Good, a group of players who are good aligned, mostly deal in epic storylines based around ancient orders of good doers. For example, they might seek to redeem ancient knights of untold power who have been corrupted. Neutral-aligned characters pretty much go their separate ways. Evil characters have been inducted into a dark secret society by one of James's NPCs, a group known by the moniker Team Evil. Team Evil is sent on missions to fulfill their own selfish, dark aims, to collect all twelve shards of an ancient evil blade, for example.

The creation of Team Evil, James says, was born out of necessity. Over time, he noticed that evil characters left to their own devices will engage in PvP, player-versus-player combat, out of boredom; they'll kill other player characters. Not all games allow evil characters or PvP. Permitting PvP has its up- and downsides. To ban it strains cre- dulity—people do fight each other sometimes, even in the real world. If I'm drinking "beer" (represented by Kool-Aid, for liability reasons and because many sites do not permit alcohol on the premises) with my buddy at the Dragon's Claw Inn, and we can't get into a friendly bar brawl, where's the fun in that? However, PvP can also lead to bad feelings between players, which can damage the community and are therefore bad for business. It's one thing to die fighting a random monster like a phase spider, but to be ganked by a fellow character who is exercising malice and forethought, that can suck, especially if one has invested a lot of time and money into a character via costuming and event attendance over the course of years. At Knight Realms, a character is allowed five "deaths" before he or she is permanently gone.

James allows evil characters to exist because they can generate interesting conflict and due to player demand—some people want to play villains. Team Evil is James's effort to direct the energy of evil characters outward, toward groups of NPCs, so that they don't murder half the town in its sleep. However, according to Matt White, a longtime Knight Realms officer, this works better in theory than in practice. Evil characters have it easy, Matt says. For starters, characters who participate in evil plots can reap powerful items and other benefits. And while James's evil NPC is supposed to kill anyone who steps out of line, in reality, Matt says, James is too softhearted to do that. Still, game play is not a bed of gold coins and infinite power for evil characters. In some sense, their work is Sisyphean, since they will never be able to win the game and take over the town—even if they did, it wouldn't last more than a month or two. Just as the Storytellers avoid allowing plots to run that would cause the annihilation of the world, so too is it impossible for evil to triumph permanently over good—to do so would be to do away with the foundation of the in-game world. Good must ultimately win the day.

Random encounters spice up each event. Unlike the main plot or open plots, these encounters are often unplanned. Monster marshals create them on the spot to fill in slow moments between mods. There are about thirty-five monster marshals on staff who ensure that Logistics is staffed and leaking monsters almost around the clock, save for three hours early Saturday morning and four hours early Sunday morning. They create character cards for the random NPC monsters, sending out bands of goblins to raid travelers, kobolds that hide in the woods, or patients with strange illnesses the townsfolk must figure out how to cure. If it is dark, they might create bands of skeletons, zombies, or rogues who raid cabins and attack unsuspecting travelers on dark paths. Sometimes these monsters are part of the weekend plot. If dark elves are this month's enemy, dark elves might harangue the town instead of the more usual goblins or trolls. The monster marshals also send out whatever plot encounters the weekend storytellers tell them to. A storyteller who needs NPCs for a scene will simply come and grab them from Logistics. These encounters keep the action pumping throughout the weekend and create the sense that there is something evil lurking in the woods and waiting to attack.

Character-driven plots are the final type used at Knight Realms and crop up only occasionally. Certain storytellers read through player-submitted character histories and create mods based on them, often for lower-level characters who have come to town, for example, to find their brother/father/sister/lover, or because they are running from their lover/business partner/parents. Some character plots are not driven by the storytellers but by the characters themselves. For example, the alchemist Rudolf von Kruetzdorf wanted to kill his wife, who ended up a horrible vampire. So he betrothed himself to my character in hopes of enraging his wife and tipping her hand. Eventually, the storytellers noticed, and his wife—played by an NPC—showed up for a final confrontation.

James estimates that between 100 and 150 people show up to each of his events, and between the set-up, the crowds, and the different plots that run each weekend, the potential for chaos is high.

I followed James one weekend, walking where he walked, trailing behind him in the garb of a generic townsperson—boots, flowy white shirt, satchel, scarf. James put a couple miles on his boots during that event. He was everywhere at once. Early, before lay-on, he brought his interior decorator's eye to the inn, the monastery, the Mages' Guild, and the count's manor, directing volunteers to decorate these spaces and then tweaking the results before the game began. In the Mages' Guild, for example, he artfully moved the leather-bound *New York Times* bestsellers along a ledge so that they appeared casually placed instead of rigidly stacked. At the inn, he arranged carelessly placed leather-covered bottles and battery-operated candles into a still-life arrangement with rubber grapes, while in the monastery he did the same thing with a selection of crystals. As we walked from building to building, a constant stream of people ran into James, saying hello, asking if we'd seen so-and-so, and confirming details for the weekend's plot.

Generally, after set-up is finished, James runs check-in, shaking each player's hand. He meets with the various marshals and coordinates with whoever is running the weekend plot to make sure they have everything they need. Somewhere in the mix he calls lay-on, gets into costume, and ensures that the first shift of monsters is ready to come out so that players have something to fight immediately. Over the course of the weekend, he switches costume at least six times, more on a hectic weekend, in order to play his continuing NPCs. As Jonas Kane, he smokes a fake cigar and serves as the proprietor of the Dragon's Claw Inn. In this role, he is able to interact with a wide variety of players, especially new players, and chat them up like a bartender would, giving them a shot of "whiskey" on the house. Jonas also organizes the evil characters. As the Count of Winterdark, James wears a deep blue coat and a wire circlet for a crown. The count fuels political plot and intrigue, mostly for high-level players, although he is also tied into a plot run for low-levels and will help wrangle some of them out onto that mod. As Cardinal Haigan, he wears white robes and entertains the priests and clerics who worship the light gods, bringing them together, organizing them, and in doing so, reinforcing the way characters who worship light gods should roleplay. Cardinal Haigan has the weight of the world on his shoulders and a mental illness. James plays him only sparingly, because taking on Haigan's personality makes him feel exhausted afterward. James plays several other NPCs whenever they are needed.

If one of James's NPCs dies, he simply rolls up a new character. He used to play Kartagus Kane, the previous owner of the Dragon's Claw Inn, who also happened to serve as the head of the Thieves' Guild. When the town found out about Kartagus's criminal dealings, they killed him, and ownership of the inn passed to Kartagus's brother Jonas. Similarly, about five years after Knight Realms was founded, the evil characters in town assassinated Baron Klarington Everest, also played by James, in his sleep. The title of baron then alternated between player characters and NPCs, and a player currently holds the title. The higher-level NPCs that James plays are his way of keeping his finger on the pulse of the game; sometimes he uses them to introduce weekend plot, sometimes they provide a failsafe to save a plot that is going badly, but most often he uses these NPCs to entertain players who want different things out of the game, to engage in political intrigue, for example, to preserve goodness and justice, or to learn about the town's history.

So much goes on during an event that there's no way James could handle it on his own. Fortunately, he has a staff of fifty-eight people, all of them unpaid volunteers, who keep the game running smoothly. Six of these staff members are officers, each with a major responsibility to the game. For example, the character card officer updates character sheets in between events, while the technical officer manages the website. Some officers oversee certain sects of volunteers. The rules enforcement officer, for example, deputizes rules marshals and clarifies vaguely written rules. Knight Realms has several different types of marshals who help keep the game running smoothly—many of the volunteers hold multiple titles, so while there are fifty-eight total staff members, there are six officers, twelve storytellers, twenty-six rules marshals, eight kitchen marshals, thirty-five monster marshals, and thirty-two role-play marshals. Most immediately, the storytellers generate modules for the players. The kitchen marshals make sure there's a hot feast on Saturday and keep the kitchen organized and stocked. Rules marshals answer rules questions and watch combat and role-play to make sure people are being honest. They also perform spot card checks to ensure players are marking down their used skills and defenses on their cards. Monster marshals staff Logistics and send out beasties. Finally, the role-play marshals try to engage people who are behaving in an out-of-game (OOG) manner and return them to the medieval age.

Role-play marshals also bolster community pride, both by doling out role-play points to people who are portraying their characters well—accumulate ten and earn an extra build—and by judging the monthly contests, which include character of the month, NPC of the month, and cabin of the month. Role-play points and the monthly contests aren't Knight Realms' only way of building community pride and support. Knight Realms also has a system of service points. Players earn service points by donating time or goods to the game. Service points are awarded to players who help clean up after feast, who help set up before an event, or who donate items such as costuming, makeup, or latex weapons to the NPC stash. Service points may be cashed in for all sorts of goodies, from build points to trinkets, limited-use spells, or special magical items. This system encourages players to contribute to the game, and, in doing so, it creates a congenial atmosphere of helpfulness that sets the tone for the community.

Ultimately, James is responsible for everything that takes place in Travance. It's his baby and one of his two sources of income, the other being a house he owns and rents out in New Jersey. While he wouldn't say how much income the game generates, it's enough for him to live on without having another day job. The fact that James earns money through Knight Realms is the source of some grumbling among the player base, especially since everyone else who works on the game does so on a volunteer basis, because they're his friends, because they want to contribute to the community, or because, depending on the type and amount of work they do, they are able to receive benefits such as free admission, service points, or magic items in return for work they put into the game. As James puts it, among the players, there is the sense that he sits at home with his moneybags twirling his moustache. But the fact that the game is managed by James alone, and not by a committee of people with day jobs, is partly responsible for its long life. James is quick to give credit for the game's success to his volunteer staff, but behind that volunteer staff, he's there, with an I-need-to-make-the-rent incentive to ensure that the game succeeds.

James works hard for the game. Before anything, he thinks of Knight Realms as a social network, and he'll sacrifice almost anything to keep that network happy. People get really invested in the game. If James is considering a rules change to make the game more balanced—to prevent one race or class from having an unfair advantage built into the rules—and a player he respects really opposes the change and decides for some reason to leave if that change is enacted, James won't make the change. For him, the game's social aspect trumps its technical aspect. Sometimes that social aspect can be a big headache. Any community with a couple hundred members is likely to generate gossip and drama, and at Knight Realms, this effect is, perhaps, heightened since a large contingent of players, now in their mid-twenties, grew up playing the game, starting in their teenage years. A substantial number of players have been part of the game for five or more years as well. Over the course of time, a number of people have accumulated a complicated web of friends, enemies, and exes, part of what players have dubbed the "drama llama." There are established cliques as well as burgeoning ones. James spends much of his time keeping his staff and players happy, negotiating between factions of people who dislike each other, and attempting to mediate the rare out-of-game drama that interferes with running events smoothly. That's the worst part of his job, he says.

However, in return for prioritizing people and relationships over game mechanics, James inspires loyalty in the friends and associates who help him, many of whom said that they help primarily him out of friendship and concern for the game. As the director of Knight Realms, James wields his power softly; if he is a dictator whose word is law within the universe of the game, he's a benevolent one who cares deeply for the well-being of his staff and players.

However, James's desire to please everyone can mean that he doesn't take a clear stand, which can be confusing for staff. From time to time, too, over the course of Knight Realms' existence, he's stepped away from the helm, gotten distracted by a new project, acting classes and the dream of acting professionally, for example, or the drive to write a novel based on the game world.

In 2010, James had his shot at finding a permanent home for Knight Realms—one of the Girl Scout camps that Knight Realms used was up for sale. It was a stretch to think he could purchase the two-hundred-acre camp, and dozens of banks rejected James's loan applications. But he and his fiancée, Misha, kept trying until they found one who didn't. He was lucky. A Knight Realms player put up a fifth of the loan principal, and finally, in November 2010, James's new company, Camp Sacajawea LLC, bought the Sparta, New Jersey, property from the Girl Scouts for $875,000. Now James has a mortgage on the property and dozens of ideas for how to use it to make money. Already three other area larps—two medieval boffer games and a zombie apocalypse boffer game—have signed on to rent the camp regularly, and, of course, Knight Realms will use it as well. The Society for Creative Anachronism will also hold some events there. Eventually, James hopes to start up an annual Renaissance Faire.

For now, though, James is addressing more immediate concerns of atmosphere. He wants to transform the Girl Scout camp into a Bavarian village, and the renovations began before the ink was dry on the land deal. In addition to structural improvement—the installation of insulation in the main buildings, for example—James is focusing on immediate aesthetic improvements, repainting the rooms so that they look like a stucco white with dark wood trim, for example, and removing the nailed-up tin-can lids painted by generations of Girl Scout troops. He's also creating more sleeping areas in the inn by finishing its attic space. He has grand plans for a boathouse down by the lake, lean-tos, storefronts for Ren Faire merchants, and permanent mod sites that use wire and canvas to create fake caves, for example. He also has small, detail-oriented plans, such as using black caulk to make lattices on the modern windows he can't replace, to mimic old-fashioned stained glass panes. The goal is to make the camp look like a medieval movie set, to achieve a level of aesthetic immersion so complete that anyone who larps at this camp will never want to game anywhere else.

It's a huge job and a huge responsibility, so it's lucky for James that he has an army of willing volunteers, four larps' worth, some of whom are licensed in construction management, to help get all that grunt work done.

Having a permanent camp changes the game. For one thing, set-up will be immensely easier—he won't have to cart Knight Realms props, costumes, and decorations from campsite to campsite in the trailer. Each game will have a storage shed at its disposal, and cleanup at the end of an event should be a snap. Aside from logistical concerns, there's huge potential for the permanence of the site to change things inside the game. Characters will be able to create makeshift shelters or draw sigils—symbols with in-game magical properties—in the woods that will persist over time, allowing the world to feel more genuine. James's keen eye for decoration, his ability to build a palpable world for his players, will be enhanced and expanded, proof that at least for one man, at least in Knight Realms, dreams really do come true.

The Adventures of Portia Rom

Portia Rom entered the inn with two gypsies she'd just met. She was new to town, an itinerant priest who had recently passed across the rift in search of new truths to write down in service to her god, Chronicler. The inn was barely full tonight; a handful of people lounged at a dozen wood tables illuminated by flickering candle light. Balthazar Yhatzi, one of her two new friends, ordered a bottle of wine from the bartender, and they passed it around as he told a variety of jokes. He wore a purple skull cap striped with silver, a burgundy vest over a loose blue shirt, and bells about his waist and wrists that jingled as he gestured. Portia remained largely quiet, hoping to blend in, but soon enough Balthazar drew her out, and she talked about her relationship to the god Chronicler, how she awoke one day to find herself sitting at a desk, ink-smudged, with a freshly completed manuscript she had no memory of writing sitting nearby.

Suddenly, a cluster of goblins burst through two of the doors of the inn, pinioning the little party in between. Someone yelled "Goblins!" and Portia froze for a long moment before some instinct toward self-preservation gripped her. She grabbed her borrowed staff and dove under the table, her last glimpse of the room revealing a green-faced monster slashing at Balthazar's back as he cried out in pain. Soon enough, a small horde of town guardsmen appeared, bristling with swords. They put an abrupt, grisly end to the goblins, then searched the corpses for items of value. Balthazar bled out on the table as his niece put her hands to his face and screamed for a healer.

The incident had shaken Portia. Some combination of shock and adrenaline catapulted her into slightly hysterical laugher. Her dive under the table had been an instinctual reaction to danger, but what danger had she really faced? The goblins with swords were merely men in green masks armed with foam bats. The "wine" that had made the table "drunk" was nothing more than Kool-Aid in a green glass wine bottle.

The candles illuminating the room were battery powered because this Boy Scout camp did not permit open flames inside buildings. Balthazar Yhatzi's real name was Josh, and in real life he worked for a financial services company. Portia, crouched under the table, was me, an innocent writer wearing a borrowed medieval costume. Some things were real, though: I was grateful to Balthazar for talking to me that night, when I was new to town and felt alone. And when I dove for the ground, I felt real terror and surprise, coupled with delight, like some people feel watching ax murders at the theater.

The genius of the goblin attack had been that in the moment the green-faced men came at me with spears, in that moment of shock and surprise, Portia's goals and Lizzie's goals had merged; we both had the instinctual human desire to move to safety. The fear I felt overcame my natural newbie urge to feel ridiculous; it shocked me out of myself and into the game. Unfortunately, once the moment was over, I reverted to feeling slightly silly.

I had wanted to try a campaign-style boffer larp for a variety of reasons. On a surface level, the style of combat interested me. I'd talked to a number of larpers who preferred boffer combat to other forms of combat resolution on the grounds that it is more true to life. During a throw-down in the Avatar System, for example, players first draw cards to determine what order they'll attack in, and then one at a time, each player and monster draws cards to determine the strength of the attack and then describes it verbally to everyone. It often took twenty minutes of real time to figure out the result of a fight that would have been over in seconds in the in-game world. In a boffer game, what you see is what you get, for the most part. If Elawyn hits you with her sword, she actually hits you with her sword and yells out what sort of damage she is doing. If someone hurls a fireball at you, they throw a small, biodegradable beanbag filled with birdseed at you, and if it hits you, they yell the spell effect. This speeds up combat, especially in large groups, and is more visually realistic.

I figured that realistic surroundings would help me become a better role-player, since I'd be able to focus less on imagining the scenery and more on getting inside the head of my character. Many larpers prefer campaign games with multiple installments, because over long periods of time it's possible to develop a robust character, one that becomes personally meaningful. Some campaign larpers told tales of the ultimate character-player meld, in which playing a character could yield a personal epiphany. A few even said that when they got the flow just right, for a brief moment they ceased to control their characters; instead, their characters controlled them. No wonder a great many larpers describe the hobby as the ultimate vacation. I wanted to experience that level of intensity, and as a self-conscious, slightly awkward role-player, I didn't think I could achieve it at a convention.

At first, it wasn't easy to keep a straight face. I spent my first main mod laughing hysterically, half in fear and half at the sight of so many adults pretending to kill one another in the dark. The plot for my initial Knight Realms weekend concerned a super-powerful vampire named Pesmerga, and on Saturday night, the town, some fifty to seventy players, searched him out, traveling deep into a cavern with sentient walls—a tunnel that the GMs constructed out of garbage bags, lined with NPCs who put their boffer-wielding arms inside and smacked at us. The tunnel dead-ended into a largish cabin, which only a few of our number could fit into. The rest of us waited in the tunnel. I am told that the GMs executed a spectacular physical effect inside the cabin, making the ceiling rain blood using some tactful red lights and a poor, sweaty man who crouched in the rafters for hours and poured water down into a makeshift sprinkler system of PVC pipe, as our villain yelled, "I will make the walls rain blood." Finally, some mystic ritual was activated, and for the sake of safety, the monster marshals called a time out, or "hold," and everyone—all hundred of us, monsters and players—moved into a large clearing behind the cabin. And with everyone in position, "Three . . . two . . . one . . . lay on!" was called, and the chaotic battle began. A tall guy dressed in rags wildly swung an imitation dinosaur bone while yelling threats in a loud, guttural voice. Legions of painted zombies oozed from the trees near the border of the clearing and attacked. A man with blood around his mouth used some skill that allowed him to cut a bunch of us down with his sword at once. I dropped to the cold, leafy ground and began my death count, and someone touched my shoulder, whispered a few words, and cast a healing spell that had Portia back up. I took more care after that, but the monsters were everywhere in the darkness. Tens of people lay on the ground, dead or awaiting a healer, and dozens more were embroiled in pockets of fighting around the clearing. It was difficult to know who was a friend and who was a foe. The air filled with cries of "Four damage!" "Break limb!" "Dodge!" and the dull thud of boffers against flesh and shields was all around me. I periodically stopped to watch the fight, thinking that this was ridiculous, all these grown men and women in chain mail or other armor underneath their cloaks. And just as this thought would occur, some shadow would flicker at the town's flanks, or right behind me would appear some monster out for Portia's blood, and suddenly, a flash of genuine fear would come over me, and I'd flee, laughing hysterically because although it only was make-believe, it was still frightful. It was terrifying, delightful, and ridiculous all at the same time.

That evening, the town was hopelessly outclassed by the monsters, and we fled from the baddies, leaving some of our own to die on the "cave" floor in what was really a small clearing in a forest in Pennsylvania.

Over time, I adjusted to the newness of the experience. I stopped running into the inn shrieking whenever I saw a goblin, to the tired sighs of older, jaded players. I expected knife-wielding assassins to come at me in the woods at night and consequently never walked anywhere by myself. I learned some of the lingo, including the words players used to refer to out-of-game items in an in-game way. Since cars didn't exist in Travance, if we saw them we called them "caravans"; if someone had a cell phone out, a frowned-upon practice, we'd talk about it as a strange device of gnomish design. In-game, the now-extinct gnomes had been tinkers of unparalleled ability. No one went to their NPC shift, they went to do "baronial paperwork," and if someone cast a protective spell on you, they'd ask for your "soul," your character card, to record the benefit. I acquired a winter and a summer costume, made to my measurements by other players in the game, and it no longer seemed odd to see, for example, the thirty-six-year-old Geoffrey Schaller running around in purple breeches and jingling with gypsy bells as Carlos. I became immune to large-bosomed women squeezed into corsets, to men in kilts who spoke with Scottish accents of varying authenticity, to people wearing satyr horns, to women dressed as cats, and to portly ogres who made terse jokes with their single-word sentences. I became so used to the idea of adults in costumes that it actually unnerved me to see these people in their street clothes.

The older players were the first ones to truly welcome me to Travance. According to conventional wisdom on the larp scene, the hobby draws participants of all ages but has a demographic hole among players in their thirties. Essentially, kids grow up playing and play until they get married or have kids or some other real-life thing happens to draw them away from the scene. Those players aren't lost forever, though. Many return after their kids are old enough to attend events. At Knight Realms, the demographic is a little bit different. A large group of players began playing the game in their teens and are now in their early to mid-twenties. Some of them have dated one another, and a few have gotten married. This group is devoted to the game they came up in. One long-time player married a woman who wasn't a gamer on a weekend that coincided with a Knight Realms game. He, some of his groomsmen, and a number of wedding guests spent Friday night, the night before the wedding, playing the game.

A number of older players have an unofficial mission of adopting people who are new to town. Most prominently there was Geoff Schaller, a long-time larper who was in his late thirties. Whenever other players wanted to prove to me that larpers weren't nerds living in their parents' basements, they'd point to Geoff as their poster boy. He had entered Cornell as an electrical engineering major but graduated with a degree in theater arts. Geoff had been a gamer and a larper for more than two decades and joined Knight Realms in 2001. He was completely immersed in the gaming community. He helped Double Exposure put on their yearly conventions. He had larper roommates who played the Avatar System, a game in which he used to be more active, and a larper girlfriend, Diane, who played Avatar and Knight Realms and who had been a second mother to Gene and Renny Stern in their early years at Lunacon, where she had run the anime room. Geoff wore his profession proudly. He held a lucrative job as a systems administrator at a small hedge fund in Manhattan and used his disposable income to buy costuming the way a golf hobbyist might buy fancy clubs or a cooking enthusiast might spring for all-copper cookware. If Geoff has a spare grand burning a hole in his pocket, he buys custom-made latex weapons or a new suit of armor. During college, Geoff had specialized in costuming, and now he was famous for his characters' garb, from Carlos's swishy purple outfit to the elven smith Gideon's scale leather armor and glow-in-the-dark shield to the puma-like facial prosthesis he wore as Garrun, who was a member of the Jaxurian (great-cat) race. Part of what attracted Geoff to larp was its creative energy. Knight Realms allowed him to practice his old costuming skills and to step outside of himself to play, for example, the flamboyant gypsy Carlos. He got a rush from playing a character in the same way some people get a rush from watching an action film. Larp fed his creativity of dress and of spirit.

However, while Geoff loved Knight Realms as a creative outlet, that attraction paled in comparison to the friendships he formed within the larp community over his many years of involvement. These larpers were his people, and the bonds he'd formed with them over the years ran so deep that the group felt more like family than like friends to him.

Aside from his costuming, Geoff was known for his service to the game. Out-of-game, he served as Knight Realms' technical officer, putting his IT knowledge to work creating and maintaining the game website. In-game, his characters always performed some service to other players—Carlos the gypsy read fortunes for people, while Gideon, as a smith, constantly fixed weapons broken during battle. When I was new, he helped me "roll up" Portia—a character-creation term derived from Dungeons & Dragons but used in many larps and other role-playing games. In Dungeons & Dragons, new players roll up their characters by rolling a set of dice to determine starting character attributes. At Knight Realms, of course, there are no dice. New players start with ten build points, which they can use to buy skills before the game starts. On Geoff's advice, I put a point in staff-fighting, so that I could wield a boffer, some points in literacy, so my character would be able to read and write in the common tongue, and gave myself a basic healing prayer and a few extra career points so I'd be able to cast it repeatedly. Earlier, Geoff had suggested I play a priest of Chronicler, the god of truth and knowledge, since Chronicler's faithful are supposed to follow people around and write things down, which would provide a convenient camouflage. He arranged for me to sleep in a cabin that had electricity, in case I should want to plug in my computer to write. He lent me a lovely latex staff and an air mattress with an electric pump, and he arranged for me to borrow Renaissance dress from Avie of Avatar fame. Before the game began, he gave me a fancy blank notebook covered in brown paper and decorated with straw so my character would have a period-looking journal to write in. In-game, his character Carlos taught me how to use my boffer to prevent attack, introduced me to a variety of players, and most importantly, let me hang out with him when I was new and frightened and didn't know anybody.

Early on in my days of Knight Realms, perhaps the oldest player in the game, Charlie Spiegel, fifty-six, a retired entrepreneur and game designer, adopted me as well. He played Father Edwin, a priest of Valos, the god of justice and head of the pantheon of good gods.

Father Edwin wore a long, crinkled white shirt, a gold-patterned vest, and numerous rings, necklaces, and bracelets. Charlie often said that since it wasn't socially acceptable for him to wear jewelry in real life, he wore it in-game. Charlie and Edwin were both bald and had puff-balls of gray beards on their chins. They each exhibited a streak of wicked humor and loved to pontificate. I was a willing listener. As I listened, the bond between our characters grew, and it was from Edwin that Portia learned how to be a proper priest. One lesson in particular sticks out for me. I wanted to learn the skill "willpower," a useful mental defense, so I sought out Edwin, who had the skill "will-power" and the skill "teach," to be my teacher. We role-played for nearly half an hour. As Edwin pointed out, having willpower meant saying "no" to whatever one had a weakness for. For some people, it was money; for others, chocolate. He asked Portia what her weakness was, and I explained to Edwin that my drunk, murderous husband, who might be searching for me at this very minute, still held allure for me. "I suppose my weakness is dangerous men," I said. He told me that if he was to teach me willpower, I'd have to get rid of that husband.

We debated for several minutes until I eventually agreed to divorce my husband, thus exercising willpower in the face of Portia's most compelling temptation. Edwin promised to petition the leader of the church of Valos for a divorce on my behalf. It was a poignant moment for my character, giving up that tie to the past, and after the event we corresponded as Portia and Edwin electronically through the game's forums and through e-mail. Finally, Charlie asked for my address, and a few days later I was surprised and delighted to find an envelope in my mailbox containing a handwritten piece of parchment sealed with red wax ending my "marriage." As with any kind of pretend, having a real prop can make things seem so much cooler. Charlie had talked with James to make this happen for me; they invented the divorce language, and Charlie drew up the document and sent it. Over time, as Portia cemented her place in town, Charlie and I encountered each other in-game less and less frequently. He adopted other young characters and gave them the gold, protection, and items that I no longer needed.

For me, the perennial problem at Knight Realms was what to do during the game. Sure, action continually erupted over the course of a weekend. After the first fifty times I got jumped by NPCs while walking around the camp, that genuine fear and adrenaline-generating surprise stopped having its effect. I was uninterested in monsters and mods that ended in a brawl. I learned quite early on that I didn't really enjoy fighting with a boffer and that Portia was a social character, not a sword jockey. In fact, one of the tenets of her religion was to "avoid interfering with the course of history," which didn't exactly jive with fighting in battles. This meant that I would have to spend most of my time actually interacting with other characters and having conversations with them, a duty that seemed dreary and difficult at first, just as it had at DEXCON when Verva Malone had made anxious cocktail chatter. I simply didn't know what to say, and I wasn't well versed enough in the in-game world to make conversation about the local nobility or the amazing Jaxurian hot chocolate being served in the inn. Plus, talking about such things seemed silly if not downright embarrassing, until I realized that, in fact, everyone else was in-character and I would seem silly or embarrass myself if I did not play along. Several developments helped me overcome this self-conscious feeling.

First, Frank, Gene, and a whole bunch of other people involved with FishDevil began attending the game. I would ride up with them and stay in a cabin with them, and we'd do a late-night NPC shift together. NPC shift was an education in itself, as one had to learn the rules around picking pockets or throwing fire balls if one was sent out as a wandering rogue or a mage. Lucky for me, the Fish-Devils absorbed the rules like a sponge absorbs water, and they explained them to me carefully. Their rotating cast of four to eight people constantly joked with one another in-game and out, taking evident pleasure in playing around with their language. Over time, from watching them, I began to figure out which topics were safe for improvisation—I could make up where Portia had been and what she'd been doing between feasts, for example, as long as it didn't have world-altering implications. I could say that I'd been traveling and had lost my luggage after a roguish mage made off with it, for example, and then that fact would be a true fact about Portia. I couldn't say that I had saved Travance from a giant spider-demon, or at least, if I did, it would be taken as a joke. The FishDevils also expanded the number of people who could serve as "home base" to me. If I was feeling awkward or out of place, I could find one of them or Edwin or Gideon and hang around for a bit.

The second advance, for me, came in the form of advice from two larpers, Geoff and another Knight Realms player, Brendan O'Hara. Geoff strongly encouraged me to pick up a trade in-game. After learning that I had written my master's thesis on traditional fermented pickles, the kind preserved with salt, not vinegar, he arranged for an NPC to be sent out to teach me "Trade: picklemonger," and I began selling homemade pickles in-game. At Market Faire I hawked sauerkraut, kim-chi, salted chilies, pickled lemons, and gingered carrots—which I made at home and then lugged to the game—for in-game money. This transaction, real pickles for fake money, gave me moments of genuine pleasure—like any cook, I enjoy watching other people eat the stuff I've made, even if they dislike it. For me, the pleasure in seeing others sample my wares worked the same way as my adrenaline-driven reaction to danger: for a moment, Portia's pleasure and mine were one and the same, and I was fully in-character. Furthermore, as a Market Faire merchant, I talked to a variety of people as they walked by my quirky booth, picking up gossip and meeting many characters I might otherwise have missed.

The second key piece of advice came from Brendan O'Hara, the new player officer, while we were chatting at DEXCON. I was complaining to him that I never knew what to do in-game and that I was particularly frustrated by my inability to use out-of-game knowledge, which severely restricted the types of small talk I could make. At the time, I was writing news summaries for *The Daily Beast*, for example, but it's hard to work knowledge of Berlusconi's most recent exploits into 1209 Travancean conversation. Brendan told me that my gripe had no merit, that players used their out-of-game knowledge constantly. I just hadn't figured out how to use it in the correct way. Technically, using out-of-game knowledge in a larp is called metagaming. Some metagaming is acceptable. For example, if two players are dating out-of-game, their characters may stay together in-game, not because their characters are in love but because it's convenient and because couples often want to sleep together, especially in the cold mountains. However, such situations are the exception and not the rule. If Gene lists the members of Team Evil during the car ride to camp, it's not appropriate for Portia to run to the authorities, for example, to report them. But if Portia accidentally overhears one of their dread meetings, if she finds out in-game, the knowledge is considered fair game for her to act on, and any repercussions her actions have will be "canon," part of the game world. In order to reduce unintentional metagaming, sometimes a player asking a question like, "Who killed Magnus?" will receive the answer, "FOIG," which means "Find out in-game." When Brendan told me I could use my out-of-game knowledge at Knight Realms, what he meant was that I should use my personal skills and strengths in a way that made sense for my character. A music major might play a bard and sing for everyone during feast. A fencer might play a warrior, and a witty conversationalist might make their character a diplomat. Someone who researched pickles might become a picklemonger. Brendan's comment helped me think about my strengths as a person. I'm not great at improv, I'm not agile or strong, and I'm not particularly witty, but I'm tenacious, and I'm a writer. I decided to start an in-game newspaper, a periodical called the *Travance Chronicle*.

The *Travance Chronicle* changed the game for me. At every weekend event, come snow or heat, I had a purpose, and one that could be fulfilled over and over again—I had a newspaper to fill with Travance's stories. Writing a paper meant I felt entitled to ask questions of anyone, nobles included. I wrote breaking news ("Queen of the Highlands Curses Residents"), crime stories ("Shantytown Shanker Strikes Again!"), reviews, investigative pieces such as a history of Travance's magnet for evil, the Inverted Tower, court stories ("Gypsies Charged with Theft, Treason"), obits for fallen characters, and profiles. Everything I wrote in the *Travance Chronicle* I learned about in-game or by sending in-character messages to other players via the online forum. For example, during one weekend a couple of the Fish-Devils and their friends went out for an NPC shift, resulting in this *Chronicle* article.

A FORCED FASHION FAUX PAS

One of the strangest crime waves in this town's history continued in January, as a band of miscreants subdued at least ten
citizens, forced them into dresses, and then magically or psion-
ically coerced the victims to extol the gowns. Victims were
forced to say, "I love my new dress," "Oh, so pretty," and other
similar phrases.

In November, at least four members of town reported similar incidents. None of the victims were robbed or otherwise
harmed, and all managed to recover their senses within an
hour of the attacks. However, the so-called "Dress-up Bandits"
remain at large, with victims unable to agree on what the per-
petrators look like, or even how many there are.

There has been no word yet on whether the dresses were of
the latest fashion, or last season's bargain holdovers.

I especially enjoyed writing profiles in a series dubbed "Better
Know Your Neighbor" because Travance was filled with colorful and
interesting characters, from Dr. Hix, a goblin who moonlighted as a
breakfast chef at the inn, occasionally slipping magical potions into
his food, to Ming Na, a tea-selling racketeer from the East who chap-
eroned new players and served as the town's unofficial employment
office. There was Malyc Weavewarden, an effeminate sorcerer of
untold power who preferred to sleep on a soft pile of women; Dame
Mixolydia Hartwoode, a genteel, British-accented bard with a flair for
negotiation and famous for both her fondue and her squire, one Victor
Sylus, a silver-tongued Don Juan who always had a ready compliment
for the ladies. Zahir ibn Hatim al Nawar, a deeply philosophical Bedouin smith, had an ongoing rivalry with Father Edwin. The talented
surgeon Dr. West took too much joy in keeping her patients awake
during complicated medical procedures, while the cowardly Dr.
Maxwell fled from battle. And of course there was Hamish, a simple-
minded Celt played by a FishDeviler, a character who had learned
how to count on his fingers thusly: "One, two, many, a lot, many
more, second hand one, second hand two. . . ."

As the *Chronicle* grew, I developed a stable of advertisers and sustainers, from Rudolf von Kreutzdorf's Alkhemikal Kandies & Apothecarium to Father Edwin and the Church of Valos. Every month I published a vocabulary word, such as *perambulate* or *jejune*. Most wonderfully, I gained a columnist, Blade the Ogre, played by Michael Smith, a portly high school physics teacher who had been a larper for several decades and had an affable, easygoing manner that made him popular at any larp he went to. He had spawned the viral "doba" chant, so popular at Double Exposure conventions. At Knight Realms, his primary character, Father Osred, was also a follower of Chronicler and mentored Portia. As his secondary character Blade, Michael painted his skin yellow, sold cigars, and spoke in one- to three-word sentences, no easy feat and one made entertaining due to his endless supply of wit. Michael had a unique ability to brighten any scene with his cleverness and his commitment to role-playing. Blade wrote two columns for the *Chronicle*, one called "Get Edge," a weather report, the other an advice column called "Me Know." Here are his first columns.

GET EDGE! LISTEN BLADE! FOR DECEMBER 1209

Weather cold. It snow. Still Cold. Next Feast, me think still cold. Me see you no gloves, you no smart! Me see you no thick clothes, you no smart. Get smart, listen Blade, wear clothes.

———

ME KNOW

Dear Blade,
  Are women good for anything else than being barefoot in the kitchen?
  Chauvinist in Green Dell

Green Dell,
  Woman good at barefoot many places! Shoes in snow good or you lose woman to snow. Woman good for protect young, smash bad bear who want eat young. Woman good for mother.

You want good woman, you get goblinoid woman! She cook, she clean, she strike down enemies good! Me meet some nice other woman too. Maybe you like barefoot woman, you like hobbit girl. Hobbit girl also like cook in kitchen. Me think you like hobbit. Me like kitchen too, but you think outside of kitchen and woman good more!

Blade

Dear Blade,

Why does my father try to ruin my life through booze and dreams? Why does he run off on crazy quests only he can see and leave our family home for days at a time?

Signed,

Worried Son in Kaladonia

Worried Son,

No easy being no father in life. Blade knows. Fathers leave, many reasons, some good, some no good. You grow up good. You learn make family. You learn stay, even if he go. You not father. No let father run life, you run life. Father maybe crazy, Father maybe secret stuff. No matter you! If Father love when here, let Father love. If Father no love, let Father go. You make own life. Booze a sometimes fun. Dreams good if you make true. Tell Father you love Father, tell Father you want him stay, but in end, Father do as Father do and it not about you.

Blade

You buy Father cigar maybe he like cigar, then tell him you buy from Blade, then maybe Father buy cigar.

Aside from the pure joy of reading Blade's columns, the paper had other benefits; it enmeshed me in Travance politics. I joined the land of Drega'Mire, one of the four main regions of Travance, ruled over by in-game lords, and became its minister of information shortly after. One fine spring day, right after I published a piece about the gypsy Tobar's recent arrest for besmirching the nobles, I walked, arm in arm, with the sassy Aerin Feist, Drega'Mire's minister of trade. As we passed the count's manor and the forge on our way to the inn, I saw Dame Evadne, a knight of Drega'Mire and high inquisitor of the barony, running down the graveled path, unmistakably headed for me. "I've got to talk to you right now," she said, putting an arm about my shoulders and steering Aerin and me away from the crowds that always milled close to the Dragon's Claw. Evadne said I was going to be brought up on charges of besmirching the nobles. One of the baron's inquisitors was going to question me about my recent article and its use of anonymous sources, who had suggested that Tobar had a powerful and shady benefactor. I thought the sources had been talking about the Fence, the head of the Thieves' Guild, but the nobles thought the sources had implied that one of them had shown shady favoritism to Tobar.

To be wanted for besmirchment was exciting—and annoying. On the one hand, the paper was making an impact. James liked it as a role-play tool and printed out copies on fake parchment that were distributed around town. New players knew who I was after reading the electronic version of the paper printed on the Dragon's Claw Inn "bulletin board." On the other hand, because I was a writer in real life, any slight toward the paper, be it besmirchment charges or allegations of inaccuracy, cut my real soul like a +20 knife of slicing. If a character wouldn't talk to me in-game, I felt genuinely angry and upset—and foolish for feeling this way over what was, after all, a game that was supposed to be fun. It took me some time to separate what happened in-game from my real life emotions, and eventually I learned to enjoy the secretive characters—I thought of them as Portia's nemeses.

Besmirchment charges against the *Travance Chronicle* were never formally filed, although I received a stern talking-to from the inquisitor. The kerfuffle over anonymous sourcing was only one of the journalistic controversies my in-game paper generated. I reported, wrote, and nearly published an expose on the destruction of the old Druid's grove—it would have been Portia's Pentagon Papers—but the twin arguments that to publish such a piece would jeopardize the grove's security and hinder my ability to get more information out of a select set of nobles persuaded me to stay my hand. I held the story as a cudgel, promising to publish it if more information on Travance's secret war was not forthcoming.

Despite the *Chronicle*'s ability to engage me in the game, I ended up feeling mixed about it. While I loved the reaction that it got from the locals, it was hard work to write and report, and sometimes it felt like a chore. I wasn't escaping my reality in-game, I was simply re-creating it. I viewed the paper both as service to the game and a way of being upfront about my out-of-game purposes. Since I couldn't put in the time to really fact-check stuff for a fake paper, I worried that Portia's semi-accurate writing would affect the way players viewed me as a journalist. When I posted to the forums about my book con-tract, I made a point of noting the fact-checking differences between the fake and real me. Sometimes I think that playing at my real-life profession inhibited my ability to really create a character, that I iden-tified with Portia too strongly, which hindered my ability to become her because it raised the personal stakes for me. If Portia screwed up, that meant that I had also screwed up.

While I found the weekend plots somewhat predictable, focus-ing around rituals or finding monsters and killing them, I became deeply fascinated with slow-burning plots that couldn't be solved in two days, like the mystery of who was overloading Travance's heal-ing focus with energy and what the result of that would be. I also enjoyed plots that centered around particular players who were try-ing to accomplish specific goals, such as Dame Mixolydia's desire to cure a deeply corrupted sorcerer. These plots, which advanced unpre-dictably and by inches, held my interest because I could not predict the possible outcomes. Apparently, I liked to investigate mysteries.

To me, larp feels more real in the dark. Out in the hills of Penn-sylvania or New Jersey, the darkness is tarry, black, and deep, more intense than anything a city-dweller normally experiences. To walk down a path lit only by the moon and hear the trees rustling in the wind, your ears alert for any sound of a hiding enemy, to know that you could be ambushed, ganked (killed, particularly by another player character), or tortured at any moment is the essence of adventure. Boffers suddenly seem a reasonable defense against ene-mies, invisible spider webs, and quite possibly larper-eating bears.

Shadows from flickering candles indoors play across faces, making them seem more dramatic and meaningful than they would in full light. I prefer to larp after dark, ideally in the hookah tent. Zahir ibn Hatim al Nawar, a Bedouin smith, runs the hookah tent, and when the weather is nice he brings a portable outdoor gazebo with mesh sides to events and decorates its walls with blankets. He jokes that it's one of the safest places in Travance, because its magical door has something called a "zipper" on it, a strange device that requires opposable thumbs in order to open and is therefore impregnable to were-cats, dire wolves, and other malicious woodland creatures. The tent floor is covered with rugs and cushions, which direct a newcomer's focus to the tent's centerpiece, a large hookah water pipe made for smoking flavored tobacco. For the price of a few gold (and provided you are of legal smoking age in the state of New Jersey or Pennsylvania) Zahir will give you a mouthpiece tip to use when the hookah hose comes your way. The real reason to come, though, is for the conversation.

My most cherished memories from Knight Realms derive from times spent gathered around this hookah with Zahir, played by a union organizer named Chris Ayala who was in his mid-thirties, and with the ambitious but retired mage Marcus, played by new player officer Brendan. Over a good hookah, the three of us talked philosophy together, mulling over the nature of truth itself. Zahir was a priest of Brazen, the god of craftsmen and, like Chronicler, a member of the neutral pantheon. Marcus played the skeptic or devil's advocate, pushing Zahir's and Portia's positions through careful questioning. As a Chroniclerite, Portia thought truth was knowable only through the experiences of others and that obtaining the maximum number of experiences brought one closer to it. Zahir, as a craftsman and Brazenite, believed that true knowledge came through practicum, in the doing. If Portia viewed knowledge as the world's chief good, then for Zahir, it was quality craftsmanship and performing to one's highest ability. That got us onto the nature of goodness. What about an evil artifact? Marcus asked. Would Zahir seek to preserve such a thing? Yes, he said. If an object was made with true craftsmanship, it was worth preserving for study, no matter if its use was for the sake of evil. From there, prompted by the snow falling around us, we talked about water and its importance to each of our lives.

I was surprised at the philosophical turn that the conversation among the three of us had taken, but what surprised me more was that our talk captured all my attention. In college I had been a philosophy major, and I used to love arguing to no end about truth and goodness and whether women had essential qualities with nearly anyone who would listen. After I completed my education, my desire to debate ended abruptly, much to the disappointment of my debate-loving boyfriend (now husband). It was as if, at the age of twenty-one and after those philosophy classes, I had finally uncovered the philosophical positions that made the most sense to me, and, having done so, having figured out my personal philosophy, I had no more use for debate. Instead of the joyous exercises they had once been, philosophical arguments became dreary and unsolvable to me. At the beginning of a debate, I felt I could foresee the final, petty underpinning assumptions we would end up squabbling over before agreeing to disagree.

Knight Realms reignited my joy in philosophy. My personal opinions about free will weren't on trial. Rather, the beliefs of Portia, who felt the direct influence of a knowable god on her life, were under discussion. I had to rethink myself through philosophical hoops I'd jumped through as a real person years before. The context of the game made that rethinking fun, and as I sussed out Portia's philosophical positions, she grew as a character to resemble something closer to a complete person.

Time in the hookah tent wasn't always serious—on the contrary, we spent most of our time laughing. Periodically invading goblins and woodland creatures provided amusing interludes, particularly since most of them lacked the opposable thumbs or intelligence necessary to figure out the befuddling "zipping" mechanism. When he was in town the ridiculous Malyc Weavewarden, one frizzy-haired Jeramy Merritt, would lounge in the hookah tent—he and Brendan and Chris were all friends out-of-game—and make foppish comments in his British accent. One evening, very late, around stupid o'clock, he hovered his gloved hand just out of sight behind one of my ears and said in a low, creepy whisper, "It's the tickle monster, Portia. It's got five limbs, and they're all hungry." I turned to see what he was referring to, and the closeness of his hand to my head surprised the heck out of me. We all laughed for some time.

Little by little, as I got to know people in-game, I began to know them out-of-game as well. At the beginning and end of events, it became difficult to walk too far without running into someone, a fellow actor, someone I'd shared a scene with, who wanted a hug, to exchange a quip, or to say hello. At events, before lay-on, I began to have a queer feeling that reminded me of attending church with my mother as a little girl. Everyone knew one another, and most everyone was friendly, even to people who dressed or seemed odd at first. They tried to help one another out. When one player lost almost everything she owned in a house fire, there was a drive on Facebook to get her garb and gear so that she could come to the game and unwind after all that stress. This game was a community, one that prided itself on being welcoming and fair. People I knew only slightly called me by name—well, my game name at least. When I returned to Knight Realms after a brief hiatus, I walked into the inn right before lay-on to cries of "It's Portia!" That simple reception, the recognition of who I was, warmed me, especially since as a telecommuting writer, I didn't get out all that much—my idea of a social exchange with officemates was buying a cup of coffee from the taciturn cashier at my local shop.

It wasn't easy to pry myself away from the community. For one thing, my character never died. I tried to die—I wanted to know how it would feel. At Knight Realms, of course, there's a mechanic for death. Once your hit points drop below zero, you fall to the ground. It's advisable to fall loudly, to let out a gasp or a cry—that way someone is sure to notice you—and on the ground, you begin your death count. There are two rounds to the death count, each of which lasts five minutes, counted off silently. During the first round, called negatives, any simple healing spell or prayer can bring you out of unconsciousness. During the second round, one of four higher-level spells must be used, and you can only benefit from each of those spells once during the weekend. After ten minutes have passed, you rise and tie a blue headband around your head to signify that you're now a spirit. From that point, you have three hours to find a physician to reanimate you or a priest or healer to bring you back through the healing focus, which, depending on the healer and how many people she— for it is usually a she—is raising at one time, you either get a scene of phenomenally powerful role-play or something quick. During these processes, it is possible to get an insanity, which you must role-play for a certain amount of time at every subsequent event.

I wanted to die, and Portia, being naturally curious about the last great adventure, wanted to die too. I didn't realize how hard it would be. Portia has only four health points, which means that one hit from pretty much anything drops her into unconsciousness. During battles, I learned to stay behind the main lines, and so I almost never got hit. I couldn't run out and invite a skull bash because, first, that wasn't in Portia's character to do, but second, in group battles there are a dozen healers around, and I would have simply been healed back to consciousness. The best way to die, I concluded, is by skulking around in the forest by oneself. Surely some goblin or other NPC might find Portia and then gank her. By the time I'd figured this out, I'd gained a number of friends in-game who kept me buffed with valence armor, which bolsters a person's armor points for the weekend (armor points are used up before health points in combat), with displacements, which allow a player to ignore the next attack that lands on her by saying "displacement," and with other spells. On a more practical note, I'm a sort of paranoid person. In college, my dorm played Assassin once, a game in which each player gets an assassination assignment carried out by putting a Post-It note on his or her target. I spent that week glancing over my shoulder, taking alternate routes home, and walking around my dorm in my bathrobe because it was off limits to kill someone going to the shower. When my assassin finally chased me down in the Boston snow, I felt a sense of profound relief. I'd known who he was before he killed me, but the jumpiness at seeing him lingered for days. To put it another way: as Portia, yeah, not as Lizzie, but as Portia, I didn't want to walk through the creepy woods alone in the dark. The idea that things were lurking to possibly kill me freaked me out. I usually walked with a party, so

I never got killed. What can I say? My *Chronicle* didn't even generate enough ill will to warrant assassination.

I would have preferred some martyred death, but instead I simply stopped coming after a year and a half of regular game play. At first I felt a profound sense of loss. I missed seeing those friendly faces and engaging in some first-rate banter. I also had to walk away from Portia's many projects, from the *Chronicle* to her post as Drega'Mire's minister of information. I'd wanted to purchase an altar to better cater to the growing number of Chroniclerites in town and had persuaded a secretive family of witch hunters to let me station it on their land. I'd gotten engaged to one of the *Chronicle*'s advertisers as part of a ruse to draw out his undead ex-wife. At Knight Realms, the story seldom ends tidily or poetically because it seldom ends—there is always another phase spider to kill or article to write or business venture to embark on. Like a junkie searching for my next fix, after the first event I missed, I cruised the bulletin boards reading the highlights of other players. I read the postings on the in-game boards and sighed at missing a weekend plot that intimately involved members of Chronicler's church. As the months wore on, the game's hold on me weakened, and although I rarely missed the game itself, I missed the people.

My husband had missed me, away so many weekends, spending our precious income on skill points for the imaginary version of myself. He was glad to have me back.

Closeted Gamers and the Satanic Panic

We all "know" what the stereotypical gamer looks like. He is a white male between the ages of fourteen and forty-five, either comically skinny or egregiously fat, an inveterate mouth breather with bad skin who never leaves his parents' basement, where he lives, and who is constantly geeking out, if not to Dungeons & Dragons, then to Halo or World of Warcraft. He's forgotten more about Captain Kirk than we will ever know, and when he's not doing 2d6 damage to an orc while eating Cheetos and drinking Mountain Dew, he's dreaming that one day a real live woman will talk to him. While it's cool, or at least acceptable, to wear sports jerseys to the big game, American popular culture does not regard adults who dress up like Superman in the same light. And then, of course, there's the insane idea that role-playing games like Dungeons & Dragons are a gateway not to drugs and alcohol but to real-life witchcraft and Satan worship.

Given the stigma surrounding gaming in general and larp in particular, it's understandable that some larpers don't want the world to know about their heroic alter egos.

The stereotype about gamers tries to have it both ways. On one hand, there's the powerless buffoon of a man, good at math but a social failure, and on the other hand, there's the satanic priest who is covertly trying to recruit children into his coven. Before writing this book, I'd never encountered the idea that role-playing games are recruiting tools for the devil, but many gamers, typically those in their thirties and forties, took great pains to assure me that they were not, in fact, Satan-worshippers, a testament to the intensity of the Satanic panic of the 1980s.

While larp's geeky image derives, in part, from the geek culture of the sci-fi conventions that helped create Dungeons & Dragons and other role-playing games, its image as a tool of the devil and cause of teen suicide derives from a small handful of events that took place in the late 1970s and early 1980s.

The most famous case is that of James Dallas Egbert III, a kid genius with an IQ of over 140. He finished high school at age fourteen and went straight to Michigan State University afterward. That's where the trouble began. On August 15, 1979, the sixteen-year-old boy went missing from the university campus in a case that quickly excited national attention. His parents hired the flamboyant private detective William Dear, who related the story of Dallas's disappearance and discovery in his book *The Dungeon Master.* Among the peculiar clues that Dallas left behind were a note that read: "To whom it may concern: should my body be found, I wish it to be cremated," and a cork bulletin board that held a strange arrangement of pushpins.

As William Dear investigated, he discovered that Dallas had been involved in the local gay community, that he reportedly synthesized PCP in his dorm room, and that he was an avid player of Dungeons & Dragons.[1] According to *The Dungeon Master,* when Dear investigated Dallas's Dungeons & Dragons group, he discovered that the community physically acted out their dungeon crawls in the vast maze of steam tunnels beneath the university in what sounds like a primitive larp. The group's GM would hide treasures for her players in niches in the steam tunnels, utility tunnels surrounding the campus's heating pipes. An anonymous member of the gaming group told Dear that Dallas had recently been booted from the group because he was always high and because at age sixteen he wasn't emotionally mature and the team feared for his safety during their games. The private investigator became convinced that both the cremation note and the pushpins on the corkboard had something to do with Dungeons & Dragons. He pressured the university administration to search the eight miles of steam tunnels.

The media emphasized the incident's possible connection to Dungeons & Dragons. At the time, D&D was relatively new, popular mainly among college kids, and not very well understood. A September 8, 1979, *New York Times* article by Nathaniel Sheppard Jr. said officials believed Dallas might have gotten lost in the steam tunnels "while playing an elaborate version of a bizarre intellectual game called Dungeons & Dragons," while a September 14, 1979, Associated Press article chronicling Dallas's discovery noted he was "feared to have been an accidental victim of an intellectual fantasy game."

The real story was far more banal. According to Dear's book, Dallas had grown depressed due to pressure from his family to succeed in school and his young age, which isolated him socially. He ran away into the steam tunnels to commit suicide and meant the mysterious cork board as a map to the location of his body. In the tunnels, Dallas attempted to overdose on quaaludes and then spent a few nights at friends' houses before taking the bus as far as his money would get him, to Morgan City, Louisiana, where he worked in the oil fields for a few days before calling the private investigator. A month after Dallas disappeared, Dear flew a plane to Louisiana and retrieved the boy.

Unfortunately for Dungeons & Dragons fans, Dallas asked Dear to keep the details of his disappearance "our secret," partly because he was embarrassed about the incident and also because, as Dear wrote, "he did not want [his younger brother] Doug to endure cruel asides from his classmates and friends about his 'faggot brother, the dope addict."[2] Dear kept his promise, telling media outlets that the boy's disappearance had nothing to do with Dungeons & Dragons but declining to give further details. The damage to the game's image was already done. The troubled Dallas shot himself a year after his first disappearance and was declared brain dead several days later. After Dallas's brother Doug graduated from high school, the private detective wrote his book, but the connection between Dungeons & Dragons and teen suicide remained.

Dallas's disappearance excited the popular imagination, inspiring Rona Jaffe's 1981 novel *Mazes and Monsters* about four college students obsessed with a fantasy game, which was turned into a made-for-TV movie of the same title starring a young Tom Hanks in 1982.

Three years after Dallas's disappearance, another teen boy, Irving "Bink" Pulling Jr., killed himself in Virginia. Bink had been in the gifted and talented program at his high school and was a huge fan of Dungeons & Dragons—his room was full of paraphernalia. At school, his teacher served as a GM for a whole group of kids; sometimes they played in school as part of the gifted and talented program. Bink was also troubled. One classmate remembered him writing "Life is a Joke" on the blackboard in one of his classes, while another said that he had "a lot of problems anyway that weren't associated with the game," according to a *Washington Post* article on Bink written by reporter Michael Isikoff. On June 9, 1982, Bink went home and shot himself in the chest.

Bink's suicide created a powerful anti-gaming activist in his mother, Patricia Pulling. Pat claimed that her son had been normal before he started playing the game and blamed it for his death because during a session hours before he killed himself, another player put a death curse on Bink's character. According to the *Washington Post*, in 1983 Pat sued the school district for $1 million in damages and legal expenses on the grounds that the death-curse placed on Bink was "intended to inflict emotional distress" on a boy who was under "extreme psychological stress and emotional pressure" thanks to the game. The Pulling family lost its suit in 1984, although by then Pat Pulling had formed Bothered About Dungeons & Dragons, or BADD, an advocacy group dedicated to getting the game out of schools.

Interestingly, Isikoff's article on the lawsuit mentions that Dungeons & Dragons "has received publicity in connection with several bizarre incidents and deaths in recent years," and alludes to Egbert's disappearance and suicide. It goes on to quote Robert Landa, a lawyer for an anti-gaming group named SALT (Sending America Light and Truth), who calls Dungeons & Dragons "a lifestyle that uses witchcraft and black magic."

As for BADD, it became the go-to anti-gaming organization for media outlets. Patricia Pulling's 1997 obituary in the *Richmond Times-Dispatch* mentions that she appeared on *Geraldo*, *60 Minutes*, and *Larry King Live* to talk about teens and Satanism. Pulling believed that Dungeons & Dragons was a gateway to evil. As she told the Associated Press in 1988, "The majority of teenagers involved, people say, 'They're just dabblers.' I say, 'My God, the dabblers are the ones committing the crimes. They're kids, and they're killing people."[3] In a *Phi Delta Kappan* article on Satanism and adolescents, Patricia Pulling's out-of-print book, *The Devil's Web: Who Is Stalking Your Children for Satan?* is quoted as saying:

> Law enforcement officials and mental health professionals now recognize the fact that adolescent occult involvement is progressive. The child who is obsessed with occult entertainment may not stop there, but he often moves onto satanic graffiti and cemetery vandalism. From that point, he easily moves into grave robbing for items needed for occult rituals, and he is just a step away from blood-letting. Blood-letting begins with animal killings and mutilations and progresses to murder if intervention does not take place.[4]

Even Tipper Gore was not immune to BADD's dubious claims. In her book, *Raising PG Kids in an X-Rated Society*, she calls Dungeons & Dragons an "occult fad" and states:

> According to Mrs. Pat Pulling, founder of the organization Bothered About Dungeons & Dragons, the game has been linked to nearly fifty teenage suicides and homicides. Pulling's

own son killed himself in 1982 after becoming deeply involved in the game. . . . A fellow-player threatened him with a 'death curse,' and he killed himself in response.[5]

While Dungeons & Dragons had many opponents in the 1980s, both small-scale and national, BADD and Patricia Pulling were among its most vocal adversaries.

At core, the game's opponents made two different claims: that Dungeons & Dragons was an occult activity that could lead children into witchcraft and that Dungeons & Dragons created an immersive fantasy that could lead children to dissociate themselves from reality, a fantasy that could be used to manipulate children into performing abhorrent acts.

The claim that Dungeons & Dragons promotes witchcraft rests on several assumptions, namely that witchcraft truly exists and that it can be caught like a cold from a game. These beliefs seem silly; most adults discard the belief that magic is real along with delusions of Santa. Even if one believes that magic exists, it's not the sort of thing people learn in a larp. Sure, my character card says I have "learned" to speak High Elven, to heal people with my hands, and to fight with a staff. But that doesn't make it true. This is not to say that larps can't help promote learning, but in my experience, players tend to pick up general life skills, such as problem-solving techniques or leadership skills, not topical knowledge. After all, most conversations at, for example, Knight Realms, pertain to the imaginary world of the game—I might become an expert on the inverted tower or Kormyrian court etiquette, but that doesn't get me very far in real life (although Kormyrian court etiquette might bear some similarities to good dinner party behavior). Suffice to say, though I spent three years on the role-playing scene, I was never once invited to a ritual sacrifice.

The bizarre belief that role-playing games initiate children into satanic cults isn't limited to the hysteria of the 1980s. One only need do an Internet search for "Fundamentalism and Harry Potter" to see that such beliefs are alive and well. Some Christian fundamentalists launched campaigns against Harry Potter on the grounds that reading the books would draw children into witchcraft. As for myself, I prefer to hew to the defense offered by sociologists Gary Alan Fine and Daniel Martin in their essay "Satanic Cults, Satanic Play: Is 'Dungeons & Dragons' a Breeding Ground for the Devil?" Fine and Martin write, "Our belief that fantasy role-playing games are not, as a rule, havens for Satanists, is not proven, but is based on our faith in the secular character of middle-class, adolescent leisure in late twentieth-century America."[6]

The claim that GMs could use their authority to lead children into perdition is at least technically possible, but it's not unique to role-play. Any adult with authority—a teacher, a priest, a scoutmaster—could abuse that status.

The fear that a larp might attain such a level of reality that a player could conflate reality with fantasy is not entirely unreasonable on its face, but in three years of observing larp and other role-playing games, I haven't seen it happen. Every larper I've met has understood the difference between reality and fantasy; after all, the fantasy is what makes larp fun. Furthermore, larp groups like that division to be as razor sharp as possible. An individual who really believed he was a dwarven warrior would constitute a danger to other players, not to mention a liability risk. No larp wants that or anything close to it. A few larpers have confessed to me that at one time they were too into the game, but this is usually followed by "and so I left the game for a while to get my priorities straight," or "and the GM told me I was too into it and asked me to take a break from playing for a few months."

The argument that violent behavior in a game setting creates violent behavior in real life is familiar to fans of video games such as Halo, World of Warcraft, or Grand Theft Auto. Unlike a mechanized video game, however, in a larp or other role-playing game there is a human on the spot in charge of setting up the system of problems and solutions, and death in-game has actual consequences. Many of the GMs I spoke to find violence a boring way to solve a problem, and if players try to fight their way out of every situation, they'll create a scenario in which fighting has a negative effect, such as the end of the world.

Whether they're groundless or not, the stereotypes surrounding gaming keep some larpers closeted about their hobby. At parties with norms, closeted larpers would sometimes tell me that "the first rule about fight club is that you don't talk about fight club," their special way of reminding me not to out them as larpers. Some larpers tell their offices that they are "going camping with a big group" on weekends, and some say nothing at all, either out of embarrassment or because larp is complicated to explain and they don't want to go through the rigmarole.

Then there's Derrick, who went to great pains to erect a wall between his gaming hobby and the rest of his life. He asked that I not provide his last name in order to help maintain this division.

Derrick does not resemble the stereotypical gamer. He's tall, has the powerful physique of a former athlete, and dresses in oversized T-shirts and loose jeans. He's in his early thirties, has a young daughter, and has been playing the same character at Knight Realms since its inception in 1997. His manner is easygoing and open, as if he could get along fine at any social gathering. To meet him is to feel that the two of you share some old inside joke together. Once, I drove him a couple hours to a Knight Realms event, and he gamely endured a full five minutes out of my husband's avant-garde noise collection, about five more minutes than I can stand. And, of course, unlike the typical larper, Derrick is black.

Derrick's upbringing can account for both his congeniality and his love of gaming. His father was a military man, so Derrick and his five siblings grew up all over the world, in their New Jersey hometown, and in Florida, Spain, and Japan. The constant moves meant that Derrick had to make new friends almost yearly, and he became adept at introducing himself to new people and finding a place for himself within the school yard pecking order. The world travel also exposed him to a variety of different people, locations, and ways of living, which he says helped him learn to respect people who are different from him. Of all the places he lived as a kid, he remembers Japan the best, in part because of his age—he spent his early and mid-teen years there—and in part because the family stayed a relatively long time, five years.

Derrick first began playing imaginatively in Japan. Around age twelve or thirteen, Derrick and two of his friends spent hours fashioning cardboard boxes into mazes and castles. One of these play-mates knew an older kid with a Dungeons & Dragons set, and every Saturday they'd go over to the older kid's house and he'd GM games for them. Derrick liked being someone else, someone heroic, a knight in shining armor astride a winged horse, battling dragons. Japan also left him with another somewhat geeky hobby—a devotion to anime.

When Derrick was fifteen, his family returned to New Jersey, and everything changed for him. Before returning to the States, he hadn't realized there was a stigma associated with playing Dungeons & Dragons. Now, with his reputation at his new high school on the line, he developed two lives and two different sets of friends: one for Dungeons & Dragons and one for sports. In one life, he hung out with white boys, playing war games with miniatures for hours on end, and enjoying mini-campaigns of Dungeons & Dragons in which everyone rotated GM duties. In the other life, he was a track star who made it into the state-wide, and later the national, rankings for high-jump. At a national meet during his junior year in high school, he placed in the top ten by clearing a jump six feet six inches high.

The weight of expectation hung heavily on Derrick. His parents expected him to do well, in part because they had six kids and they wanted him to get a scholarship to college. As a track star, he felt like a minor local celebrity and feared that if he got into trouble, it would appear in the newspaper—it would be a big deal. He felt he had to maintain his image, and gaming didn't fit with "star athlete." If he were discovered, if his status as a gamer were made public, Derrick knew he would face ridicule. The fact that he occasionally hung with "geeky white dudes" baffled his athletic friends, including his best friend, prom king and star basketball player Dave.

It was hard to hide such a major part of himself from both his friends and his family. Derrick kept his game books in his closet so that he could close the door and lock away that part of his life when necessary. One day, though, fate intervened. For some reason, he had put his gaming manuals on his desk. As Derrick tells it, Dave came into his room, saw the books, and said something to the effect of, "What in the white bullshit?" But Dave kept an open mind and kept Derrick's secret, and the friendship survived.

Years later, one of Derrick's gaming buddies showed up for a session with a pamphlet about a new game called Knight Realms. Derrick went to the first event, which took place in a park and involved a lesson on how to make a boffer and a few tactical battles. He loved it. But the still-teenaged Derrick was involved in track at college, and it would be a big deal if he were injured. Derrick enjoyed the new hobby so much that he thought, "Track be damned, kill the vampire!" He didn't tell his coach about his new hobby; he made up stories any time he was bruised or tired from a weekend battle.

Eventually his family found out what he was up to. Derrick never told them, but his siblings deduced his secret from the equipment he kept in the house—they saw his boffers and started asking questions. The news spread like wildfire through his large but close-knit family. Derrick's devout, church-going parents still believe that Dungeons & Dragons is a devil's thing, that his gaming hobby is neither healthy nor holy. While he disagrees strongly with that attitude, he also respects his straitlaced parents and tries not to bring it up or make an issue out of it in front of them.

In his late twenties, Derrick made a brief attempt to come out of the larp closet. He admitted to Dave that he is not just a gamer but a larper, 'fessed up to two friends he's had for more than a decade as well as the on-and-off girlfriend who is the mother of his daughter. He had what he dubbed the "I'm-not-insane conversation" with them. Sharing his hidden gaming life with his friends hasn't been easy. His non–Knight Realms friends are, as he put it, "urban" and come from a certain mindset; getting them to understand larp and the desire to larp is like getting a fish to ride a bicycle.

Derrick has tried to keep news of his secret life from spilling beyond his immediate close circle of acquaintances, because he still fears the consequences of making his hobby known. He's negotiating the realm of geekery and the complicated expectation placed on him by family and society, the expectation that he be a strong black man. On one hand, American society sees black men as scary and intimidating, potential criminals, he says. That racism works in myriad subtle ways, the way someone in a car might lock the doors when he draws near, for example, because they see his race first and foremost. His family and his culture expect him to rise above that, to prove to the world that its expectations of him are wrong. A black man is supposed to be hard, he tells me. A black man is supposed to be strong. A black man like Derrick is supposed to work his butt off to prove to the world that black men can be hardworking, can provide for their young daughters. What a black man does not do, he says, is go into the woods on the weekend to engage in the childish activity of dressing up. That's soft. And he can't let it be known that he's soft. In fact, he says that as far as black culture goes, being unemployed, drinking booze on a downtown stoop would be more acceptable than being a larper.

For Derrick, Knight Realms is a huge stress reliever, a place where he doesn't have to live up to expectations, a place where he feels like he doesn't even have to be black, and a place where he can let his imagination play. Nevertheless, the way race plays out inside the game is complex and, at times, problematic. Most directly, Knight Realms, like many games, has a sort of pan-Asian race, in this instance called the Khitan. The race attracts players who are fond of anime and Asian culture, people who want to portray samurai, tea men, and maidens, wear kimonos, and behave as if dishonoring their people or their families is the highest evil. Derrick's longest running character, Shen, is a Khitanian and allows him to pay homage both to his love of anime and to the time he lived in Japan. On the other hand, such roles amount to essentially racial dress-up and, with it, the potential to be insulting. One Asian American player, who plays a garden-variety human, is constantly asked if he's Khitanian, his out-of-game appearance confused with an in-game race. It is insinuated, in one set of the usual pregame rumors posted on the Internet before an event, that the Khitanians have been killing cats and selling them for food at Market Faire. Is this racism? The Khitanians may be a fictional race, but they function as stand-ins for Asian people. By proxy, dragging up this old racial saw was offensive enough that several players posted on the boards calling it out as a cheap, racist shot.

"Racism" is permitted and encouraged in-game between the races that exist in Travance, which further complicates the picture of race at Knight Realms. In the rules, bigotry is written into certain race descriptions. Elves think humans are beneath them, for example;

humans distrust Khitanians; and of course, everyone is afraid of dark elves. These ingrained likes and dislikes make the world of the game more complex and realistic, a closer mimic of the flawed world in which we live. The stipulated bigotry of the rules can help new players develop their characters. A good-guy paladin who hews to the societal dislike of Khitanians, for example, has certain unique blind spots in his way of approaching the world, and a player then has to suss out that complexity.

It's all fine, so long as the racism stays completely inside the world of the game. When humans are racist toward goblins, for example, the racism seems abstract and permissible to me. On the other hand, dark elves are a common racial trope in fantasy games and one that plays uncomfortably on racism in the real world. Dark elves in Knight Realms have coal-black skin and white hair, and they live underground. They have a tightly knit society; those who go aboveground are branded, effectively excluded from the society, which seems an interesting reversal of the real-world risk Derrick feels he would run if his underground hobby were discovered. Marked dark elves are also commonly feared in-game; the race is considered terrifying and mysterious. In order to portray a dark elf, as a character or an NPC, all players, regardless of race, must cover exposed skin with jet-black makeup and either wear a white wig or spray-paint hair white. Literally, players must put on black face.

Derrick is famous for running dark elf plots in the game. I fondly remember NPCing for him at night in the rain once. He led a herd of us, dressed in and painted black, toward a clearing where we would ambush the town. He held a boffer shield over his head to block the rain. I was soaked and shivering on that autumn night and not exactly looking forward to hitting people. I needed a pep talk. Before we arrived at the clearing, Derrick turned around and said something like, "OK people, it's the weekend, and we're all out here in black face paint in the woods. We're all big dorks. Now let's go have fun."

After eleven years playing this game, he knows what he's talking about.

Derrick's not the only larper who doesn't want to be discovered. Meet "Brian," a police detective in his mid-forties who is slight of build and full of fear. Brian is terrified that his coworkers might discover his weekend hobby and asked that I withhold his real name and the city where he works to help maintain his anonymity. For the last three and a half years, he's been attending a larp with one of his sons.

Like many larpers, Brian played Dungeons & Dragons throughout high school and college. After college, he began attending area gaming conventions, and in 1997, at one of these conventions, he tried out a vampire larp, in which, at random, he was cast as a police detective investigating the occult. Brian enjoyed the game so much that when the GMs decided to run it on a long-term basis, he kept attending. The game, part of White Wolf's Vampire: The Masquerade franchise, relied on the premise that vampires keep up the "masquerade" by concealing their presence from humans. The game that Brian attended met in public places, from bars to go-go nightclubs, with the idea that if a player attracted the attention of the general public he or she could be penalized for revealing the masquerade. No one ever noticed Brian's group. Brian became fast friends with some of his fellow players, who recommended that he try out the game he now attends regularly.

At first, Brian attended this game at the behest of his middle child, and he's continued going with his younger son, "Peter" (not his real name), who is currently a tween. Brian credits the game with helping Peter break out of his shell. When they first started attending, Peter didn't feel comfortable talking to high-level characters. Now he's not only comfortable talking to high-levels, he's also started making friends of his own. As a father-son activity, Brian says the game has deepened his relationship with Peter, that it has provided the opportunity for father-son talks, that his son is now comfortable asking him questions about how to flirt, for example. Brian also seems to enjoy the game for its own sake and spoke to me fondly about leveling up his character and practicing his improvisational skills. Sometimes, he even attends the game when Peter can't come.

The way Brian describes it, a police department is gossipier than a supermarket tabloid. When they're transferred, officers are checked out on and off the job, and if you're involved in any controversy, it follows you from post to post. I met Brian a few blocks from his office, and we walked in the opposite direction to get a coffee. As a police truck drove by, he mentioned that this single sighting might open him up to gossip that he'd been seen with a strange woman in the city. Much as Derrick described the confines of what it means to be a black man, Brian described the confines of being a police detective. Officers are supposed to be all business all the time, whether they're on or off duty. They're supposed to be serious, sober people with serious, sober hobbies. Certain games, like card games, fantasy football, and family board games are acceptable, but nothing weird would be. And "weird" is a pretty large category for police detectives. As Brian put it to me in an e-mail, "There are coworkers who play computer games and even *they* are considered geeks, so you can imagine what a larper would be called. Psychotic comes to mind." Larp is at odds with the machismo of police culture, a machismo that manifests itself through endless teasing. In Brian's office, for example, if someone found an old yearbook photo of Brian with a mullet, they might tack it up on his desk. And if Brian removed that photo, he would have lost the challenge—to remove such a thing would be to prove that it had gotten to him. To this culture, the idea of a grown man "frolicking in the woods playing dress up" as Brian put it, would be downright preposterous, a trace of blood in the water to the circling sharks. If Brian's hobby was ever discovered, it would spread around the office rapidly, and he'd never be able to live the jokes down. As he wrote to me, "In police subculture, one is only known for his last screw-up. Meaning that no matter one's reputation, a cop will be known for a foul up, either on duty or off duty. I could not deflect any razzing I got related to larping. It would follow me FOREVER! All of my good arrests would be forgotten. Think of grade school bullying of a nasty variety and you may get the idea."

While Brian's extended family is well aware that he's a larper, only two people at his office know. One is a computer geek who understands, Brian says, because he's a computer geek. The other person who knows was surprised at first but calmed down after Brian explained the hobby in detail. He's not as sure of her silence, though, and worries that if she gets angry with him she might let it slip one night after too many drinks. That's just how Brian's department catches criminals.

James Dallas Egbert and Irving Pulling, through their suicides, enshrined the idea that gaming was geeky, dangerous, and bizarre in American culture, and it's kept men like Derrick and Brian firmly closeted at work and home and ensured that scores of others hide where they're going on the weekends behind such euphemisms as "camping" and "family time." In doing so, the stigma against larp forces some gamers to adopt secret identities, forces them to compartmentalize their personalities in order to live up to the real-life roles thrust upon them by circumstance. All this raises the question: when is a closeted larper not larping? Is Derrick more himself in real life, where he is forced to hide his love of fantasy because it doesn't conform to some role that society has scripted for him, the role of the strong black man? Is Brian any less of a detective or any less of a man because he enjoys harmless dress-up? The societal pressure to fulfill a certain role at the expense of any other desire ensures that the only place where a closeted gamer can be emotionally whole is that place where his or her personality and profession are both accepted: namely, at the game.

The Unwritten Rules

To say that the land of Travance has problems is a drastic under-statement. Mummies! Deadly plagues! Malevolent floating eyes! Heroes have managed to quell all these evils with swords, spells, and cunning, and yet, they have not been able to defeat one insidious foe, so inhuman and barbarous that even the greatest minds of our generation have struggled to subdue it: inflation. Even fantasy is subject to the laws of economics and, as it turns out, to modern political sensibilities, sexism, and the unknowable rules that govern the real emotions of players.

Travance suffers inflation because players have too much money and too little to spend it on, according to Matt White, a long-time staff member at Knight Realms who is deeply interested in the in-game economy. Matt likened Travance to a gold rush town, except instead of mining gold, its inhabitants kill monsters, loot them, and find hidden treasure vaults. This labor doesn't produce anything concrete, just heroism; characters are simply foraging for gold and introducing piles of previously uncirculated money into the game economy. The supply of monsters is inexhaustible, and while the monsters occasionally have problems with cash flow—sometimes there's no gold in the game kitty so they leave Logistics empty handed—still the adventurers who hunt them can't help but become wildly rich.

When the Knight Realms staff introduced Market Faire, it gave form to Travance's inflation, Matt theorizes. Market Faire takes place in the inn on Saturdays. Characters sell pickles, knitted scarves, hand-blended tea, candy, and much more—it provides a marketplace where loot may be spent. In addition, it's something to do on a Saturday afternoon during a natural lull in the game, and a player who has forgotten to bring food can purchase actual lunch with fake coin. However, the idea of selling real food for the fake money intoxicates some players—on both ends of the transaction—making prices exorbitant. A basic sword may cost one to two gold coins to purchase in-game, but at Market Faire that will hardly buy a steak sandwich. Of course, a poor character won't go hungry—most everyone is generous with their food, whether a character is paying for it in-game or not; the transaction simply makes it seem more realistic.

The formal trade system was a failed attempt to provide an additional set of potential purchases to players. The system is essentially a game within a game—the aim of which is to collect a full set of commodity cards and earn an extra point of build. Here's how it works: players may spend build to acquire a skill called "trade." Trades come with a specialty, so for example, Portia has Trade: Picklemonger on her character card, while other players have anything from Trade: Taxidermist to Trade: Cobbler to Trade: Winemaker. Each trade produces one type of commodity—wearables, durables, consumables, or luxuries—symbolically represented by commodity cards given to players with the requisite skill at check-in. Players may learn up to two trades and can spend extra build to pick up trade proficiencies—essentially advanced merchanting skills—which increases the total number of commodity cards received at check-in. Portia is a pickle maker and a soap maker. Her pickles are classed as consumables, while her soap is classed as a luxury, so at check-in I get a set of commodity cards emblazoned with "consumable" and a set emblazoned "luxury." A character with a trade such as tailor or cobbler would get "wearable" cards, while a character with a trade such as wheelwright or carpenter would get "durable" cards. Spend build on trade proficiency +1, and you get a larger quantity of cards. Though it is not required, many players choose to represent their trades in-game by selling real-life items for gold at Market Faire. So in addition to the symbolic pickles and soap (the consumable and luxury cards) I carry around with me, I also sell real pickles at Market Faire for gold coin, which enhances my ability to role-play Portia. The aim of this game-within-a-game is to collect a full set of commodity cards (one of everything, but three luxuries, for low-levels, double that for high-levels) by trading or paying other merchants. So, for example, Portia produces all the consumables and luxuries she needs, but she swaps her extras to other merchants in exchange for the commodities she needs—durables and wearables. Turn in a full set of cards to James, and you gain an extra build.

The idea was that some players, generally noncombat characters, would want to pick up trades and produce commodities, while adventuring types would use their gold to pay for the cards in cash to get that free build point. Plus, according to Geoff Schaller, the trade system enhances the realism of the game, because realistically, adventuring is an impractical occupation for so many people to have. It's much more reasonable to think that the battling bard is really a cobbler during most of his waking hours—the ability to acquire a profession provides an opportunity to fill in a character's backstory. The cost of acquiring the cards also simulates real expenses that a character would have each month, the expenses of food, clothing, and shelter. As a role-play tool, the system is successful, although it doesn't serve its intended purpose of creating an additional market where gold is spent; players who have commodities mostly wheel and deal among themselves, using the cards as currency, while players without trades move on with their weekend.

The staff partially controls inflation through price-fixing. For example, according to the rules, one minute of smithing costs one silver. It takes five minutes to make a basic dagger and ten to make a basic sword, so the costs of these items are five silver and one gold (equivalent to ten silver) respectively. There are similar regulations for the cost of sorcery. These checks are in place so that new players without much coinage can afford to have equipment fixed and created.

However, price-fixing isn't universally successful because black markets arise. Certain spell ingredients and materials needed to forge weapons and armor are very rare in-game. Take mithril, a nearly indestructible metal (borrowed from fantasy literature, most notably, J. R. R. Tolkien's work) that enhances the ability of armor to protect the wearer. Mithril armor is immune to destructive attacks and cannot be pierced by attacks that would normally bypass armor. In addition, it enhances the "soak" of a piece of armor. A soak rating basically allows the wearer to take less damage—if you're hit for five and have a soak of four, then you take only one damage. Thus, at Knight Realms, where long-term, continuous protection is rare, mithril is incredibly valuable. A character who wants mithril armor has to find a bar of mithril and pay a smith to turn it into armor. Although the laws of the barony fix the price of a bar of mithril at twenty gold, scarcity combined with a glut of currency has more than doubled the material's street value. To help alleviate the problem of scarce materials, players are now able to purchase them with service points.

Another solution to inflation is to remove money from the economy. The staff accomplishes this through taxes and fees. Each character owes five gold in taxes each year, payable to an in-game tax collector, and anyone who wishes to sell goods at Market Faire must pay a five gold fee to obtain a yearly trade license. The staff also removes gold from circulation by charging for certain items. For example, the Dragon's Claw Inn serves coffee, hot chocolate, and instant lemonade for a nominal in-game fee. If a smith wants to establish a smithy or a priest wants to purchase an altar, plenty of in-game gold is required. NPCs sell trinkets and other items in exchange for gold. Some coinage also goes missing when players leave the game either permanently or for extended periods, for example, while going to college in another state. Real-world economies usually suffer from hoarding or inflation, but Travance's economy suffers from both hoarding—because characters don't have to spend money on essentials—and inflation—because characters can potentially afford the high prices and because the merchants don't have perishables they must sell, which usually triggers steep price declines.

Cash-flow problems also plague the game, since hoarding is part of the larp mentality. Some players love carrying jingling bags of loot and will hang on to their coinage. James buys silver and gold coins for use in-game, hands them out to new players as starting money, and doles them out to NPCs to serve as "treasure" should their lifeless goblin corpses be searched. When players hoard coinage, a liquidity problem develops; there is no physical treasure for the monsters to carry into the woods. The game bank helps ameliorate the cash-flow problem—players withdraw and deposit their physical funds at Logistics. The changes in bank balance are recorded on character sheets, and the recovered coinage is sent out into the woods in the pockets of monsters. Matt speculates that this may actually exacerbate the problem of inflation as in-game money is not tied to the actual coinage available. Using deposited money as monster loot pumps an unlimited amount of money into the game economy, money that does not have anything productive backing it.

At Knight Realms, inflation isn't only a problem in terms of money but in terms of levels. Characters who have been around for all or most of the thirteen years of Knight Realms' existence—and there are many—are powerful and fearsome. The challenge for staff is to entertain both the level 60 and the level 1 characters with monsters that are interesting and fun. Send out an NPC geared toward the higher levels, and the low-levels, or lowbies, will have no chance to hit it and will die in droves. Send out a smaller monster that the low-levels can affect, and a high level player can kill it with one blow. In the latter situation, it is considered good manners for an upper-level player to stand to the rear, letting the lowbies do the job and helping only if they get themselves in serious trouble. Knight Realms attempts to manage level disparity by sending out different sorts of plot, plot that can be resolved through role-play, for example, as well as plots that are geared for high- or low-level characters. During main mod, the town might fight a powerful boss with a bunch of minions, with the idea that the lowbies will take care of the minions while the higher-levels take care of the boss. It's also common for an NPC to roll into town, say, "We've got to fight the goblins in the cave," and then add something like, "The enthusiasm of the inexperienced will be most useful in killing them." This translates to, "This mod is geared for people who are level 15 or under." In this circumstance, an experienced NPC uses his out-of-game knowledge to help select the low levels. It's a safe bet that those barbarians he's never seen before are lowbies, so they're asked to join the quest. Likewise, an NPC might go to a seasoned player and say, out-of-game, "I need people under level 10. Can you help me?" and together they'll round up whatever low-levels are around the inn, using role-play. High-level mods are denoted in the same way, with characters being told that it is "very dangerous" or "only for the experienced." Sometimes during the speeches before lay-on, a GM will advise players that main mod is going to be broken into two parts, one geared for people of level 30 or higher. Sometimes during main mod or other large mods, a magic field will suddenly appear that only allows characters of a certain level or higher to pass through to fight the monster or monsters inside. At times, the lowbies feel excluded by this type of mod entrance, but ultimately, it's the staff's way of controlling the crowd, creating interesting monsters for the higher levels, and preventing mass character death.

The economic situation of players also causes conundrums. Knight Realms has a diverse player base. There are tweens who arrive with parents, a lot of teenagers and twenty-somethings, a smaller but devoted contingent of players in their thirties and forties, and a few players in their mid-fifties. The occupations of these players include retired entrepreneurs, IT professionals, lawyers, union organizers, high school teachers, and waitresses, plus a number of high school or college students. Along with these differences in age and profession comes some economic disparity, and with economic disparity comes the risk that some players might be able to buy in-game status, and that doesn't play into the notion of fairness. It wouldn't be fair, for example, to walk into Knight Realms, lay down $5,000, and expect a level 50 character—that is something that has to be earned over time.

On the other hand, Knight Realms is a for-profit business, and so, as a sort of compromise, it is possible to pay to advance your character slightly faster than usual—James allows players to purchase one point of build at each event for an extra ten dollars.

James manages disparities in wealth through several channels. It is possible to "buy" certain in-game items with actual money, using Market Faire as a money-launderer. A player can turn out-of-game cash into food or other goods and then, through Market Faire, turn those goods into in-game gold. For this reason, Knight Realms has a rule: if it costs more than ten dollars, you can't sell it for in-game money. Players can also purchase an in-game benefit through armor, which provides a defensive benefit. Players receive armor points, according to the Knight Realms rule book, "based on the armor's type, craftsmanship, and looks." Wear a great-looking suit of full body armor—which can cost upward of $500—and you get more points. Of course, when players wear real plate or chain mail, the immersive atmosphere of the game is enhanced; the rule is there as an incentive to raise the standard of costuming, not to punish those who can't afford armor. Donations of money and time are also rewarded with service points, which evens the playing field. If a player can't donate money or latex weapons, perhaps she can make some time to organize the costume trailer or clean up after feast. Finally, with a large mortgage and a new camp to trick out, James has offered pledge projects to players—donate money in increments of $250, $500, or $1,000 to help improve an aspect of the camp and receive thirteen, twenty-five, or fifty build and a magic item.

Even the fantastical world of Knight Realms is subject to the laws of economics and, of course, the laws of nature. In an obvious physical sense, gravity still exists at Knight Realms, although for druids, turning into a bird and flying is possible. The laws of physics have been somewhat preserved inside the rules system as well. To weave a spell or pray to one's god for aid, a player must expend mental energy, for example, and a character's physical prowess is a combination of a player's natural strength and agility and skills bestowed by the rules, for example, the ability to deflect any one hit. A high-level fighter likely has several advantages over a low-level fighter—a lot of health points, a weapon that hits for a lot of damage, and so-called tag skills that allow him to disarm his opponent, resist certain attacks, or provide other benefits. However, a clumsy player will blow through these advantages faster than a skilled and agile athlete.

Unlike the rules of economics or physics, however, the rule of law in Travance is inconstant and disturbed by the modern sensibility of its players. Knight Realms is set in the 1200s, and a hereditary monarchy rules the land of Kormyre, though none of Travance's nobles inherited their titles. Rather, Travance's lords earned their titles, working their ways up from squire to knight to lord.

The medieval realism of Travance has limits. Unlike the real denizens of the 1200s, Knight Realms characters bathe, get their vitamins, and abstain from bubonic plague. Lords do not behead everyone who displeases them. And the townsfolk have suspicious tendencies toward democracy and the press, suggesting that everyone's voice ought to be heard, defending beleaguered Chroniclerites from censure, and grumbling about the directions the nobility shouts to them during battle, many players taking a "you're not the boss of me" attitude because during the week everyone spends time pleasing their bosses and aren't we all here just to have fun?

In-game racism also produces liberal-minded anxiety. Although racism is written into the game, the concept that all men, dwarfs, and gypsies were created equal is hard to shed. The rules might stipulate that most people in the Kingdom of Kormyre think that wild mages are part demon and should be killed on sight, but apparently only the most tolerant citizens in the country have arrived in Travance. In other words, few players practice the racism dictated by the rules, maybe because tolerance is so ingrained in players out-of-game, maybe because racist assumptions—even imaginary ones—create real-life discomfort.

This discomfort is heightened thanks to the fine line between portraying an emotion and feeling an emotion. Larp, with its alter egos and complex imaginary worlds, can create confusion between a player and a character. Sometimes it's unclear where the character ends and the player begins, particularly if a larper has really thrown him- or herself into the role. When a character tells Portia he hated a story in the *Travance Chronicle*, sometimes I have a gut reaction of anger and disappointment, which Portia channels in-game. Perhaps I'd be better able to separate the two if I were a more experienced gamer. Add the racism written into the game to the emotional mire, and the potential is explosive. It's possible to use the prejudices ingrained in the rules to be mean to a player one dislikes, but it's also possible to use these prejudices to heighten a scene or a rivalry between characters. Over my two years at Knight Realms, I most often noticed racism between players who were friends or at least long-time acquaintances out-of-game; in other words, racist role-play most often occurred in a friendly context where it had the least chance of causing permanent offense.

Sexism also plays a subtle role in the game's social dynamics. Chivalry and its sexist assumptions are part of knightly culture, and that culture is part of what draws gamers to larps such as Knight Realms. The rules of the game make no distinction as to gender— men and women can and do play characters of every class. While the population of larpers appears—based on my anecdotal experience of the community—to skew heavily toward men, Knight Realms has a surprisingly large population of women, one that has grown over the years, according to James. He hasn't kept track of the numbers, but I'd estimate that not quite half of his player base is female. And yet, despite the game's strong female population, few women have achieved titled in-game power. In the course of the game's thirteen-year history, there have been only a small handful of female knights—six out of about forty knights—and only two women have been appointed ladies of the land, out of about twenty-five appointed lords, though five women have married into noble titles in-game.

After discussing the in-game hierarchy with a variety of Knight Realms players of both genders, three reasons for the paucity of female leadership emerged. Generally, the lord slots are filled by characters and players who have been fixtures in the game for many years, and in the early days, Knight Realms skewed more dramatically male, so the pool of experienced male players is significantly larger than the pool of experienced women. Second, many women in the game play "support-class" characters, roles sometimes denigrated as "scenery" or "girlfriend-class," characters such as healers or priests, not the frontline fighters favored for positions of power in a medieval-esque setting. Perhaps related is the fact that many women in the game do not appear interested in amassing power or politicking their way into court.

Kristen is one of a handful of women to attain political power at Knight Realms. She asked that her last name be withheld since she works in a small academic field and thought an easily Googled connection to larp might hurt her chances of becoming a professor of comparative religion one day. Kristen began playing Knight Realms while she was still in high school. She had been a fan of fantasy literature and movies growing up, a love that grew to encompass tabletop role-playing games. In high school, a coworker at the pet store where she worked invited her to a one-day Knight Realms event, which she attended with her boyfriend. She remembers the flirtatious environment of the game; it'd been the first time anyone had really hit on her, and she found it flattering. Soon she was coming to the monthly events as the druid Elawyn, and she'd broken up with her old boyfriend and gained a new one. The split, like many romantic splits in a small community, earned her some enemies. For several years Kristen floated along in-game merely understanding the rules that directly applied to her. She thought of knowing the rules as a guy thing. She wasn't a great fighter either. The friends she'd made at Knight Realms encouraged her to do better, she says. They told her that she could do it, that she was capable; and as it turned out, she could and she was. Kristen wanted to move up in the in-game hierarchy, so she worked hard at memorizing the rules and became one of the first female rules marshals. For more than a year, her longtime boyfriend would run her through weapons drills to help her learn to fight better, and now she's known in-game as a frontline fighter.

Kristen has long brown hair, a girl-next-door face, and a trim, graceful body. On occasion, I've heard men fondly describe her cleavage. Although Kristen is all smiles, Elawyn is brash and intimidating, the personification of Kristen's hidden temper. Inside, Elawyn's character goal is to make her dead mother proud. My first encounter with Kristen occurred when Portia interviewed Elawyn for a story in the *Travance Chronicle*. I walked away from the conversation weak-kneed, intimidated, blood pulsating in my face, and with the fluttery feeling that some real-life catastrophe had befallen my family out-of-game. After the weekend was over, I e-mailed her through the game's bulletin boards to break the tension. Elawyn was made a knight of Pendarvin two years into her game play. Kristen says serving the town as a noble is hard for anyone but perhaps particularly hard for a woman due to the way our culture perceives women leaders. Many of the women I interviewed echoed this sentiment, noting that women who yell to corral the town during battle sound "bitchy," while men who loudly direct their troops sound "magisterial."

Over her six years at Knight Realms, Kristen followed a traditional path to power—she entered the boys' club on its own terms, by working to improve her command of the rules and her ability to fight—and in doing so, she gained enough respect to be named a knight in-game. Out-of-game, in overcoming the challenge of learning the rules, she gained confidence as a woman and as a person.

If Kristen followed the battle prowess route to power, Jen Wolfson amassed it through spectacular role-play, or RP. In a game like Knight Realms, combat and RP are two sides of the same arcade token, two ways to enjoy the game, pleasures that often overlap. Some people really enjoy the sport of boffer-fighting; they play to whack monsters with swords. Other players love politicking and talking philosophy in-character. Jen is one of the latter; she's got role-play deep in her bones. It began with an intense love of medieval fantasy fiction. By her junior year of high school she'd gotten a job selling fish and chips at the Pennsylvania Renaissance Faire, and from there she worked her way up to running the archery booth. During these five years she worked on her improvisation skills, perfected her British accent, and assembled a variety of Renaissance wear, which the community sometimes refers to as "garb." Her friends from the Ren Faire involved her in their D&D group, her first experience gaming, and finally, after she finished grad school, a friend of a friend persuaded Jen to attend a larp called Equinox. Jen instantly fell in love with the hobby. For her, larp was an extension of novelistic escapism; instead of losing herself in a book, she could physically immerse herself in a fantasy setting, becoming a character instead of reading about one. She found the game a good way to take social risks, to try on different personalities for the weekend, to give new conversational tactics a try. In-game, there might be consequences, but out-of-game, the risk was very low. After a few years she did a brief stint as one of four directors of another larp called Nocturne, and after she left Nocturne, she joined Knight Realms, where thanks to her role-play skills, her character quickly advanced.

A plump lawyer in her mid-thirties with shoulder-length orange hair, Jen radiates confidence in- and out-of-game. She named her bardic character Mixolydia after a musical mode, a throwback to her early college years as a music performance major. Mixolydia is unfailingly polite, quietly feminist, and determined. Somehow, Jen is able to role-play Mixolydia in such a way that it is clear that she is not Mixolydia and vice versa. I think the secret lies in her voice, in the way she uses her excellent British accent. Many players, myself included, talk casually with their regular diction and in their normal tone of voice as they role-play—they sound like themselves in a costume, which can create a conflation between player and character. Jen's accent and mannerisms make it clear that she is playing a character and not herself, which lowers the stakes in terms of in-game interactions with her. Hurl a racial epithet at the elf Mixolydia, and she'll respond, but Jen will not get offended. Not all role-players are able to create such a consistent and clear character.

Mixolydia quickly became a knight of Winterdark, serving the count. Although Jen's command of the rules is sketchy and Mixolydia is not a brawny character in-game, she'll feed, protect, or advise nearly anyone, and the goodwill she's generated is Mixolydia's biggest asset. I got an up-close view of Jen's role-play during an NPC shift late one January night. One of James's NPCs heard a chance comment from Mixolydia to one of her friends, the barbarian Tieg, and he made up a mini-adventure for the two on the spot. In the NPC cabin, he tagged me and another guy on the late shift to play the parts. We were young lovers, and as Mixolydia and Tieg came upon us in the woods they'd see me poison a cup and hand it to him. They'd probably stop us, and then they would have to uncover the backstory; my lover's father had killed my brother years ago, causing my father to die of grief and my family to crumble. Now, I was trying to avenge my family. James put a bench into the snow and lit the two of us with a red flashlight. I mimed tipping a small vial of "poison"—a tiny makeup jar—into a mug. Not so fast, James told me, he wanted me to tip the poison slowly and more obviously, so the players would be sure to see it. Eventually, Mixolydia and Tieg neared the scene, and as I handed the cup to my lover they interrupted us. I thought the scene would quickly end, but Jen became very interested in the well-being of my NPC. She arranged to speak to my lover's horrible father on my behalf, ensuring that I'd be sentenced to banishment instead of death. Her companion, Tieg, gave me marvelous advice in three-word sentences, and by the end of the scene I felt as though this throwaway NPC had undergone an important life transformation. Tieg and Mixolydia had addressed the situation with earnest serious-ness, and Mixolydia in particular was intense, willing to go the extra mile to talk to a character we hadn't even cast—my lover's father, played by James after a swift costume change. She made a convincing diplomatic effort to smooth the whole situation over. Jen's realistic role-play made me a better role-player and made my stint as this NPC fun and meaningful. Jen's ability to convincingly play a scene, and in doing so to elevate the game experience of her peers, definitely helped her character move up in the ranks of power. Her out-of-game talent as an actor helped improve her in-game status.

It's not always easy for women to get ahead in-game—Jen and Kristin's stories are the exceptions that show that it is possible, not the rule, possibly due to social pressure. As one female larper pointed out to me, fantasy games have a fairy-tale aura, and many fairytales fea-ture the passive princess and active knight, roles imprinted upon our culture and psyches, roles that are not so easy to discard, in real life or in-game. While the written rules of Knight Realms are neutral, the community itself enforces certain unwritten standards of behavior in ways that differ for men and women. Dressing up in costumes is part of the appeal of larp for many players of both genders. For men, the act of dressing up and paying close attention to fashion has the whiff of transgression about it. In order to become the proverbial hero, these men engage in an activity that is traditionally thought of as feminine, an activity that breaks free of restrictive ideas about masculinity. Many women take advantage of the costuming opportunity that larp offers by wearing provocative clothing: leather halter tops, corsets that make their décolletages impossible to miss. For women, costuming doesn't offer as great an opportunity to break out of gendered expectations; rather, it offers the opportunity to control the state of their own femininity by skewing further toward the Madonna or the whore side of the equation. Women are sometimes subject to male and female members of the bodice police, who comment, at least to one another, on who looks particularly slutty or bang-able.* In larp, as in everyday life, an unwritten code of rules governs the behavior that is acceptable for men and women, a code of rules that, as many feminists have pointed out, includes plenty of double standards.

The first thing one notices about "Claire" (not her real name) is that she is beautiful, tall, and statuesque. Her eyes are blue, her hair gold-blond, and she wears a ready smile. She is polite to everyone but uses that courtesy to shield her inner self from the casual observer, giving her a slightly cold or distant aura at times, as if she is cautious about revealing too much of herself. She gives the impression that there's a lot going on behind her smiling eyes. At Knight Realms she plays the modest elf Nina, a devotee of the earth-mother Gaia, and a healer type. Claire lives in Canada, and for five long years she'd make the eight-hour drive down to Pennsylvania or New Jersey to attend Knight Realms events. She first tried the game after the local larp she'd been participating in folded. She and her friends were shopping for a new game when they came across the Knight Realms website. Claire remembers being impressed at the level of stagecraft evident in the photos on the website—the latex weapons, the decorated sets,

---

* Officially, the game's policy on costuming for all players is that it be "publicly decent," and the costuming rule admonishes players not to "dress in a manner that is overly revealing or provocative," giving rules marshals the ability to "insist that you change into different clothing or costuming." My sense is that this rule exists mainly to keep the game PG-13 and players un-naked. I've never seen a marshal enforce this, probably because truly indecent dress occurs so rarely.

the high standard of costuming. In 2005 she road-tripped to an event and fell in love with the game. The fantasy fiction that Claire loves and Knight Realms offer the same escapist benefit to her—both allow her to experience situations far removed from the reality of her own life. In real life, people never get upset about dragons, so in a larp it's possible to have fun with that anxiety and to be silly about it. For Claire, the problems set in when her real and fantastical lives started to collide.

Claire always seems to have a boyfriend. She has dated several men at Knight Realms in succession, about four in five years, with brief breaks in between. The short lead-time between boyfriends revved the rumor mill, which speculated that Claire started cruising for a new guy before leaving her old one. Whether or not it's true is immaterial—the fact is that these speculations generated ill-will toward Claire, ill-will that often emanated from the protective friends of her exes.

One such situation came to a head in-game during my tenure at Knight Realms and involved two love triangles, one in-game, and one out-of-game. In-game, Nina was then Lady Nina, a title she gained through a politically motivated marriage to one of the lords of the four lands. The lord was absent from the game for a long stretch, and in his absence he asked his squire Darren, played by a man I'll call "Miles," to be Nina's bodyguard and companion. Claire and Miles decided to play out the relationship between their characters as brotherly and sisterly, and Nina and Darren were often seen together in-game. An evil-aligned character wanted to stir up trouble for the goody-two-shoes Lady Nina and wrote a letter to Nina's husband suggesting that Nina was adulterous. The letter circulated for some months, and the plot simmered.

In the meantime in real life, Claire was dating a man I'll call "Leo," also a Knight Realms player who portrayed a lord in game, though not Nina's husband. When they broke up, Claire started seeing Miles. Their fling was short-lived, and they soon split, in part, Claire says, due to intense social scrutiny.

At the next event, the adultery plot went public, and the baron held a public trial during which he asked the assembled townsfolk if they could vouch for Nina's chastity or if they'd seen Nina and Darren venturing off together unsupervised. Some of Claire's friends, who also played Nina's friends, spoke up for Nina in-game, and a couple characters played by friends of various exes spoke up against her. Lady Nina said, pleadingly, that no one had asked her what happened and that she'd gladly submit to inquisition to prove that she was telling the truth. The trial proceeded, her request was ignored, and it ended with honor combat between a knight of Nina's husband and Darren, Nina's champion, who ultimately won the battle. Claire felt that she, and not Lady Nina, was on trial and left the scene in tears. Miles, Claire, and Leo were all incredibly reluctant to comment on what had been a miserable occurrence for all three of them. James, who had permitted the trial with good intentions, as the resolution to an in-game, player-created plot, published a public apology for allowing it to happen. In-game, he also tried to minimize the damage—the count organized the honor combat for a time when the vast majority of the town was out fighting monsters and thus unable to watch. The count also passed a law saying that anyone found even speaking about the matter would be severely punished.

Clearly the circumstances around Lady Nina's trial got quickly out of control, as real-life events gave what was meant to be an in-game plot a different context. That such a scene was played out to its conclusion is proof that even very experienced role-players make mistakes. Whether or not the people involved intended this as a result, the trial read as a public inquiry into Claire's virtue—a slut-shaming, a way of enforcing a restrictive code of female sexuality in-game and out-of-game, a public commentary on a situation that really was nobody's business but Claire's, Miles's, and Leo's. Since that event, Claire has been on hiatus from Knight Realms. If she returns at all, she says, it will be after a substantial amount of time has passed, after everyone's tempers have cooled. In the meantime, she's started killing zombies with boffers as part of Dystopia Rising.

Lady Nina's trial is an extreme example of what can happen when real life bleeds over into larp, although usually, the out-of-game affects the in-game in smaller, less explosive ways. After all, any community of a couple hundred people is likely to produce some sort of drama and gossip. But in a larp, that drama has the potential to be reenacted, echoed, and explored in public. To me, that is the chief danger of larp, that life will imitate art too closely, and that once everything is out in the open, once the fiction is stretched to its breaking point, there is nowhere to hide.

Playing War

Everything boils down to war for Jeffrey Mclean. It is the common denominator of history for him, the core act that defines the world we live in. Jeff studies it now as a college student, but as a veteran, he lived it for more than a decade. And he's spent most of his life playing war as a larper and a World War II reenactor. War, for Jeff Mclean, is an inevitable consequence both of history and of leisure.

The collusion between Jeff's real and fantasy lives is not unusual in larp, where some aspect of the player appears in every character and the game world always mirrors facets of the world we live in. Occasionally this leads to explosive situations, as in the case of Lady Nina's trial, but more often the mixture of the real and fantastical is a good thing, proving that larp can be more than an escape or vacation from real life, more than a flimsy shell behind which a player hides his or her true intentions. Sometimes, larp is a profound expression of identity, a vehicle for self-discovery, and a therapeutic outlet.

As a child in suburban New Jersey, Jeff and his neighborhood friends would get together and declare, "Let's play war." Kids with fatigues would put them on, and they'd creep through the woods with their toy guns, shouting "bang bang" at one another. The wounded dropped to the ground and counted to sixty before rising miraculously to rejoin the fight. When his dad brought home a set of big boxes, Jeff used the cardboard to make a helmet, shield, and sword covered with duct tape. They weren't very realistic, but Jeff played knight with them, pretending to be a hero.

Around age ten or eleven, he began playing D&D, and a few years later he started his lifetime love affair with miniature war gaming, a style of game in which players pit armies of tiny figurines against one another on a game terrain. Jeff particularly enjoyed painting his own figurines, finding satisfaction in assembling his own army. In his early teens he played paintball and laser tag, which tapped into something written into his own DNA, the desire to become a soldier. With so many gaming hobbies, it was perhaps inevitable that Jeff would become a larper. When he was fifteen or sixteen, with a head full of J. R. R. Tolkien and the old movie *Excalibur*, he visited his local hobby shop and picked up a black-and-white pamphlet for NERO NJ. His first character was a warrior, and he arrived at the game looking for an authentic medieval atmosphere. Like so many other larpers, his first event hooked him. He couldn't describe quite why. Larp for Jeff was the roar of the crowd for a basketball player or the quiet of the woods for a hunter—something about the atmosphere drew him, made him feel this game was the real thing, not a mere dress rehearsal. As a kid he'd always wanted to be a hero, and now, as a warrior at a larp, he had the chance.

NERO, which later became LAIRE, introduced Jeff to the larp scene and its denizens, people he'd still be hanging out with years later. The future founders of Knight Realms played in the same game and floated on the periphery of Jeff's social circle. The high school–aged Jeff was a shy wallflower, and the way the larp forced him to interact with so many people, even to speak publicly on occasion, changed him. He became more outgoing, brash even, and comfortable improvising. He landed a role entertaining people at a local Renaissance Faire. Most importantly, though, through LAIRE Jeff acquired a circle of close friends. For a time they played a crew of evil knights—Jeff always preferred to play someone with a clear set of values, whether a good guy or a villain. Villains were easier, since they didn't have to follow so many rules. Jeff and his friends didn't do the bad guy thing halfway—at one point, they ganked the entire town.

Jeff didn't slack on costuming either. In the 1980s and 1990s, he says, players could assemble high-quality costuming—fake scars, cloth tabards, and fancy worked belt pouches—to express their character concepts. They could make everything appear authentic down to the smallest detail, but they'd still be walking around with homemade boffers, plumbing supplies covered with duct tape. It just didn't look right. Today players buy much of their costuming and weapons through eBay, boutique websites, and Etsy, but back then, in the early days of larp, during the Internet's infancy, such sites were years away. Then his friend found an ad for foam latex weapons in a magazine and ordered a sword from Europe to see what it looked like. While it wasn't up to today's standards of realism, Jeff says, it seemed awesome compared to what they had. Very sword-like. They sparred a little with the new weapon—a hit tingled more than one performed with a boffer, but not too badly. Over the next few years, Jeff cruised some nascent websites, and he bought a latex sledgehammer, which he showed to James, who agreed to allow its use at Knight Realms, which Jeff and his friends began attending in 1998. Jeff thought to himself, Damn. I want to see what they do for every type of weapon. His apartment became a veritable storeroom; he bought daggers, hammers, maces, pole arms, staffs, bows, even throwing daggers.

The same heroic impetus that drew Jeff into larp also helped drive him to join the army. At the time, it seemed like the natural next step to him. He had a strong military tradition in his family. Every male relative he had had served in the military for at least a couple years. Jeff thought of the military as a place where he could learn morals and develop a work ethic, a place that would help him mature, give him a focus and direction. At eighteen, he didn't feel ready for college and

was all set to enlist, but an accidental knee injury kept him from join-
ing until two years later, in 1995 at age nineteen. He bucked family
tradition by enlisting in the army—most of his relatives had joined
the air force or navy. In retrospect, he says he was naive about what
it meant to be a soldier. Many people who served in the 1980s never
saw combat.

Although he began in an armored unit, Jeff soon switched to
Explosive Ordnance Disposal, or EOD, essentially the army's bomb
squad. These troops neutralize bombs, land mines, and other explosives. After Jeff switched fields, he discovered that his grandfather had
worked in a similar unit, defusing underwater bombs during World
War II. In 2000, after five years in the army, Jeff wanted to use the
skills he'd spent so long practicing, to prove to himself that he could
do the job he'd been training for. The army tries to mimic reality, but
like all simulations, it fell short. Some of his instructors had been in
Operation Desert Storm and had advice and observations about how
it would or wouldn't be in the field, but Jeff wanted to witness the
reality himself. He switched into a new EOD unit that was deploying
on a peacekeeping mission to Kosovo, during which he got his first
real taste of war. He remembers visiting a Serbian base on top of a
hill and observing the bunkers below—there were about twenty of
them, each one bombed out, with a hole in its roof. His team helped
keep the roads clear of mines and submunitions—the components of
cluster bombs that scatter on impact—dealt with old weapons caches,
and marked minefields. His team blew them up in situ or collected
weapons for detonation elsewhere.

Kosovo was his first of four deployments. He went to Afghanistan
in 2002, in the wake of the September 11 attacks. His unit ended up
supporting Special Forces, which meant he got to see the countryside
and interact with locals, in part because Special Forces were helping
train the Afghan army. He saw combat. He helped deal with huge
caches of weapons the Russians left after the Soviet Union disinte-
grated in the 1980s and stuff left over from when the Mujahedeen
fought them. He saw rooms full of twenty thousand mortars that
almost overwhelmed him. He saw a lot of things. He doesn't like
to talk about it. An April 21, 2003, Army News Service article about

three EOD technicians and a Special Forces soldier killed in an explosion on the job quotes Jeff, who helped dispose of the fatal cache a year after the accident, as saying, "Everyone felt their loss. We're a very tight-knit community so when someone dies in the line of duty, their name doesn't just go on the memorial. We all remember them, whether we knew them from school or through friends."

When he returned home in 2003, he and his wife, whom he had married before his first deployment, divorced. In 2004 he deployed to Afghanistan again, destroying more weapons caches and working with the marines, and then in 2006 he had his fourth deployment, this time to Baghdad, where his team did a lot of post-blast analysis of destroyed vehicles.

Throughout all these deployments, Jeff always returned to his home larp, Knight Realms. His friends played a family of good-aligned paladins, the Tellinghasts, who were dedicated to the in-game deity Valos, the god of justice. Jeff played Aradiel Tellinghast, a knight templar of the church, a heroic character bound by the rules of morality. One of Jeff's friends says that Aradiel is Jeff, but better, something Jeff takes as a compliment. Aradiel had to go, though. Somewhere around Jeff's second or third deployment, the character became less fun. The fantasy world echoed the reality Jeff experienced during deployment. Certain aspects of the character—the way he stood in a doorway, protecting a family, for example—roused unpleasant feelings in Jeff, memories that he didn't care to relive. Aradiel, as a dedicated Valosian, saw the world in black and white and made decisions based on the courage of those convictions rather than on facts. Aradiel tended toward zealotry, and Jeff had seen the effects of zealotry firsthand. At first he didn't understand why the game suddenly created uncomfortable feelings in him. It took him a while to acknowledge that he had PTSD and to receive treatment for it. He mostly stopped playing Aradiel because he didn't want such terrible feelings to infringe on his fun.

The feelings, Jeff says, are the most real things about the fantasy fights that take place in Knight Realms. Boffer battles hint at the reality of combat: the anxiety that unknown bad guys wait quietly in the darkness, the adrenaline rush of danger, the flash of brotherly love that pushes one's body out of the attacking line after a friend falls, and the momentary emotions of doubt and loathing as the enemy rushes forward. While the quality of emotions might be similar, the intensity isn't. Boffer battles provide the sort of rush that a scary movie might, the secondhand rush of someone safe in a theater seat; the battles are only a taste, a pale reflection of what it means to have your own life and the lives of your compatriots on the line. At the end of the day, Jeff said, larp is imaginary combat. There might be bitter emotions about who got "killed," but nobody dies, and there's no blood.

When Jeff returned from his first deployment to Afghanistan, he became interested in World War II. He watched *Saving Private Ryan* and Steven Spielberg's TV miniseries *Band of Brothers*. These weren't his childhood war movies—they didn't show the Hollywood glamour of war; they showed the nitty-gritty dark emotional stuff, the complexity of what happens to soldiers during combat. There is no closer bond than the one between people who have held each other's lives in their hands, Jeff says. For the first time, he began to relate to the individual soldiers portrayed on screen. He started to study World War II. It attracted him not simply because of the films made about it but because this war had it all: technical accomplishments, individual sacrifice, and epic proportions. It had a morality to it. Best of all, it was well-documented, with plenty of material available right down to the mundane details of life in that era, details Jeff could really sink his teeth into.

Years later, after returning from Iraq—his fourth deployment— Jeff was stationed at Redstone Arsenal in Alabama. Before he left for the South, he did some web searches for larps in the area but hadn't found anything that wasn't three or four hundred miles away from where he would be stationed. He decided to investigate World War II reenactment units on the Internet and found a lot of active groups near his base. He had to decide what sort of soldier he wanted to play, and initially he went for aesthetics. German SS soldiers are notorious of course, but they also had the sharpest-looking uniforms. Jeff dropped that idea after investigating the price of a basic "kit," the minimum required costuming and props, which he estimated at $3,500. In addition to wanting a sharp uniform, Jeff didn't want to play a run-of-the-mill soldier but someone with a unique and special job. He decided to play an American paratrooper. The kit was cheaper, since it was made of canvas instead of wool. A group at a nearby fort in Tennessee was reenacting the 506th Parachute Infantry Regiment of the 101st Airborne Division, Dog Company, the same regiment that *Band of Brothers* had followed. Jeff joined up.

Military reenactors from whatever era, be it Revolutionary War or World War II, participate in two basic types of formal event. Most obviously, they refight known battles in front of the general public; they are living history. Many reenactors also participate in improvised private battles, sometimes called "tacticals," which have an outcome not determined by history. Tacticals are not open to the public and are akin to larp, with participants getting killed or injured based on the honor system. Like a boffer larp, Jeff says, some guys are there to fire blanks and act macho, but most are deeply into re-creating the look and feel of a particular moment in time.

Jeff, of course, was in it for the atmosphere. He did a lot of research because he wanted to be authentic and realistic so that he would understand what it had been like. He assembled his basic kit for about five hundred dollars and had it shipped to his office. When it arrived in its big box, his coworkers gathered around him as he opened it. They ooh-ed and ah-ed over the uniform, feeling the fabric and talking about how durable and tough it seemed. After fourteen years in the army, Jeff had become accustomed to his equipment—his gear felt like a second skin, completely natural for him to wear. As a reenactor, he had to get used to different equipment. For one thing, it wasn't warm. As winters go, the ones in Tennessee aren't bad, but spending the night outside with his reenactment unit, wearing only what World War II soldiers had worn—a T-shirt, shirt, jacket, and a scarf, maybe some gloves—he felt cold. In *Band of Brothers*, there were soldiers in blankets in their foxholes. Jeff read interviews with guys who had been through World War II in which they talked about how cold it got. This was the common experience of soldiers: the cold. He remembered how cold he'd been at times in Afghanistan, tried to imagine how soldiers in World War II had stood it in this flimsy gear, powered by sheer will. Reenactment was a way of appreciating other soldiers and what they'd gone through.

Jeff learned a lot about the war from the 506th unit. He made some buddies who invited him to shows put on by and for collectors of war memorabilia, some of them very high end. They treated the shows like museums, going to look at gear and photographs as historical research that might help them reenact more accurately.

At an event, two forces would meet. They didn't tend to reenact Pacific battles with Japanese because a lot of those fights were naval, and therefore logistically difficult, and because the landscape of the South mimicked Europe far better than the tropics. The Americans would set up on one side of the field, with the opposition, generally reenactors playing German soldiers, on the other. Most of the time the two sides didn't talk but simply stared each other down, Jeff said. But someone had to play the enemy. A couple guys in Jeff's unit were friendly with some German reenactors and introduced him. The German reenactors talked about Eastern Front battles, tacticals between Russian and German forces, battles held on private land that had trench lines dug for this very purpose.

Tacticals fought in realistic trenches interested Jeff, though only German or Russian reenactors could participate, so he'd have to change units. German reenactment appealed to him more than Russian reenactment, in part for ease of research, since the Germans had left behind so much paperwork. Over time, Jeff got to know some of the German reenactors, one of whom portrayed a *Fallschirmjäger*, a German paratrooper. The uniforms were interesting, but Jeff wasn't convinced that he wanted to join the unit until he researched the *Fallschirmjägers*, learning that they viewed themselves as chivalrous. He found photos of these German paratroopers giving first aid to enemy troops and initially believed that their record was completely clear of war crimes, though recently he learned of some documented misdeeds, which he has started to research. Like members of the EOD in modern times, the *Fallschirmjägers* volunteered for that duty and weren't conscripts. He bought a basic German kit, lucked into a reproduction Mauser rifle, and joined the unit.

His German unit commander was a mechanic, and people who owned era-appropriate Jeeps or *Kübelwagens* would come to him because he knew how to service these ancient vehicles. Reenacting with vehicles was difficult—a Sherman tank, the type the Americans used, isn't easy to transport to and from events.

The details are important to most reenactors. Those who aren't into ensuring that their clothing has period-correct dye color, for example, are sometimes called "farbs."* As Jeff pointed out, some people are lazy and will watch a couple movies and think they know everything they need to about reenactment. Jeff wasn't like that. He researched it.

Reenactors of any historical period can be insane about details; there's a common term across reenactment for people who are too intense about the minutia of costuming: stitch counters or thread Nazis. But when it comes to certain historical details, there were some unspoken rules for Jeff's unit. Websites for various units of *Fallschirmjägers* across the United States and Europe contain disclaimers at the bottoms of their pages stating that the groups are non-political historical societies who don't support or promote the Nazi regime in any way. Most pages also specify that neo-Nazis and other people with extremist political views are not welcome to join. And at core, Jeff isn't into Nazi reenactment because he's into Nazi ideology any more than a player portraying a necromancer at Knight Realms is into necromancy. For Jeff, reenactment is about simulating the feel of a historical period and imagining what World War II era soldiers went through on a daily basis. At the same time, Jeff's *Fallschirmjägers* never said *"Sieg Heil"* or did the Nazi salute because some boundaries are not meant to be crossed. The intent of reenactment, Jeff says, is not to offend but to entertain, enlighten, and educate.

---

* No one quite knows where the word came from, but as Tony Horwitz pointed out in *Confederates in the Attic*, which explored Civil War reenactment: "'Farb' was the worst insult in the hard-core vocabulary. It referred to reenactors who approached the past with a lack of verisimilitude. The word's etymology was obscure; [reenactor Robert] Young guessed that 'farb' was short for 'far-be-it-from authentic,' or possibly a respelling of 'barf.'"

Similarly, at Knight Realms, he remembers going out with a band of evil NPCs and one of them saw a village in the distance and said, "Let's rape and pillage it." Jeff quickly asked the player to come up with something else. They could pillage the town and cut off the right hand of everyone in it, or pillage the town and do something else, but that idea of rape, no matter how off-the-cuff and fictional in this setting, was off limits. What if there were a rape survivor among the players? It was unacceptable to even joke about.

Jeff moved back to the East Coast and retired from army life in 2010, entering college in upstate New York. He is a history major and plans to focus on European history and military history and to go on to grad school one day. It's a new chapter in his life. He still attends Knight Realms regularly and intends to return to reenactment now that he's found a German unit nearby.

Jeff spent sixteen years in the army, attaining the rank of sergeant first class. It's clear he has complicated emotions surrounding his service. He took pride in his work while he was enlisted, says he took care of "my guys" and his duties, exercised the skills he took so much care to learn, and felt that brotherhood with his comrades. But the wars also cost him his peace of mind. It took him years to come to terms with his PTSD. He sometimes talks about how the propaganda whitewashes the job of a soldier, which is to kill people.

Politically, he says he is confused but loyal. He has an idea of what Vietnam might have been like. He gives the distinct impression that he is glad to be out of the army. His close friend Joe Bondi, who has larped with him for the last twenty years, says that feeling is new for Jeff, that it was hard for him to retire and leave the bomb disarmament to someone else. Given his mixed emotions about the army and war, it's curious that all of Jeff's hobbies—miniature war gaming, larp, reenactment—have to do with war, fighting, or violence in some manner. Joe tells me that Jeff painted war-gaming miniatures while deployed abroad and that he suspects that they served as a tether to the here and now for Jeff. Jeff himself talks about his love for larp, which predated his long stint in the military, and how it introduced him to so many great people, like Joe or his roommate, Terry. He says this old guard sometimes laughs that in twenty years of larp, no one has died. Sure, people have had asthma attacks and twisted ankles, but in all that time, no one has fallen off a cliff or died of exposure or been mauled by a bear.

Maybe World War II reenactment offers Jeff a safe space in which to relive and deal with what he saw on deployment, a way to revisit it in an environment where he has some control over circumstances and outcome. Maybe he games for the simple pleasure of it, because he loves stories and has always been fascinated with war. Maybe he larps because in a synthetic reality, everything has meaning, and heroism is still possible. At Knight Realms, he started out as the hero paladin Aradiel, but now, twelve years later, he can't play that role anymore. Instead, he's created a new character and a new history for himself, a man named Radu Dragovic, a gravedigger.

Larp as Training Tool

A thick, putrid smoke permeates this place. Broken Jersey barriers and other rubble cover the ground. Lit-up oil barrels offer flickering light in the darkness, and in the distance, bright lights flash at irregular intervals. Machine guns fire continuously, and the cry of "More ammo!" sounds periodically. A small team of soldiers in fatigues and with guns on their backs has dragged two of their bleeding fellows into a cinderblock room, attempting to stabilize the patients while one of them calls in the injuries over the radio.

But the man with the book and the flashlight that gleams so brightly in the darkness is only calling someone in the next room to report mock injuries. This isn't real, but it's not a game either; the simulation, which helps soldiers practice lifesaving techniques under stressful battle conditions, is part of Combat Lifesaver Training at Fort Indiantown Gap, Pennsylvania, a National Guard training center. I spent a day visiting the site to examine how the army uses something very like larp to prepare its soldiers for real battle. This particular training simulation is realistic—these rooms have roused vivid memories for some veterans preparing for deployment.

It's not just the darkness, the rubble, or the flashing lights that give soldiers flashbacks, says Captain Adam Bickford, the medical operations officer in charge of the Medical Battalion Training Site at Fort Indiantown Gap. Most particularly, it's the smell that sends some soldiers back. According to Captain Bickford, the training area is equipped with smell generators that send out smoke that smells like war—like blazing diesel, sewers, or burning human flesh. The smell generators aren't military grade—they come from a special effects company. Captain Bickford's least favorite odor is the eau de sewer, which we're enjoying together. The smell is faint at first, unfamiliar, with a hint of rotten, and after ten minutes I'm still not used to it; its unpleasantness has become pervasive without becoming more intense, a fragrant backdrop to the action. Captain Bickford warns me that the smell clings to clothing. If they don't open the doors and fan out the room, it can linger for weeks. Sometimes after training, he says, they run a coffee odor through the smell generators to help clear the rooms.

The tapes of machine gun fire are less high-tech. I wonder if they are recordings taken during battle, but Captain Bickford informs me that they're audio tapes from a Hollywood sound website.

He takes me and Major Corey Angell, the post's public affairs officer and my escort for the day, into another room, this time one with the lights on, although it is also filled with sewer smoke. Captain Bickford says that they must have just finished up training in this room. When we walk through the doorway, we appear to be standing on some sort of porch. In front of us, a door leads into a shed-like structure with windows cut into it, a mock house made with drywall and two-by-fours. A poor legless, armless dummy lies on the ground inside, rubber lips open. To our right is a deck with a banister and steps that lead down to the ground, out into a large open space. There is a human hand lying on the banister—well, a firm rubber hand with realistic modeling and a wire loop coming out of the wrist.

Captain Bickford says that the army, and sometimes teams of state and local first responders, including the Veteran's Affairs emergency medical response team, practice house rescues here. The army sometimes uses amazingly lifelike moving dummies controlled by computer for training, he says. In fact, for Halloween he is thinking of dressing up this area as a haunted house and inviting military families inside. We all laugh. For a moment, he's thinking like a larper instead of an army captain.

As we're leaving, another door opens, a door down the deck stairs and across the room from us, and several soldiers in fatigues enter. Apparently they've forgotten their poor patient's hand and have returned to retrieve it. We leave quickly to allow them to complete their exercise in peace.

These simulators are a part of the training for combat lifesavers and combat medics at Fort Indiantown Gap. Of course, the army trains medics before deployment, but it also trains many ordinary soldiers in a variety of EMT-like duties, from controlling bleeds to chest decompression to treating a collapsed lung. Training begins with classroom instruction and practice on dummies, and soldiers work their way up to the elaborate scenarios filled with stressors. The goal for combat lifesavers is to make the techniques so automatic that they can perform them under pressure. The lights, the smoke, and the smell are all part of increasing the stress a trainee is under. In advanced scenarios the army also uses moulage kits, essentially makeup kits, to make realistic, stomach-turning wounds on live patients in order to help combat lifesavers and medics learn to assess injuries. Moulage simulates any kind of visible injury, including bruises, burns, compound fractures, open wounds, and, at the highest levels, amputation. Combat lifesavers learn basic techniques, while medics require a more complex and deeper understanding of injuries, and the intricacy of moulage used to simulate wounds varies accordingly. At its simplest, moulage is fake blood purchased from a Halloween store, but if there's the budget for it—and at Fort Indiantown Gap there is—it includes high-quality fake blood, makeup, and latex prosthetics. Captain Bickford says that he's got some guys with art backgrounds who help create prosthetics and a couple who have been trained at the military's moulage school, where they learn to create and apply realistic moulage.

When it came to moulage, I knew what Captain Bickford was talking about—it's possible he and my larpers bought their supplies from the same theatrical company. During my brief tenure at the zombie apocalypse larp Dystopia Rising, I'd seen "infected" characters with gross open wounds on their necks or bullet wounds created from bits of latex and fake blood. Players created these looks by either buying premade latex wounds or using liquid latex to create their own prostheses. They would attach, for example, the circular ridge around a bullet wound to their skin with spirit gum, camouflage the edges with a flesh-toned makeup, and paint the oozy parts with bottled fake blood. It's probably not as realistic as army-created injuries because, well, zombies aren't realistic, but the wounds are made of the same core ingredients.

As it turns out, the army and a larp game have much more in common. They're both communities with their own strange activities intended to bond participants: basic training in the case of the army and larp in the case of larpers. Larpers wear costumes; soldiers wear uniforms. Larpers come from different walks of life, and so do members of the National Guard. Soldiers learn tactics, while many larpers enjoy tactical games.

The army and a larp both constitute subcultures with their own distinct languages, based heavily around acronyms. For example, larpers enjoy talking OOG (out-of-game) and IC (in-character) with NPCs (nonplayer characters). But in the land of acronyms, the army is truly king, or perhaps should I say HRH (His Royal Highness). It has departments like the PTAE (Pre-mobilization Training Assistance Element), which organizes a lot of role-play and teaches TTP (tactics, techniques, and procedures) to soldiers according to their MOS (military occupation specialty). One sergeant even joked to me that the army is full of TLAs—three-letter acronyms.

But at the end of the day, larpers play at going to war while soldiers actually go. The point of larp is fun, and the point of the army is to win wars. Yet the army jargon for going to war, for deploying, is being "in theater," a phrase that suggests performance and playing a role. Given the army's training activities, the word *theater* is oddly appropriate.

Fort Indiantown Gap contains a fake Arab town called the Combined Arms Collective Training Facility, or the CACTF (pronounced cack-tiff) for short. It's on a small paved hill in the middle of the woods. It's got a mosque that peculiarly resembles a New England country church, complete with a graveyard filled with round cement gravestones. Next to the church, there's a pile of rubble ringed by a round asphalt drive. The rest of the town consists of about three blocks of buildings, including residences, half-finished cinderblock structures, a police station, a hotel, and an open-air market with stalls made of timber. A short distance away lies the shell of a burnt-out car. Underneath the words "Police Station" and "Hotel" their translations are stenciled in Arabic lettering. Inside, the hotel is sparsely furnished with desks in some rooms, bureaus, the odd stack of mattresses, and bookshelves.

First Sergeant William Hyatt is an instructor with the PTAE, which manages, runs, and coordinates training at Fort Indiantown Gap, and he shows me around the CACTF on my visit. Like most of the people in charge of training soldiers who are about to deploy, he has recently returned from a tour of duty; he returned from Iraq in July 2006, shortly before taking the post. The theory is that soldiers recently returned from deployment will be up on the most current insurgent tactics and therefore able to help train deploying soldiers accordingly, Major Angell says.

At the CACTF, Sergeant Hyatt shows me the little details that make this fake town mimic the real ones he fought in abroad. He points out the thousand places where an enemy could be hiding. For starters, the buildings are rife with sniper nests, tiny holes in some of the interior and exterior walls at about knee height, some of them covered with tape or cardboard. He informs me that insurgents use these both visually, to watch people approaching the building or inside it, and as sniper holes, akin to the narrow arrow-slits in medieval forts and castles. In the basement of the "hotel," a bookcase hides a tunnel that leads underneath the town, into a sewer system. This part of the design makes the CACTF a truly three-dimensional training facility, he says, since enemies can be stationed on top of buildings, inside them, and below them, like a real city. In one of the townhouses down the street there is a weapons cache set up with mock trip wires and traps, like real weapons caches are. Rush to discover what's inside the cache, and a soldier could end up "dead." The graveyard outside the church is important, Sergeant Hyatt says. Sometimes during exercises they stage burials there, because insurgents have been known to bury large caliber weapons and rockets in fresh graves.

During scenarios, the military used to use laser guns to simulate live fire but has since ended the practice since laser guns aren't realistic enough. Plywood stops lasers, for example, while a real bullet rips through to whoever is standing behind it. For this reason, most training scenarios use real weapons, to give soldiers the experience of feeling the recoil of a gun. Usually, the guns fire blanks, with an honor system determining who dies or is wounded, along with a set of observer-controller trainers who monitor the fight and tell soldiers when they're out of play or wounded. Sometimes the soldiers use rubber bullets, which hurt when they hit but don't do permanent damage.

Toward the rear of the town, behind the hotel, the wooden remains of a mock open-air market flank a paved road. Sergeant Hyatt conjures the image of a training exercise for me, lots of soldiers dressed in flowing robes and head-wraps pretending to be locals, while one of them, one bad guy, needs to be winnowed out. Nearly everyone is a civilian in that scenario, and there's only one bad guy. How do you tell who's who? That's realism, he says.

The CACTF is a $10 million town, finished by the government contractor ECI in 2008, and it has been wired within an inch of its fake life. It contains seventy-two cameras, which can be moved to different areas of the town depending on which parts of it are "in-play" during a training exercise. The cameras can shoot during the daytime and have infrared settings for night. The town is also wired for sound, with speakers capable of generating noises from dogs barking to kids crying to gunshots, helicopter rotors, and the Muslim call to prayer. Some of the furniture has outlets under it where the HUTs, human-urban targets, basically remote-controlled dummies, can be wired.

All of these speakers, cameras, and dummies are controlled from the Range Operations Center, a small building perhaps a mile away that is staffed by Raytheon Technical Services Company, another government contractor. David Moyer, a forty-something veteran of the first Gulf War, works in the control center as an electronics technician. At the end of a training session, Moyer and his team edit the video footage and screen it for the trainees. The camera gives an objective picture of what goes on during training scenarios. Soldiers who didn't learn what's being taught correctly can actually see where they went wrong, and it's hard to deny one's own mistakes when they're caught on tape.

The CACTF isn't only used by the military. Federal, state, and local first responders, including SWAT teams, police, and EMTs also use the facility to test their preparations for emergency situations. A group might practice setting up decontamination tents in case of a nuclear explosion or coordinating between a SWAT team retrieving "bodies" from the rubble, in reality dummies stamped with numbers indicating their injuries, and medical teams decontaminating and treating the bodies.

Not every training scenario is high tech. Sergeant Hyatt also takes me to see something called lane training, a battle drill designed to help a single squad, a collection of about twelve to fifteen soldiers, put together several tasks it's learned. The point of this exercise is not to simulate combat but to show the squad what to do in combat, Sergeant Hyatt says. Today, two squads from the 131st Transportation Company will be "walking the lane" and will practice responding to direct and indirect fire, responding to flares, moving around an obstacle, and several other tasks. This exercise will be "dismounted," or on foot. The 131st Transportation is not primarily a fighting unit; rather, its function is to supply other troops with fuel, water, food, ammo, and anything else, using trucks. Because their function is not necessarily to fight, they are what Sergeant Hyatt calls "soft targets" for insurgents, as opposed to the "hard targets" of infantry companies, for example. But due to the number of improvised explosive devices (IEDs) that insurgents are using in Afghanistan, these support units are now very likely to face combat, and so training is geared to hone their basic soldier skills. They may not be kicking in doors, but it's possible they'd face small arms fire with a disabled vehicle. The two squads that I will watch are relatively green and have not worked together before—this will be their first foray into battle conditions as a team.

We begin at a shanty town the size of a city block, set around a central square. The town consists of a collection of giant steel shipping containers that have doors and windows cut into them, some stacked two high to create buildings that have stairs leading to a second story. Everyone is milling about outside, waiting for instruction.

The two squads are briefed on today's mission. The mansion in town, one of the two-story buildings, is a known Taliban stronghold, and there may or may not be Taliban there when they arrive. Each of the squads will walk the lane on its own. We all drive up to the start of the lane, about three-quarters of a mile away. Each squad has its own leader and divides into two teams, each one with its own leader. The squad leader establishes a chain of command; if he should go down, or his second should, there is a third person in charge. Everyone jumps up and down to make sure his equipment—his flak jacket, helmet, water, ammunition clip—is secure. They must be wearing at least fifty pounds of gear. For the most part, they are armed with rifles that have a yellow block screwed into their barrels, which creates a seal so that when the gun fires a blank it will recoil as if firing a real round. The soldiers talk among themselves, doling out numbers that will determine how they will cover doorways once they get to town. They receive cautions not to fire at someone's face and not to fire at civilians. They psych themselves up, saying things like, "Let's do this together. Let's get home together."

They walk two by two on the road down to the town, a gravel lane that wends its way through woods and fields. Two veterans follow behind. They will give hints and suggestions if the squad really seems stuck. They will also tell a soldier when he or she is "out of play," should one be felled by fire. The first squad to walk the lane encounters an enemy on the hill, hiding behind a tree below them and firing up through a field of tall grass. The squad drops to the ground to avoid being hit and in hopes that the enemy may not have seen all of them, Sergeant Hyatt says. He and I are strolling behind them. The soldiers gather behind one section of the grass and scrubby brush and perform a flanking maneuver, with one group establishing a base fire and another, mobile group flanking to the left, pinning the OPFOR, the opposing force, between them. The enemy is wearing a headdress and a long robe over his army fatigues for the role. One of the soldiers gets left behind. When the team splits, he doesn't go left or right, and so he's told that he's now "out of play" and he mock limps down the road for a stretch and then returns to his team to get practice with the next obstacle, which is a line of razor wire stretched across the road.

Such wires can be trapped with explosives, Sergeant Hyatt tells me. The squad takes positions on the ground on either side of the road, and one member takes a grappling hook on a long rope, swings it, and sends it sailing toward the wires. As soon as he's thrown it, he hits the ground. The hook misses the wire, so he stands up and does it again, pulling the razor wire toward him. Nothing happens. A nearby piece of carpet is placed over the wire so that everyone can walk over it and on toward town.

No sooner is the squad across the wire than a rocket-propelled grenade is fired at them from afar, in this case represented by a small-ish, pale yellow football fired out of a grenade launcher. The soldiers again hit the ground. Sergeant Hyatt picks up the rubber projectile and hands it to me.

Finally, after a few more trials and tribulations, the squad reaches "town," where a group of soldiers awaits them. There are three men in the main square, wearing their army tops inside out to denote the fact that they are, essentially, NPCs. One of them sits on top of a couple benches in front of a door that leads into the mansion courtyard, while the other two mill about with loose joints, pretending, perhaps, to be drunk. As the soldiers enter, these NPCs keep attempting to interact with them. The one in front of the courtyard door offers to sell them bullets in a mock Arabic accent. The other two do anything in their power to distract the soldiers, from walking into their personal space and gyrating to falling down in front of doors. The first group of soldiers negotiates all this with a little fumbling but eventually makes it into the two two-story buildings and successfully "kills" the hiding Taliban who are firing on them. When the second squad approaches the end of the lane, they choose to enter town through its main entrance, and one of the NPCs, one of the mock-drunk ones, runs at them, and they fire on him, killing him. He says something like, "Jeez, guys, not good. I'm an unarmed civilian!"

Sergeant Hyatt speaks quietly into my ear, telling me that if a guy ran at him like this in a situation like this, he probably would have fired too. One of the realistic portions of this scenario, Sergeant Hyatt says, is that there aren't many people around in the mock-town. Soldiers in theater call it the ghost town effect—when a town empties out during the day, it often means that the locals have gotten wind of an impending attack and fled. We watch the second squad successfully displace the man selling bullets and cover the doorway into the courtyard. One man checks it for traps by hovering his hand a few inches away and tracing the doorjamb in the air. Someone inside the mansion fires at the soldiers in the doorway, but they make it through, one by one. Doorways like this are called "fatal funnels," Sergeant Hyatt tells me.

With the lane successfully completed, the soldiers gather for an AAR, an after action review, a sort of mini-workshop where the officers who watched the scenario give feedback to the squad and review what happened.

In some ways, the army and larpers have similar aims when it comes to role-play—they aim at realism. In larp, this can mean a reality populated with magic-wielding elves, but it's a world with consistent laws, while in the army it means simulating battlefield conditions as closely as possible. For larpers, the simulation is as much art as it is science—James pats leather-covered books and wooden casks into shape at Knight Realms in hopes of making the game seem more real. If he's trying to mimic anything, it's something that only exists in fantasy novels. The army, on the other hand, takes a more scientific approach. It examines the physical realities of life on the battlefield—the sights, the sounds, the smells—and tries to mimic them for soldiers with fake towns and moulage, smell and smoke generators, soundtracks, and recoiling guns. The less tangible portions of reality on the battlefield—the stress of having one's life on the line—can't be physically replicated, although the army does its best by adding a time clock and shouting instructors to medical "trainees" in hopes of amping up the stress. Larp is all about feeling the emotions of a character, while army training seeks to make certain potentially life-saving skills reflexive so that in an emergency, the proper procedures are followed in spite of the emotions a soldier might be feeling. In this way, although the army's training simulations do have the element of fun in them—the "NPCs" have a good time laughing and cavorting during lane training—it's fun with a deadly serious bent. It's absurd and hilarious that some trainees leave a fake rubber hand on the balcony, until it's a human hand lying in a combat zone. While the army's training simulations have some hallmarks of a game—a defined beginning and end, an intermediary filled with puzzles, and a set of victory conditions—they fail the ultimate hallmark of games, that they be without purpose and exist for the sake of themselves. Larp's purpose is an escape from reality into a more interesting world; army training simulations aren't an escape, but they do introduce soldiers into a reality that is hopefully more interesting than anything they'll see in real life.

The armed forces aren't the only institutions that use larp-type techniques for training purposes. Medical schools hire fake patients to help new doctors learn to diagnose illness and to train them in the fine art of the bedside manner. The FBI has a town, similar to the CACTF, called Hogan's Alley, where its agents practice drug busts and learn to interrogate "criminals," and law schools have mock trials and moot courts. These simulations help people practice skills they've learned in a low-stakes environment, and the settings of these scenarios mimic the world we live in. For new units walking the lanes in the army, these training simulations are essentially drills intended to hone physical skills. However, role-play can also be subtle, its unreality used to reveal functioning truths of human interaction and to help workers practice less concrete interpersonal skills.

Stephen R. Balzac has just this aim. He is the president of 7 Steps Ahead, LLC, an organizational consultancy company. On occasion, when the situation calls for it, he runs larps for clients aimed at helping

uncover and change office dynamics. Stephen has a lot of practice creating complex games—he's been writing and running them for more
than two decades. In 1983, while he was in college, he started the MIT
Assassins' Guild, a live role-playing group that helped shape theater-
style improv on the East Coast, together with Harvard's Society for
Interactive Literature (SIL). After receiving a master's in computer
science from MIT in 1987, he moved to California and started a satel-
lite branch of SIL called SIL West.

Over the next decade, Stephen continued to write and run games
with SIL West, which had a lot of members from high-tech industries.
Stephen noticed the connection between in-game and out-of-game
behavior when his players began commenting that some in-game
events reminded them of things that had happened at their offices.
After playing Stephen's games, some players mentioned that the scenarios made them recognize what was missing from their jobs. One
woman quit her job as an attorney after a game that made her realize
she hated it; instead, she became a corporate counselor at a high-tech
company. Another lawyer ended up running for judge, having met
his future campaign manager in-game while they were trying to rig
an election.

Stephen didn't have his eureka moment until 2001, when he ran
a game called Secrets of the Necronomicon. Stephen had written the
game in 1992, basing it on the writings of H. P. Lovecraft, a gothic
horror writer of the early 1900s, best known for the story "Call of
Cthulhu." He'd run this game successfully three or four times before,
so what triggered his epiphany wasn't the game but the people who
played it. Stephen worked for a bioinformatics company at the time
and invited a bunch of his officemates to participate, and a whole
group of them came out and played. In the weeks afterward at work,
where the game was a topic of conversation among his coworkers,
Stephen noticed that they behaved in the same way at the office as
they had at the game. The quiet guy who had run his team ineffec-
tually during the game had trouble coordinating and working with
other people in the office. The statistician who had methodically figured out how magic worked in the game was very analytical at work.

The CEO who used loopholes to bilk his colleagues out of the raises he'd promised behaved in a sleazy manner in-game.

After Secrets of the Necronomicon, Stephen realized that there was a strong correlation between behavior in a larp and at work. He left his job and returned to school for a master's in organizational psychology and founded his consultancy company after graduating. Now he is also an adjunct professor of psychology at Wentworth Institute of Technology and sits on the boards of the New England Society of Applied Psychology and the Society of Professional Consultants.

For Stephen, creating a game to help solve a business problem is more art than craft. First and foremost, the game must have a good story, because a good story keeps people interested. Second, this good story must be constructed in such a way that the issues, whatever the group wants to work on, arise organically; otherwise the game will feel forced, like an after-school special. Finally, while the game world must be consistent and operate in a logical fashion, its setting should be somewhat fantastic, transparent enough that players can see themselves and their problem behavior in their characters, but far enough removed from the reality of the actual office that a player has the ego-saving excuse of, "It wasn't me who did that; it was my character." For Stephen, every simulation tries to evoke an emotional reaction or reveal an emotional truth about how coworkers interact with each other. Whatever the dynamics found in an office, Stephen finds that they will come out in a game. The game functions as a sort of Rorschach inkblot—when put in an unfamiliar situation, a group of people will revert to doing what they feel most comfortable doing. He says that it's not important which patterns manifest but rather that something will manifest and allow for later discussion.

While Stephen has some standard games that he runs for offices to correct standard problems—too much conflict, not enough conflict, managers who don't know how to manage, teams that can't accept delegation, teams that are too uniform, teams that don't know how to debate—he also caters games to his clients. If an office has trouble with too much conflict, he might write a game with a lot of factions, some of which are at odds with one another, or he might write a game in which the players have to collaborate, choosing between many attractive alternatives and developing strategies to achieve them. He usually writes games for fifteen to forty people—any fewer and there isn't a sufficient level of complexity and politicking to keep the plot interesting and moving, but more than forty players and it becomes hard to maintain control of the situation. At the end of the game, which usually lasts no more than four hours, everyone gathers for a debriefing, during which they discuss what went right, what went wrong, and why. The compressed time frame of the game allows players to see the consequences of their actions immediately, whereas in real life, the consequences might take months to appear.

Stephen ran one of his games, called Long Ago, for his colleagues in the New England Society of Applied Psychology. He assigned the characters semi-randomly to the participants. The set-up was simple: the king's family and advisors are fighting to take his place and to control what happens in case of his continued health or early death. Stephen also gave the characters their own small goals and subplots. The golem, for example, wants to become a person, while the genie trapped in a bottle of gin for a thousand years wants to avoid sobering up and help as many people as possible. Each character began with a commodity such as money, connections, skills, or influence. To simulate the passing of time, Stephen divided the game into four rounds. In real life, each round lasted fifteen minutes, but in-game, each round represented one hour of time. Executive coach Kevan Norris, who played one of the king's advisers, had an overarching goal of seducing the king's daughter and avoiding the king's son. He'd just gotten down to the former, surprising a colleague who thought he was asking, "So, are you seeing anyone?" in seriousness instead of in-game. They both joke about it now. As an executive coach and a psychologist, Kevan felt the game reflected the core personalities of himself and his colleagues.

Stephen's rules tend to be simpler than those that govern boffer games—instead of hundreds of pages of Byzantine rules, his longest set of guidelines was about fifteen pages, although he does write out character backgrounds for all his players. He says that his rules sets are small because his games focus on player interaction rather than on building a specific game world. In a short, one-shot game with fifteen to forty participants, he doesn't have to write rules to cover every possible situation, in part because the game is small enough that someone could simply find and ask him. Knight Realms, on the other hand, as a campaign larp with more than two hundred players, needs a consolidated rules set for every eventuality.

The game must have a sufficient level of complexity in order to mimic real life. People know how they are supposed to behave in theory but often don't do it in practice. It's easy to say you'd help an old lady cross the street, but what if you come across her while you're in a rush to get back to the office? Part of Stephen's job is to help people practice making the right choices in difficult situations and to make them aware of what causes them to make incorrect choices. Whereas Knight Realms players have years in which to develop and sustain complexity, as a consultant, Stephen has to create games with emotional complexity right out of the gate.

He ran one such training for the Department of Homeland Security in 2006, a game geared toward uncovering problems with preparation in the case of a virulent flu pandemic. Rather than having the participants speculate about the best plans around some boardroom table, Stephen made them put their theories into practice. Some one hundred players, including local and federal officials, military officers, local doctors, and business representatives, gathered in an auditorium at George Washington University in Washington, DC. According to the scenario, the people inside the auditorium—doctors, government officials, businessmen, and concerned citizens—were attending a conference on bioterrorism. Many of the players were playing themselves, partly at their own insistence and partly because Stephen was brought into the project six weeks before it ran and didn't have the time to write one hundred characters. As a panel on bird flu began, the cell phones of the audience started ringing, and some people stepped out to answer the calls. Stephen's GM team was calling the "doctors" with news that a British tourist had collapsed in nearby Dulles airport, ill with bird flu. As it turned out, the British tourist wasn't the only one who had it. One of the doctors at the fictional conference was infected, although he was not yet showing symptoms. Stephen had worked with an expert to model the speed with which the flu would spread, basing the spread of the game's virus on the 1918 flu pandemic. They had several possible results preprepped.

Stephen represented the mechanic of infection with blue stickers. In the compressed timeframe of the game, the initially ill doctor had twenty minutes of contagion, representative of the twenty-four to forty-eight hours a flu victim has when he or she is contagious but not yet showing symptoms. The first doctor put a blue sticker on everyone he touched, and those players in turn received a series of nested envelopes from Stephen. The outer envelope might simply say that nothing happened, or it might ask players to put blue stickers on each person they shook hands with for the next twenty minutes and then to open the enclosed envelope. The second envelope told infected players, for example, that they had headaches or felt sneezy, with directions to role-play these symptoms and then to open the next envelope in another twenty minutes. By the end of the scenario, everyone in the theater had been exposed to the deadly strain, although not everyone had contracted it.

In the meantime, this collection of experts had to make decisions about how to manage the outbreak. That the player characters were infected with bird flu themselves added an extra level of urgency to the proceedings, and when people realized they could die from the strain, it took them aback, Stephen said. The players made decisions and released information to the public through press conferences. They failed to quarantine the airports, which proved calamitous. As the players made decisions, Stephen released newspaper articles that he'd written in advance, chronicling the spread of the epidemic and responding to the various decisions the players made during the game. A second, smaller group of players stashed off-site mimicked the reaction of a small local community, the fictional town of "Rocketville," which got all of its information about the epidemic from newspapers and press conferences and via cell phones. They responded to the trickle of information that members of the conference let out accordingly.

The players' response to the mock pandemic failed spectacularly. Because officials didn't quarantine the airports, the virus quickly spread to cities across the nation. Key decision-makers sickened, slowing response to the disaster. The slow release of information to the public resulted in riots in Rocketville and elsewhere, as locals rushed stores since food and other supplies were dwindling. Hospitals couldn't keep up with the stream of sick and dying as doctors and orderlies sickened, mortuaries overflowed, and people looted pharmacies as they realized that the remaining stock of anti-viral drugs were reserved for emergency workers. As more people sickened and died, food, electricity, and Internet service became increasingly scarce. Levels of panic and lawlessness spread across the United States. There were not enough healthy police officers and National Guard members to quell the unrest, and many of the player characters died of the lethal flu strain.

At this point, after four hours of game play, simulating three weeks of epidemic, the game ended, and the players spent the rest of the day in breakout sessions discussing what happened and how to avoid it. During the wrap sessions, some players said they had gotten "caught up in the moment" and "did not consider longer-term consequences of their actions," as Stephen put it in the paper he contributed to *Ethics and Game Design: Teaching Values Through Play*.[1] His point is that it's easy to say you'd close airports when sitting around a table during a planning session, but when an official is in a room full of business owners whose livelihoods might be damaged by the action, that decision becomes much harder, and there may be horrific consequences either way.

During these sessions, the groups came to several realizations, Stephen said. One was the importance not only of first responders but of people who played supporting roles—the orderlies at the hospitals, funeral directors, morticians. If these people are too sick to come to work, hospitals can't care for the overwhelming number of patients, and the bodies of the dead can't be carted away. The group also noticed some secondary logistical worries—if truck drivers sicken, who will get heating oil to houses in the Northeast when winter rolls around? They had focused instead on the high-tech elements of keeping businesses running at the detriment of infrastructure. For some of the military players, the big realization was that civilians, especially panicky civilians, won't listen to people in uniforms and let them do their jobs unless the reason they should is explained. And finally, the blue dot stickers brought home to the crowd how quickly an epidemic can spread. Hearing the numbers and statistics about virulence wasn't as powerful as seeing it happen. During the real-life swine flu epidemic of 2009, Stephen said he saw policymakers taking some of the steps outlined during the breakout sessions, handling the epidemic quickly and rushing vaccines into production.

Unlike the army's war games, Stephen's games are aimed at uncovering the interpersonal dynamic between people, the reasons things happened as they did. Like a piece of literary fiction, they aim beyond entertainment and toward enlightenment. Stephen tries to create epiphanies for his players, eureka moments similar to his own eureka moment gleaned so many years ago during his Necronomicon game. In short, his games suggest that larp can be much more than an immersive game; rather, the hobby has the potential to become art.

10

Larpapalooza

S tan and Sylvia were searching for weed, and not in a subtle way. They asked a butcher with a blood-spattered shower-curtain apron, a small woman with pale blue hair that matched her corset, and a tall, blond man with feathery paint around his eye, to no avail. Finally, they petitioned the Merchant, the man who had drawn every-one together in New York tonight for some shadowy purpose. Stan Helsig, a pothead with an insatiable appetite for kind bud, worked in the film industry, renting videos out of a small shop in New York, while his sidekick, Sylvia Sigfried, worked at a gothic floor show on Eleventh Street as an usher and, on certain nights, as the woman who gets ceremoniously sawed in half and then made whole. She lived in a rat-infested apartment in the Bronx and took care of her sick parents. Deathly afraid of the sky, she carried a parasol with her at all times to block it out.

Both of them knew that supernaturals populated New York along-side its ignorant human population. This did not trouble them.

Two years after I made my larp debut with the help of Molly Mandlin, I returned to DEXCON with a different mission in mind. By this time I had accustomed myself to the convention experience, which involved wandering around the floor during the day, doling out smiles and obligatory hugs to people I knew from Knight Realms or from seeing them at conventions. In the evening I ambled around the hotel, checking in at room parties, and making a friend here and there.

At DEXCON 13, held in July 2010 at the Morristown, New Jersey, Hyatt, I stayed with a couple of these friends, including Brendan O'Hara, a slender man with curly black hair and short, groomed stubble over his cheeks. I had met Brendan at Knight Realms, where he played several characters, including a drunken satyr who told exaggerated tales culled from 1980s B-movies and then antiquated, and Portia's hookah-loving chum Marcus. He and his girlfriend, a die-hard larper with short, curly blond hair, were sharing the bed, while I and a mutual friend of ours, also one of the Knight Realms hookah crew, Jeramy Merritt, camped out in sleeping bags on the floor. Jeramy's flamboyant dress meant he was hard to miss. Tall, slender, and with a huge mass of curly hair that hung down his back, Jeramy routinely wore brightly colored suit jackets he'd found in the women's section of secondhand stores. His uniform also included pajama pants, often homemade, striped black and red or black and green or dizzy with paisley. Gene Stern swore he resembled a slightly sinister David Bowie, and in general, Jeramy preferred the 1980s to other decades.

As usual, this DEXCON offered more than thirty larps, along with countless numbers of board games, miniatures games, quizzes, and tabletop role-playing games. I intended to take advantage of the variety of larps and attend as many as I was able over the course of the four-day convention, in hopes that the variety of styles would reveal the essential nature of larp itself to me, offering me a perfect moment of immersion in some fantastical world. I had originally dubbed this search the Larpgasm, after the "Civil Wargasm" road trip that Tony Horwitz took with Civil War reenactors in his book *Confederates in the*

Attic, but one of my larpers told me in no uncertain terms that there would be "no gasming of any kind." Brendan named my experiment "Larpapalooza," and so it was fitting that I embarked on this journey with him, or rather, that I embarked on this journey by trailing after Brendan, aka Stan Helsig, during the Shattered larp, a game set in a world loosely based on the Buffyverse, the world presented in the TV show *Buffy the Vampire Slayer*. Although there were fairies, werewolves, and vampires, Stan and Sylvia, the characters we were playing, were simply garden-variety humans with the garden-variety desire to score some pot.

As it turned out, we had no involvement in the main plot of the game at all. Our game play consisted of asking various characters for drugs, sometimes obtaining them, play-smoking them outside of the pale function room, and then behaving as if our characters were stoned. The game had an actual plot. As Stan and Sylvia returned from smoking, explosions erupted directly behind Stan; we only knew about them because the GM announced such things and because Brendan and I could see from the way other players had gathered around the GM, character cards in hand, that a combat or other encounter was occurring. But Stan and Sylvia had no part in it, and I never took out my character sheet or called a skill, but then, since the rules had not really been explained, I probably would have been too timid to try to use my levitation spell, for example, because it's always awkward to do something you've never done before.

Even though Brendan and I were locked inside the narrow world of our characters (find pot, smoke pot, repeat), we still had a great time. The capstone of our experience, this game's perfect larp moment, resulted from the minor action of another player, Michael Pucci, a devout Buddhist in upper management at U-Haul Connecticut. He was thirty-two, of medium height, and stocky, and he carried himself with the confidence of someone who knows who he is and where he is going. Michael had been gaming and storytelling for over ten years and had recently started up a wildly popular zombie apocalypse boffer larp called Dystopia Rising in Connecticut. He also played a gypsy, one of the Yhatzi family, at Knight Realms. Tonight, at Shattered, he was playing a fairy from the winter court, complete with ear tips, in part because he thought it would be fun to discard his human-ness and play a character that was totally alien. Early on, Sylvia had tried to talk to Michael's character, Mr. Vendemere. Mr. Vendeme-re's attitude toward the humans was that the worthless flesh-sacks ought to be quivering in their boots with gratitude because the fey had deigned to make an appearance. Michael quietly told me that he looked like a normal human, say an eight on a scale from one to twenty. Then he says something to the effect of, "As you look at me, it's like a veil lifts, and for a moment, I look like a twenty-three. I am ungodly beautiful, so beautiful that it's frightening. And then the veil comes down, and I'm back to an eight." Clearly, that human body was just a disguise.

For the rest of the evening, Stan teased Sylvia about crushing on Mr. Vendemere. Later, Stan tried to hit on a reluctant woman in a light blue wig while asking her for pot. He mentioned Mr. Vendemere, and the two of us went into verbal attack mode. I began describing Mr. Vendermere's pulchritude to this woman with rapid-fire speech at the same time that Brendan began explaining how the two of us had arrived here this evening and what we'd done. At first, the blue-haired woman was confused and looked from one to the other of us in sequence. She tried to make interjections, but we steamrolled over her in tandem with our improvised ramblings, both finishing at the same moment. And then, almost as one, all three of us put our hands on our heads and laughed out-of-character. Back in-game, the blue-haired woman took a phone call from her daughter that enabled her to get away from us, and we went onward to find more marijuana.

Around midnight, after four hours of Shattered, I began to grow tired of it. I'd had a great time joking around with Brendan in-game, but our goal of obtaining increasingly potent larp drugs had gotten old. We'd taken a few breaks from the game and visited our hotel room for a discreet drink of real alcohol, and we'd taken a role-play detour to the actual hotel bar, situated directly next to the function room that held Shattered. A couple of our fellow gamers, still in-character, had ordered dinner and a beer at the bar, and we'd briefly joined them. But by midnight, and with four hours of game to go, I was ready to leave. We'd missed our opportunity to be involved in the main plot, we'd had our good time, and frankly, everything since our steamrolling conversation had been second-best. With a quiet word to one of the GMs, we departed for the evening.

Interestingly, Michael and I, the veteran larper and the novice, had similar game experiences. He'd spent Shattered embroiled in fairy politics; the winter court of fairies had tried to goad the summer court into battle. Neither of us had really interacted with the GM-run plot. Michael thought that the game's strength lay in its diversity of character concepts, from vampire to fairy, which made for interesting player interactions early in the evening. But from a storyteller standpoint, he thought it would be difficult to craft a plot appealing to any significant segment of those differentiated characters. The characters were so diversified that any one plot was only likely to appeal to a small faction, leaving everyone else to create goals for themselves.

I'd gotten Shattered half-right, reaffirmed my idea that it's good to have a concrete goal to pursue in a larp, such as scoring weed or finding your father or writing a *Chronicle*—such activity helps do away with one of the great problems of larp, which I think of as dull cocktail party syndrome, when I end up milling around a room waiting for something to happen. Hanging around a player with a strong personality also pepped up my larp experience. Brendan and Michael belong to the class of gamers that I think of as planets; the force of a planet's personality and his or her skill at role-playing creates a gravitational pull that sucks other players into orbit. I had spent the game orbiting Brendan; in pursuing his character goal, we'd had a boisterous, hilarious run, but ultimately, the fun of acting stoned and ridiculous burnt itself out. The danger of being too self-involved in a larp was you might miss your entre into the game's plot and become bored with your character goals.

On Friday night I tried another flavor of larp, a game called Deadlands, set in a Wild West that included gothic elements such as demons and magic. The game, run by FishDevil, had a hard-core following of gamers, ones who were slavishly devoted to costuming. Before the convention, I had gone over to Gene's house and rolled up my character in order to avoid the line of new players onsite. I named my character Eloise Vichyssoise, and I "rolled up" this character with a deck of cards, randomly drawing them to determine Eloise's stats and the number of skills she was permitted. In addition, a player could take "edges" and "hindrances." If you took a hindrance, you gained additional points that could be put into skills or could be spent on an edge, an advantage for your character.

I thought the hindrances were terribly fun. On the advice of Cappy's girlfriend, I took the "enemy" hindrance, which meant my character had an enemy somewhere; in this case, it was a chef who had shut down my restaurant in Paris. I also took the "grim servant of death" hindrance, which meant that bad things happened to those around me, a hilarious problem for a professional chef. The way the in-game mechanic worked, if my attempt to use a skill failed—if I drew an ace from my deck—the worst possible outcome would happen to my party.

I created a French character because I wanted to be part of Team French, consisting of Brendan, his girlfriend Liz, and a couple of their friends. Team French did not mess around when it came to costumes. Liz had purchased a tuxedo jacket with a high waist and tails for Brendan, who also donned a red vest, a cravat, and a gigantic top hat for his role as Jean-Luc LeFleur, an old-money fop who had journeyed from France to invest in Cairo, Illinois. Liz played Amalie Giroud, a woman with a demure demeanor that belied her skill with guns. She wore a tiered faux-satin skirt in dark red, with a fusty black blouse and matching red coat. A black wig covered her hair, and she pinned on a hat laden with black silk flowers and trailing mesh. I made do with an outfit gleaned from my closet. I wore my white chemise from Knight Realms and added an apron with a dishcloth hanging off the waist, a wooden spoon, and a whisk from my kitchen.

After all of us were dressed, we went down to the larp, which was held in the same room as Shattered had been. It was located right next to the bar-lobby area, and so people in costume waiting to start Deadlands milled about with wide-eyed businessmen there for a Friday night drink. In the larp community, venturing somewhere public in costume is commonly known as "freaking the mundies." But for tonight, at the convention, the freaks far outnumbered the mundanes in this hotel lobby bar.

The FishDevils had taken great pains to dress the set inside the beige hotel function room. They had set up a casino, laying printed green felt meant for blackjack, poker, and craps over a variety of tables. Xeroxes of confederate money had been cut to size to provide the currency for this evening of gambling. One end of the room had a rolling bar set up at it, complete with stools and "alcoholic" drinks that consisted of soda, since the convention's policy didn't permit alcohol on the convention floor for a bunch of reasons, including liability and to prevent underage drinking. Screens sectioned off opposite corners of the room; one concealed a special poker table, the other, a museum with framed papyri, a small African mask, a silver-encrusted dagger, and other objets d'arte that the GMs borrowed for the event.

People began free role-playing, talking in-character, although the game hadn't officially started. I soon discovered that my French accent was worse than awful. Michael was there, wearing suspenders and drinking from a flagon, talking fast, making claims, and offering flattery to the ladies. He was playing a snake oil salesman named Dr. Waites. Eventually, the FishDevils explained the rules, a little quickly for my taste: conflicts were determined by a stat level, plus a skill level, plus a card draw. The seasoned gamers caught on immediately. I felt immediately confused but figured that someone would explain what I needed to do if and when the time came. All thirty of us milled for an hour and a half, gambling and chatting, while seemingly nothing happened.

I was finding this game harder to get into than Shattered had been, in part because it was a continuing larp. Shattered ran for the first time at this convention, while Deadlands had run twice a year at the Double Exposure conventions for about five years. Many of these players had established characters with private plots they eagerly anticipated. And while my character was playing Brendan's chef, we didn't have much reason to hang out in-game—he was involved in continuing the story of his character; I was new to town and still finding my way.

In the meantime, Michael parked himself at the craps table with a few other gentlemen. He'd heard that the local union was involved with the casino, and Dr. Waites wanted to bankrupt the bank backing this new casino, in hopes that the money would be gone when the northerners arrived. He enlisted several characters with the in-game "gambling" skill to his cause, and they collectively broke several of the tables. At one point, as a combat was beginning, he scooped all the remaining money off the craps table, said thank you, and slowly walked out of the room, the highlight of his game experience, a spectacular theft hidden in plain sight. Then, for Michael, it was beer o'clock and time to head toward bed.

Around midnight, and three hours into the game, I was bored of Eloise. My horrific French accent, so amusing to attempt for the first hour or so, had grown exhausting to keep up. I had learned to play poker and blackjack in-character, both games I hadn't remembered how to play in real life, because I actually prefer not to play them. I also met an art expert and made cursory small talk with a bunch of characters whose players I knew out-of-game. I was beginning to feel as if four hours of convention larping was about all I could muster. As I prepared to slink off to bed, Eloise was sucked through a portal and into a desert near Cairo, Egypt. The six of us, including Brendan and Liz, banded together and killed two large bulls, which were really demons. Sure enough, the GM supervising our party, combined with my peers, managed to teach me which numbers to add to what type of card pull to determine whether I actually hit the bull with my cleaver. We didn't act out the fight; rather, we verbally described what we were doing, as tabletop players do, while sitting in the hotel lobby. After helping defeat the bulls and returning to the town of Cairo, Illinois, I felt I'd had enough larp for the day; it was half-past beer o'clock, in my opinion.

The strength of Deadlands, Michael said, was its immersive setting—the game space didn't feel like a hotel function room but a thriving casino, thanks to the FishDevils' decorations. Furthermore, the world of Deadlands felt as though it extended beyond the immediate realm of the game, it felt substantial, thanks to its campaign setting. After years of game play, the GMs had explored different facets of the world and of the town, which had its own history, a history remembered by the established characters that populated its landscape. Similarly, players had developed and deepened their characters over time. Players with established characters were also more likely to invest in costuming for them, as Liz and Brendan had, which added to the overall atmosphere. In contrast, Shattered didn't have this feeling of a concrete and complete world because it was a new game with all-new characters; many players of Shattered cobbled costuming together from their suitcases and rolled up a character a half hour before the game started.

The thickness and clarity of the Deadlands world made it harder to arrive as a newbie, though. I'd created my chef, but she didn't have enough depth or substance to play for more than a few hours. And whether it's school, a workplace, or an in-game community of larpers, it's always difficult to fit in as a new kid. Michael also pointed out that Deadlands's plot hooks were hard for players to pick up on. Both he and I were new to town, and both of us spent most of our game experience gambling, unaware of whether there was a plot or how we might involve ourselves in it. The difference was that he was able to find his own character goal (bankrupt the bank) while I failed to make my own fun and simply wandered around. Neither of us lasted till the end of the game.

Around one in the morning, I returned to my room to find that Jeramy, in all his faux–David Bowie glory, was already there and preparing himself for the sort of bizarrely costumed convention-ramble that so many people enjoy. You could wear whatever outrageous thing you damned well pleased around the floor at a convention like this, and people would smile, high-five you, and tell you that you looked awesome. Sometimes it happened unintentionally. Once, I'd been wearing a white shirt, black pants, and red lipstick, and some guy had taken my picture on the convention floor because he thought I was dressed up as Uma Thurman's character from *Pulp Fiction*. A great number of people in wacky outfits perpetually wandered the convention floor. I'd seen a older man with a stuffed dragon eternally on his shoulder, a guy wearing a captain's hat and a long leather jacket strutting about with a cane, a gentleman in a black and purple suit and top hat circa 1890s England, women in full Renaissance wear or wearing jeans with corsets or gypsy bangles around their waists and ten-gallon swashbuckler hats dripping with feathers. Goth kids with stringy hair and faces full of metal skulked across the lobby, while hipsters in brightly colored leather jackets hunched in their shoulders and darted glances at the strange accessories on display—tiny hats, angel wings, and spirit-gummed devil horns. Jeramy was in full effect tonight. He often purchased odd things from the estate sales that he and his girlfriend frequented—a bomber jacket made out of a bath towel emblazoned with an ad for the film *Gone with the Wind*, a cheesy framed poster of a tiger that he gave to Brendan and Liz when Liz bought a house, an absurd number of cigars he'd acquired at a steep discount. He and his girlfriend, Jenn, a graphic designer, loved stuff that looked theatrical, particularly if it was from the 1980s, and if it was awesomely tacky, cheesy, and over-the-top, so much the better. Currently, Jeramy was hunting for a keytar, a handheld piano in the shape of a guitar that hailed from his favorite decade. When I opened the door to our hotel room, Jeramy towered before me in an electric, Elmo-red flannel jumpsuit with a zipper up the front. It covered him from the neck all the way down to the soles of his feet. I realized he was wearing footie pajamas. They even had a buttoned up butt-hatch. His reddish hair, curly and shoulder-length, billowed behind him in a cloud. In one hand, he held a bottle of rum. We both began laughing hysterically, me at his bizarre, oh-so-Jeramy outfit, him at my reaction, which was pretty much the reason to wear footie pajamas in the first place—to get a laugh out of folks. We had a drink and then wandered down to the mostly deserted convention floor, in search of adventure. Since we didn't find it down there, we climbed the staircase to the ballroom level, which had been sectioned off into four different areas used for larps.

The far room had had a Cthulhu larp, a horror larp, in it; the middle room gave off the fading sounds of battle; and when I opened the door to the third room, a woman in a sleeping bag fell out of it. We had found Sleeping: The LARP, a joke made flesh. Sleeping: The LARP was part of a trend of gamers laughing at their own hobby, using it as a bald-faced excuse to hang out. After all, any social event could be transformed into a larp. There was also Bar Crawl: The LARP running at this convention. I wasn't able to attend, but at the previous convention, DREAMATION, I had gone. We had drunk in bars while only minimally following the scavenger hunt rules, chief among them "pics, or it didn't happen." The mock-event Sleeping: The LARP had this description in the convention schedule.

> "Sleeping: The LARP." Our master of dreams, none other than Mr. Sleep himself, will run this fantastic action-packed larp filled with emotion, anxiety, drama and . . . snoring. Yes, that's right, each player will have an exhaustive list of no goals what-soever other than to sleep as peacefully as he or she can. An incredible level of interactivity consisting of slumber in near proximity to other participants will surely make this an experience you won't ever forget. Players are encouraged to bring their own sleeping bags, pillows, air mattresses and Ambien. Friday, 12:00AM - 4:00AM; One Round; Bring Your Own Materials. Experts ONLY; Very Serious, All Ages.

There were perhaps five people sleeping near the door, which was opposite the wall that concealed the still-going boffer battle. As the sleeping-bagged woman explained where we were to us in hushed tones, we backed away slowly, and returned to our room, one last tipple, and sleep.

Before I'd arrived at DEXCON, I'd registered for a Cthulhu larp. The Cthulhu games, loosely based on the writing of H. P. Lovecraft and his followers, focused on investigating the Elder gods, dark monsters from the abyss that could crush humanity with a mere thought. The more you learned about them, the less sane you became. A Cthulhu game generally featured characters such as mad scientists, adventurers, mystics, nobility, and professors of the arcane. The games could be set in any historical period but typically had only one ending: everyone dies or is driven insane from facing the hideous unknown, filled with super-powerful alien beings, some of them tentacled, who will one day return to rule the earth and crush humanity like the bugs we are.

The gaming group PST Productions generally ran four or five Cthulhu games at each Double Exposure convention and had a devoted following of players that I hadn't met, primarily because they rarely ventured out to play other larps—they were all Cthulhu all the time. PST's cult following meant that it was impossible to casually show up to a game—all the slots would already be filled. So I made sure to sign up for the hotly anticipated premiere of their steampunk Cthulhu setting as soon as I had registered for the convention. I was rewarded with a detailed character history that arrived via e-mail. I would be playing Madame Blavatsky, a historical character and self-professed medium, one of the founders of new-age spiritualism who helped create the Theosophical Society, an association based on the belief that all world religions espouse the same set of core truths but that the practicum of these beliefs, the trappings in which each religion clothes those truths, differs from faith to faith and is potentially destructive.

That Saturday evening, I attempted a steampunk costume. Steampunk is a genre that grew in popularity in the early 2000s, attaining its own lifestyle conventions and forming its own subculture. Think steam power and the Victorian age, and then mix in the idea of magic as elaborate technology. Think zeppelins, gears, *The League of Extraordinary Gentleman*, *2000 Leagues Under the Sea*, Nicola Tesla, mad scientists, and *Journey to the Center of the Earth* (or bottom of the ocean). The symbol of steampunk culture is a pair of brass goggles or a bare watch gear. I threw on a dress over some baggy pants and boots, laced a recently purchased corset over it, added several necklaces, threw a black scarf over my head to suggest my "mystic" bent, and borrowed a cane with a compass in the handle from Jeramy to help me role-play Blavatsky's bum leg. Not the most steampunk costume ever, but I thought I'd pass.

Larpers from different games crowded the hallway outside the divided ballrooms. Vampire players dressed in black malingered at the entrance, waiting for their game to go off in one of the rooms. A little farther onward, toward the room where Sleeping: The LARP had been, people dressed as cowboys, football players, pop culture icons, and everything in between milled around two tables where several people with nasty skin abrasions sat, preparing for Dystopia Rising's zombie apocalypse event. All the way at the end of the hallway, I could see the brilliantly costumed Cthulhu players standing: men in half-capes and white jackets with goggles around their necks, women in ball gowns or pantaloons and corsets wearing pins shaped into cogs or trilobites, and a French maid and a man in a suit with a towel over his arm, like a butler.

I received my character history and a small character card divided into three panels. One panel bore a rainbow of colors, one displayed my character name, and one contained a list of abilities and stats. Inside the game room, we all sat down, and for the first time at this convention, I had the rules explained to me. The character card was designed to be folded into thirds and clipped onto our convention badges so that our nametags would be visible to everyone else. There were no card pulls, dice rolls, or rock-paper-scissors games involved in this larp, only stat comparisons. The rainbow on one side of the card was for a sanity check. My rainbow had Xs in the orange portion. When something horrible happened, the GM, called a Keeper in this game, would order a sanity check and name a color. If he named a color that was above orange on my card, then I would downgrade my sanity, according to the list of adjectives written below the rainbow. If I passed three sanity checks in a row, I would downgrade my sanity anyway, to represent the fact that in this universe, no one is immune to the horror of the surroundings. The Keeper asked if there were any new players in the audience, and I raised my hand. I was one of two. He walked us through a combat scenario in front of everyone, using a couple seasoned players in the demonstration. Combat occurred when someone declared it by saying, "Combat." Next, we all looked at our constitution stats. He named numbers, beginning at one and moving upward. When your number was called, you declared what action you were going to take. When he got to the top number, he counted backward. When your number came up again, you physically took your action. When he got back to one he asked, "Does anyone wish combat to continue?" and since the answer, for purposes of the demonstration, was no, we stopped.

I was reasonably clear on the rules for perhaps the first time ever. With our demonstration over, we all left the room to reenter it in-character.

We'd all been invited to the Adventurers' Guild that evening for a soiree during which a mysterious machine would be unveiled. The room was decorated with pots of six-foot-tall bamboo and organized around a set of L-shaped tables that held anachronistic gadgets. One section had a large pyramidal piece of glass set on top of what might have been an ancient record turntable. The other main part of the machine held a disk that radiated light—it had a piece of fool's gold atop it and about six wooden dowels stuck straight up around it. The whole thing screamed mad science. A footman served us hors d'oeuvres (peanut butter crackers) from a silver platter and champagne (water in Styrofoam cups). I introduced Madame Blavatsky to an archeologist attempting to fund an expedition to the center of the earth aimed at proving that the planet was, in fact, hollow. I spoke with the head of the Adventurers' Guild, the historical personage Nicola Tesla, and a young ingenue who had stolen her overprotective father's invitation to this event and broken out of the house.

The machine, as it turned out, was a time machine, and predictably, it didn't work as intended. The young man we sent into the future to retrieve a newspaper returned through the giant octagonal portal as a mere collection of organs and bones, represented by plastic props the GMs threw out onto us. We all did a sanity check. As the evening progressed, I tried out my skills. I used my mysticism and occult skill to determine that the crystal powering the machine was in fact a summoning crystal. I psychically scrutinized one of the scientists' pasts and discovered that his intention was true. I decided to bury the hatchet with my old nemesis Aleister Crowley, who discovered that the crystal in the machine had been switched out for another. Around us, chaos erupted—a woman had died in the backroom, a monster came out of the portal, people were running around in the dark. The swami I'd been studying with in India arrived, played by the man who had previously been the butler. The action reached a fever pitch. I went into the back room to conduct a séance for a woman who had died. Her husband pulled out a chair for me and executed a surprise attack, shooting the base of my skull with two fingers. Since Lizzie was genuinely surprised, Madame Blavatsky died. As I fell to the floor, I could hear the swami pounding on the door, yelling, "Blaa-vaaaa-tsky! Blaaa-vaaaaa-tsky!"

And at that moment of high drama, the game ended, and for the first time, I fiercely wished that it had not, so that I could learn what it is possible to do with a dead body in Cthulhu, so that Madame Blavatsky's story could continue. The lights came on, and everyone pulled chairs into a circle. Over the course of an hour, all thirty of us briefly explained what had happened to our characters. The intrigue and variety of plots given to the group amazed me.

Jack the Ripper was there, undercover, along with the policeman who had sworn to catch him. Several secret devotees to the Great Old Ones had slipped potions to various members of the group in order to convert them. One woman was trying to use the dimensional portal to become a god. The manservant belonged to the Assassins' Guild and had been hired to take this woman's necklace and then stab her. He did this after the head of the Adventurers' Guild had knocked her and her husband unconscious for occupying his office. After accomplishing his mission, the manservant left and was sent in as a different character, my swami. The dead woman and her husband, as it turned out, were vampires responsible for the death of Kaiser Wilhelm II. They were trying to resuscitate the Ukrainian nation, although she spent the game dead and he spent it trying to lure someone into the back room in order to kill them and suck their soul into his wife's body, reviving her. I had fallen for that one. The plots went on and on, each person gaining a small moment in the spotlight.

The Keepers had written interlocking backstories that immediately immersed the players in a plot. Because all of us were "new to town," there were no in-game cliques to exclude people. The minimal rules were simple enough that even I could understand them. The setting of this game was oriented toward investigation and roleplay, and that is exactly what I enjoy in a game, as it turns out.

I had played in six larps over three days at this convention, and finally, in my last open slot, I found the game that fit me as a player. No one I knew had attended this larp, but I'd managed to have a good time anyway. I had been completely immersed in the game for its entire duration, about three hours.

The Cthulhu game succeeded for several reasons. The prewritten characters, complete with backstories, gave each player some minor goals to accomplish over the course of the evening, in addition to reacting to the major plot. The plot hook—the faulty time machine—

had been accessible to every player and had immediately gone wrong, which provided intrigue early on in the game. The elaborate set and costuming had helped transform the beige function room into a swanky private club, and the vast amount of private plots seeded in our backstories meant that at least a few came to fruition, adding extra drama. Furthermore, the poorly functioning time machine gave the Keepers the opportunity to introduce monsters or other alien beings whenever a lull in the action presented itself. And finally, the clarity with which the minimal rules were explained meant that everyone was clear on how to affect the game's environment.

The only distraction from the game itself was the noise from Michael's zombie apocalypse larp running next door, across the thin ballroom barrier. We could hear the noise of the flesh-eating undead being vanquished with foam bats.

I would use the knowledge I'd gleaned at Larpapalooza to run my own game for a set of non-gamers. Since I'd liked Cthulhu so much, I'd run Cthulhu, and Jeramy, Gene, and Brendan would help me.

11

Cthulhu Fhtagn!*

I am not qualified to run a larp. Sure, by the time I ran Cthulhu,
I'd been larping and researching the hobby for three years, but
that didn't mean I knew how to run a game. After all, I've watched
thousands of movies over the course of my life but have no idea how
to direct a film. As a novice GM, I faced an overwhelming number
of responsibilities: I had to create a plot interesting enough to grab
my players, gather props, find NPCs, and, horror of horrors, learn
the rules. On top of all that, I'd decided to conduct an experiment.
I wanted to see if larp could bring any old group of people together
as a community; I wanted to test its universal appeal, to check my

---

* A phrase Cthulhu cultists chant in Lovecraftian tales, possibly mean-
ing "Cthulhu waits." It is an abbreviation of "Ph'nglui mglw'nafh Cthulhu
R'lyeh wgah'nagl fhtagn," which means, "In his house at R'lyeh, dead
Cthulhu waits dreaming."

reactions to the hobby against a third party. I'd decided to run a game
for non-larpers.

As a rookie GM, I immediately established a team of qualified
experts to help me with the game. Gene, a gamer from the cradle,
was my first addition. He had a knack for explaining rules systems to
other players, especially to, ahem, reporters in need of help. Among
his friends, he was the planner—even when he wasn't going to Knight
Realms, he'd arrange rides for everyone, including me, and I knew I
could rely on him to work hard prepping for the game. His large,
boisterous personality matched his physique—he was a big guy—and
usually he wore a little ponytail at the top of his head, which gave
him the appearance of a samurai with a topknot. He kept the top
of his hair chin-length but kept the sides shaved, sometimes buzzing
designs into them. As a GM, Gene excelled at creating scenes and
plot challenges on the fly. I knew, for example, that a character once
derailed the main Deadlands plot within the first five minutes of a
FishDevil game, and that Gene and the team worked together to create a new plot, written on the spur of the moment, that occupied their
players for the next eight hours. Gene firmly believed that in larp, a
player ought to be able to do anything, even if it made more work
for the GM. I liked that player-centric attitude and knew that if I collapsed in a quivering ball of stress during the game, Gene would be
able to carry on.

Brendan and Jeramy had loads of individual experience gaming, but they also worked well as a team. Brendan had been the new
player officer at Knight Realms for several years. He was responsible for running the rules and safety demonstration for new players
before each game. He often ran low-level mods at Knight Realms to
entertain newbies, and he'd run several weekend plots with Jeramy.
Jeramy spent several years as the planning officer at Knight Realms,
essentially filling in any gaps left by other staff members, and he'd
run a lot of weekend plots and individual mods during his tenure.
Together, Brendan and Jeramy were working on a sci-fi larp of their
own invention, called Doomsday. Brendan was a lot of fun. He was
the kind of guy you wanted to keep in your coat closet, retrieving
him each day for a beer on the couch and some amusing banter. He

seemed like the kind of person who would be comfortable anywhere, the sort of person who always knew what to say to a group of people to ease the tension and let others in on the joke. If Brendan could blend, Jeramy really stood out. Jeramy is weird, and he doesn't hide it, but his weird is a weird that invites people in, particularly if they happen to be standing a few feet away from the crowd, from normal, on the fringes. And although he is a creative dresser, his inventiveness extends beyond his surface. He was writing a zombie novel, and as a GM, he described scenes to players with colorful details and unexpected outcomes.

As a team, Brendan and Jeramy were full of laughter and 1980s references, playing off each other as the jokes escalated. They worked well together. As role-players, I thought they were planet-class. Their enthusiasm and commitment to their characters felt infectious, and I wanted them in my game, in part to emulate good role-playing for my newbies.

With my GM team and my flavor of game selected, I needed players, a location, and a firm date. The location was easiest—I had access to a hundred-year-old house in the old Victorian beach town of Cape May, New Jersey, a three-story pink monstrosity with a dusty basement ideal for hiding serial murderers and external decks with stairs that connected all three floors, which would provide excellent egress during chase scenes. The five-bedroom house had bed space for twelve, plus a couch, but everyone else would have to sleep on the floor. Best of all, it belonged to my parents, so I wouldn't have to pay for larp space, so long as the fake blood we used didn't stain the carpet.

My husband and I scared up a collection of some twenty players for our game from among our friends, many of whom were curious about my book topic. Our old roommate, Chip, a fiction writer I'd gone to grad school with, agreed to come down from Boston, along with a couple buddies I'd met through my work on the small literary journal *Fringe*. A friend who worked over at the *Today* show agreed to come as well. Then there were the scientists. My husband was studying for a PhD in physics at Rutgers and a slew of his peers—mostly physicists, with an astronomer and a mathematician thrown in for good measure—agreed to come. One of my younger cousins flew in from Tennessee. Unbeknownst to me, she'd been into cosplay, or costume play, for some years. (Cosplay is a hobby and subculture in which participants carefully replicate the outfit of a figure from anime or popular culture and wear that outfit to conventions.)

A flurry of e-mails and a handy web widget decided the date for us, a weekend at the beginning of October. With the logistical necessaries in place, I began to plan.

My husband, George, and I talked plot as we cooked dinner over a series of weeks. We'd run a short-lived Dungeons & Dragons campaign once, and we loved making up stories together. George was particularly interested in forcing players to make difficult decisions, and so we talked about having a band of good guys in-game who would have to do something horrible, like sacrifice a virgin or a hand in order to get a necessary something. The idea wasn't more concrete than that at first.

I had decided on a published rules system rather than writing my own rules, because it was simpler and I wanted to worry about plot, not reinventing the wheel. Writing a rules set can take weeks, months, or, in the case of large boffer larps, years of preparation and playtesting. I thought I had enough on my plate just running an event, so I had decided to use Cthulhu Live, the same system that the Cthulhu game I'd played during Larpapalooza had used. The rules were simple for a larp, and I hoped the non-contact combat would minimize breakage inside my parents' beach house.

Early in the process, Brendan sent me a series of exploratory questions: Did I want the players to feel scared? Did I want the atmosphere to be horrific or more neutral? Would I let the players write their own characters? I wanted this game to evoke the same excitement and drama I'd felt at Larpapalooza when my swami colleague had banged on the office door yelling my name, and I wanted it to evoke the atmosphere of its source text, the stories of H. P. Lovecraft and his followers, their horror and mystery. I decided to work with the basic premise of the Cthulhu mythos, the idea that powerful alien beings called the Great Old Ones exist between dimensions but can enter this world when the stars are aligned. Humans are simply the house pets who have run amok while their evil and powerful masters are away on vacation.

Two months before the event, we had our first informal GM meeting when Brendan and Jeramy and their girlfriends visited the space down in Cape May. The visit prompted many discussions of cool, scary scenes that we could stage in the house. The basement held particular interest for Brendan and Jeramy. It had a cement floor, exposed wooden pillars that supported a low ceiling, and several stubby doors with tiny windows that led underneath the front porch. Wouldn't it be cool, Brendan said, if someone looked through one of those little windows and saw a dead body laid out? We talked about drawing in chalk on the basement floor, to make some sort of ritual inscription. We counted the number of ways to enter or exit the house. There were six doors, excellent for the NPCs to surprise the players. Jeramy thought it'd be spooky if an NPC died in the bathtub on the second floor and then came through the front door a few hours later, as if nothing had happened. We immediately nominated him for that job. Although we bounced around a few plot ideas, nothing stuck. Finally, after an hour of discussion Jeramy said, essentially, that this plot didn't have to be Shakespeare. After all, we could just do the Knight Realms thing and have a couple of competing rituals. That settled it in my mind. I'd run a basic plot at my first game. After all, there were only five conflicts in literature—man versus man, man versus himself, man versus nature, man versus society, and man versus machine—but the variations were infinite.

Two weeks later, George and I sat down and brainstormed over a bottle of wine. The house would double as the Salty Dog, a boarding house in 1890s Cape May. As the stars aligned, the barrier between our world and the world of the Great Old Ones would weaken and become porous. The bad guys would do a ritual to help Cthulhu cross the barrier, while the good guys would do a ritual to strengthen that barrier and keep him out.

Over the next few weeks, I fleshed out the plot in meetings with Jeramy and Brendan and over a series of lunches with Gene. We carved out roles for each of the GMs. Brendan would play an evil doctor who wanted to raise Cthulhu using human hearts, which he would remove from the chests of the still living, turning them into evil cultists. Essentially, he would lead Team Evil and help minimize in-game death. Jeramy would play a troubled transient man with psychic powers who knew that Cthulhu was coming and wanted to warn the guests. Essentially, he was the NPC contact for Team Good. I would play Ophelia, the owner of the Salty Dog, and I'd serve as a floating GM, available for skills challenges. George, a confirmed non-larper, would play my chef and would handle the food for all of us. Liz, Brendan's girlfriend and a hard-core larper, would wear her fabulous Victorian gown and play a reanimated woman, modeling role-play for the novices, and she could also help run some skills challenges, since she knew the rules. Gene would run camp NPC from the attic, sending monsters out from a portal located somewhere in the house, which would periodically vomit beasties until the players figured out how to close it.

I'd decided to write character backgrounds for my players for several reasons. I worried that the main plot wouldn't be enough to keep the characters busy and wanted to seed secondary plots into the backstories. As a new larper, I'd also found it easier to portray a pre-written character with quirks, like Madame Blavatsky, than to create my own. Somehow, writing up a character for myself to play had felt too high stakes, like I personally was on the line, and I wanted my players to feel they were portraying someone else. At Knight Realms, it had taken me months of role-playing to come up with character quirks, but my game would run for one day only, not nearly enough time for my players to really build out their backstories. Finally, I wanted to give the players immediate reasons to interact with one another, and I knew that interlocking backstories would help make, for example, the local mobster talk to the man he was blackmailing.

Writing the backstories took me more time than anything else did. Everyone got a good, single-spaced page explaining who they were and why they were at the Salty Dog on this particular weekend. I began with ordinary characters: dilettante sons, shady business-men, mobsters, feminist big game hunters, and detectives. The more I wrote, the crazier my backstories became, as I strove to keep myself interested and ran out of stock ideas. There was the cryptozoologist whose fiancée had been killed by Bigfoot; the nun who was a member of the order of Hypatia, a secret, sacred sisterhood trying to take down the Vatican; her bodyguard, a woman who single-handedly found her way out of the African jungle as a kid. I suppose I really jumped the shark when I wrote about the poor girl who had been blown from Canada to Maine by a hurricane and then forced into prostitution. Every character had a connection to other characters. The nun had her bodyguard, the mobster extorted money from a number of people, and the precognitive artist's dead prostitute sister had been friends with the Canadian prostitute. The players and I wrote one another e-mails about character histories, and I sent tips on how to assemble a costume from one's closet and thrift stores. I encouraged players to aim at a Victorian steampunk style, although the game world didn't quite fit the genre.

CTHULHU CHARACTERS:

Genevieve Hudson, 27, artist

Genevieve was born to a middle-class Bostonian family, the oldest of five sisters, and had a close relationship with her next-youngest sister, Hortense. The five sisters went to private school where they learned to be pure, pious, domestic, and submissive (although the last lesson never stuck). They also became conversant in literature, history, geography, drawing, and music. Hortense excelled at the latter, learning to play and sing beautifully, while Genevieve became an accomplished painter and artist.

When Genevieve and Hortense were seventeen and sixteen, respectively, their father died after a fall off a horse. Oddly, Genevieve had drawn a picture of her father doing this after a strange dream the week before. After Dad's death, the family became nearly destitute, left with nothing more than their gable house and a tiny pension.

As the eldest daughters, Genevieve and Hortense found employment. Genevieve moved to Manhattan as a governess for a wealthy family, while Hortense moved to Cape May, New Jersey, to serve as a companion to an elderly aunt fond of music.

Genevieve's life in New York was difficult at first. She missed her family dreadfully. But she had the weekends to herself to paint and draw. She worked for Horace Astor, an art collector with a magnificent collection in his uptown mansion. Her big break came when he chanced across some drawings she had made illustrating architecture for the children. Recognizing her talent, Horace introduced her to other local collectors, and her work began to sell, first in a trickle but then in a steady stream. Genevieve left employment with the Astors and set up her own studio. Henry Wellington, the prominent businessman's son, was among her chief supporters.

Genevieve keeps a private set of paintings drawn from her own dreams. The queer set of images has predicted future events, among them the great blizzard of 1888 that killed so many in the Manhattan streets and a freak flood that killed hundreds in Pennsylvania the following year. Lately, her private paintings have taken a dark, sinister turn. . . .

While Genevieve's career flourished in New York, Hortense fell on hard times. Within a year of her arrival in Cape May, her aunt passed away, leaving all her worldly possessions to the church. Without enough money for a train ticket to New York, Hortense took a job as a maid at a local resort but found she could make more playing piano and singing in a burlesque show at a local house of ill repute. From there, it was a short fall into infamy, which she tried to hide from her sister. Recently, she was found murdered in the whorehouse, her heart cut out, and one of her fellow prostitutes sent a telegram to Genevieve, notifying her of the circumstances.

Genevieve has come to Cape May to pay for a grave for Hortense and to sort through her sister's meager belongings. She feels guilty that she couldn't help her proud sister and responsible for the murder. Perhaps that is why, for the last few weeks, the pictures painted on the underside of her eyeballs are horrible, slimy, tentacled things that fill her with regret and fear. . . .

Dr. Stephen Rowe, 35, cryptozoologist

Dr. Stephen Rowe is the only son of a Cleveland cooper and his wife. Though his father was not educated, soaring demand for barrels at this stop on the frontier propelled the Rowe family to middle class wealth, and Stephen was able to attend the University of Wisconsin at Madison, where he majored in zoology and received his doctorate with flying colors. Soon after graduation, he accepted a professorship at the nascent Cleveland University.

Unfortunately, a mountaineering trip to Washington State with several of his good friends derailed his promising career. One night, a rustling outside his tent woke Rowe. Across the moonlit clearing, he saw a stooped figure, standing on two legs, naked, and covered with hair. The creature looked quite savage. It had a prominent brow and an elongated jaw and appeared to be sniffing at their clothing, which they'd hung out to dry on a line. Rowe remained silent and still, not knowing how to approach the creature. When the beast loped off into the woods, Rowe followed it, afire with curiosity, his head filled with visions of the awards he'd win when it was announced that he had discovered a new species. Stephen lost the beast and his way back to camp in the dark. When the sun rose again, he finally backtracked to the tent where his anxious companions awaited.

His friends only laughed at his fantastic tale the more he insisted that he'd seen the absurd beast. Stephen's pride was hurt. The following night, he heard the rustling again, and again the beast appeared in the clearing. This time, it bared its three-inch-long fangs at him. Stephen fled into the forest, running for his life. The following morning, the sun rose, and he made his way to camp again. His fiancée, Elizabeth, and his best friend and colleague, Dr. Matthew Jameson, were mauled and dying. Stephen remains haunted by Matthew's last words, which were an unintelligible forewarning of some grave horror that he apparently witnessed during the encounter. When Stephen made his way to town, no one believed his incredible story, explaining it away as a mangy bear grown skinny and insane with hunger, seen through the eyes of a man awash with fear.

But Rowe knew what he had seen. Stephen carries Matthew's broken pocket watch, which retains the exact time when the slaughter occurred. From that moment forward, he was obsessed with finding out more about this beast and others like it. Over the last five years, he has made several trips: to Vermont to research sightings of the savage men who populate the forest of the Green Mountains; to New Mexico in search of rocs, the long-taloned birds represented on totem poles; to the Missouri River in search of carnivorous mermaids; to Mexico to see the chupacabras; and now, to Cape May after receiving reports of giant fish men.

During a trip to Manhattan in search of the fabled mentalist ear-slug, he met Duchess Ermengarde of Zutphen, a medium, and the two struck up a correspondence that has lasted for several years. The Duchess's companion, the hunter Josephine Kensington Phillips, is interested in tracking and killing new animals, and Stephen's letter to the Duchess about the fish men has brought them both to Cape May.

I handed the character histories and my rule book over to Gene, who had generously agreed to create statistics and skills for each of them according to the mechanics of the rules, a time-consuming technical exercise. In the meantime, I had a list of props to gather and create. Chief among these were ten realistic human hearts, five of them for use in the good-guy ritual, the hearts of the house, which would be hidden around the Salty Dog for the players to find. The other five hearts would stand in for the human hearts of characters— if Brendan's doctor successfully performed a ceremony on an unconscious person, he would be able to "remove" his or her heart for use in the evil ritual. Fine art is not my forte, and I didn't have a lot of money to spend on props. I cruised eBay until I found a heart-shaped Jell-O mold, which I promptly ordered for experimentation. I soon discovered that while cherry Jell-O mixed with cocoa powder makes a nauseating heart, the vomitous thing wasn't firm enough for players to toss around during a game. Instead I turned to an old grade school favorite: salt dough, a bakeable dough made from flour, salt, and water. I added red food coloring, which turned it the shade of brick. I molded, unmolded, and baked five of those to serve as the hearts of the house. Then I was out of food coloring. I made the next five hearts out of plain white dough, and George, who paints for fun, washed them with different shades of red until they looked drippy and gross.

I also needed to produce two pieces of paper, one written as a letter, the other ripped from a book, that would contain the instructions for each of the rituals. I wanted these sheets to look browned, crackly, and old. After a little searching on the Internet, I had a variety of techniques at my fingertips. Paper could be crinkled and then made flat, dipped into tea or espresso and dried out in the oven, rubbed with lemon juice and then heated over a candle. Its edges could be carefully wet and then burned in a controlled way, creating an interesting texture. I tried some of my good resume paper and some plain printer paper, experimenting on small swatches. Finally, I had a kitchen full of browned scraps and my final method. I wrote the rituals for Team Good and Team Evil on two pieces of paper and treated them. The resulting paper, brittle, spotty with water stains, and a deep brown, seemed ancient. At Gene's suggestion, I brought my yellowed sample scraps with me to leave around the house as red herrings.

The best prop, however, was not of my making. Jeramy's girl-friend, Jenn, who would be playing the artist Genevieve Hudson in-game, is an accomplished artist in real life and made a gorgeous statue of Cthulhu, perhaps five inches tall. I could only ogle his per-fection, his squiddy tentacled mouth, his long baleful claws, and his abominable dragon wings. She painted it a mottled green all over. Both rituals used the statue, which the GMs hoped would get the two teams to work together when it came time to power up the statue before its use in either ritual.

As the day of the larp approached, my blood pressure spiked from uncertainty. A larp has a great many moving parts, and of course, the actions of the players determine the outcome, like a Choose Your Own Adventure story, so I couldn't plan everything down to the last detail. What if my players ended up hating larp, as my husband had? I had brought George to a Knight Realms event and to a Dystopia Rising game, and he'd struggled with boredom and suffered from the overwhelming expectation he put on himself to behave in a theatrical manner. What if my gamers suffered the same fate? Aside from the boredom, I had put plenty of duties in other people's hands—Gene was recruiting his own NPCs and writing stats, Jeramy and Brendan would create backstories for their NPCs, plus Brendan and Liz were arranging a clock-chiming noise that we'd play, since we intended something creepy to happen at the top of every hour. The worst thing that could happen, I thought, would be boredom on the part of the players. Or if they hated it. Or too much plot. Or not enough to last a whole day. Or a logistical failure. My co-GMs told me I was feeling the typical new GM jitters, and in the week before the game, they took turns, as they put it, "sanity-checking" me.

With the food purchased, the props accounted for, more or less, the characters built, and my sanity still minimally intact, all of us headed down to Cape May for the weekend. Gene brought four friends with him, our volunteer NPCs, and after a few last-minute cancellations that got my nerves fired up, we had fifteen players, plus Liz, George, the three GMs, and the four NPCs—twenty-four people in all.

Everyone arrived on Friday, coming from Pennsylvania, New Jersey, New York, and Boston. Brendan and Liz brought their rule book, and I brought mine, from which Gene had copied quick-reference sections for the GM team to carry. We split our group of players into two. One stayed on the first floor of the house, which contained a kitchen and dining room, a bathroom, and a sort of parlor area around a fireplace. The second group went up to the attic, which had a weird kitchenette with a large area around it that would serve as camp NPC, as well as a large, in-game bedroom. Downstairs, Gene explained the rules to half the players, while upstairs, Ian and I explained them to our half.

Although he's in his early twenties, Ian resembles a grumpy old man. Perhaps it's that he wears overalls on occasion or that his long, curly hair, gathered in a ponytail, seems to belong on a southern gentleman or underneath a cowboy hat. Ian was Gene's best friend from high school, one who served, good-naturedly, as the butt of his jokes. I knew Ian well. He'd driven me to Knight Realms many times over the course of my research. He preferred to play sidekick characters that made other people laugh, and this was certainly true at Knight Realms, where he played the genial Hamish, a simple-minded Celtic bard who was the sidekick to Gene's Billiam. Hamish's simplicity belied Ian's intelligence. To play a stupid character well, you have to be smart. Hamish once told Billiam that in order to romance a woman, he'd heard you had to build her a ship, a courtship.

Ian brilliantly helped answer the players' many questions about the basics, explaining concepts like character statistics with the practiced air of someone who had dealt with newbies before. We ran the players through several rounds of combat, just as I'd been run through combat at DEXCON.

After explaining combat, Ian and I made sure to point out that what makes the game is the realistic reactions of your fellow players. If I knife Ian and he says, "Oh, I'm dead," it's lame. If I knife him and he staggers back, holding his ribs and gasping, that is much more fun.

We fielded a few questions about specific skills, and with that, the two groups rejoined downstairs. In true larp fashion, we stayed up quite late talking and drinking, and after a very brief GM meeting,

the remaining stragglers went to bed. The game would begin the following morning after breakfast.

At the crack of nine, I paired up with one of the NPCs. He and I
hid the hearts of the house in different locations—one outside in the
barbecue, two in the basement, one inside the fuse box, and one in a
drawer on the second floor. Gene had had the brilliant idea of scatter-
ing red herrings around the house. He and the other NPCs wrote on
my scraps of parchment—grocery lists, old notes, creepy, maddened
sayings—and strewed them around the house. Gene had also brought
what seemed like his entire stash of weapons—canes for walking,
baseball bats, boffers, coils of rope, toy guns—and we attached item
cards to each of them and put them in random places around the
house, some of them behind "locks," indicated with a card stating the
lock's level. One of the NPCs was Vince Antignani, a Knight Realms
player whose character was a prominent member of the Rogues'
Guild and a well-known Chroniclerite. We'd shared many scenes in-
game. When he first joined Knight Realms, Vince spent a few years
NPCing exclusively, with no real character; he was a master NPC.
True to his roguish expertise, he brought real padlocks to the game,
which we taped to some of the lock cards. Vince also owned a set of
metal lock picks, which he had brought to give to whichever character had the highest skill level in lock picking, in this case, the detective Jerome. I set up a small museum with a couple of objects, marked
with cards, in one of the bedrooms. The good and evil players each
needed a set of bones, which they'd find in this room.

Downstairs, my players had gotten into costume. For a group of
novices, they certainly looked impressive. My cousin Phoebe Hill had
one of the best. She was playing a bodyguard who was part of an
elite and secret religious order, and she looked like a member of the
Swiss Guard. She wore red and black striped pants tucked into high
boots and a sort of red tabard that hung between her legs with a smart
military vest buttoned over it. A rosary hung from her belt. Jeramy's
girlfriend, Jenn, wore a long skirt with a fusty blouse, a gold pin at its
neck, and a suit jacket. Cheri, a friend I'd met working on my literary
journal, was playing a big-game hunter and wore khaki pants tucked
into riding boots and a beige cap and came armed to the teeth with a

faux rifle and a hunting knife that caused her some consternation on the way home, when airport security questioned her about the weapons in her checked luggage. Brendan and Liz wore their Deadlands costumes. Everyone looked great.

With little fanfare, we called lay-on, and immediately the room filled with people talking loudly and animatedly. After about fifteen or twenty minutes, there was a lull. I noticed that no one had picked up anything, not the scraps of paper lying around, not the weapons, and I had a moment of panic. What if they didn't search the oversized dictionary and find the scrap of paper with the good ritual written on it? What then? I bonged the chime to indicate that it was noon and led some players on an expedition to see the house. We discovered Liz's character in one of the rooms, the first creepy thing of the day. She'd done her makeup very pale, and we found her lying unconscious on a bed. We led her downstairs, where the lull continued.

Gene came to the rescue. After I bonged the chime again, for 1:00 PM, a horde of zombies appeared out of nowhere to attack the players. Our first combat went somewhat slowly, as everyone was still getting used to the rules, but from then on, the larp went off without a hitch. In the compressed time frame of a larp, when a new GM is hyped up on adrenaline, much of the experience blurs, although for me a few select scenes stuck in my brain. I spent a lot of time marshalling various skills challenges, primarily lock-picking challenges. I and the other GMs had to prod players to get them to use their skills at first. When someone brought a locked book to me and said they wanted to open it, I asked, "What skill are you calling?" to help them along. It worked, and as the game progressed the players became increasingly willing to call skills off their character cards and role-play their actions. When players wanted to do research in the library, I told them what information they were able to find out. I spent a lot of time walking from the first floor to the third floor to coordinate the bonging of the hourly chime and the NPCs. Jeramy and Brendan were very much in the game. Brendan's character summoned a beasty in the first hour of the game to create dead bodies. When injured players were brought to his room, he Kali-Ma'd out their hearts á la *Indiana Jones and the Temple of Doom*. Team Evil acquired several members. By midday, the players had what Gene called "a case of the larps." They had picked the house dry, opened every lock, taken every weapon, and snatched up anything that seemed remotely useable. I was surprised that nearly all of the players were so into the game. The NPCs donned fake gunshot wounds and painted themselves white or green or blood red, depending on what the situation called for. The players politicked among themselves, and Team Good had officially formed up, helmed by a mystic, played by my friend Sarah, who had originally introduced me to the concept of larp. Jeramy, in his capacity as insane but good homeless guy, was able to psychically communicate with her and in doing so, eased the plot along. Freaky things happened every time our in-game chimes bonged. Dead bodies hanging down in the basement, dead Jeramy in the tub upstairs, creepy reanimated corpses in the living room. Zombies and more zombies.

While I spent most of the larp out-of-game, ferrying information among the GM team and answering player questions, the moments I got to play Ophelia were the most fun. I had a great scene with August, a physicist who worked with my husband and played Dieter the mob boss, in which we traded barbs and established that I was probably paying him protection money. As Ophelia, I also sold off an ancient artifact to Amruta, an astronomer who was playing our head nun, a member of a secret order. I also got to yell at a variety of people—Ophelia kept freaking out as players continuously picked the lock leading into her room and stole objects from her private museum.

My favorite moment occurred after lunch, when Gene sent a horde of powerful monsters to storm the first floor of the house. My former roommate Chip, who was playing a paleontologist, and I were attempting to escape from zombies by fleeing up the stairs, when Gene appeared above us, wearing armor made of skulls and armed with a large club. He nearly dropped my health points to zero, and he downed Chip, who bled out on the stairs. Gene brushed by us to engage other players. I fled into a coat closet, and while a crowd of characters rushed out the front door, I made it over to the stairs and managed to grab Chip. He, I, and three more players traveled down into the basement and out into the backyard, where the zombies flanked us. We fled up the back deck stairs into the second floor in an attempt to get our wounded selves and the dying Chip to the doctor, who had set himself up in a nearby bedroom. With four people to heal, Brendan, as the doctor, went to work. What should happen next but more zombies? They came up the stairs inside the house, chasing a collection of players. We shut the door to the room, so that our motions could be outside of the combat count. As we locked the door, we heard Gene's voice calling out the numbers, going up and down. Silence fell. Then it rose again—another zombie was attacking characters in the hallway, and the counting started once more. The battle had been raging for more than half an hour. Finally, silence fell. I heard one of George's colleagues say, "Does anyone want to continue combat?" and everyone inside the doctor's room, all five of us, plus everyone in the hallway, dead monsters and players included, broke out in hysterical laughter. "Ah, gamer humor," Brendan said: "It's universal."

He doctored each of the four of us in turn, using a fascinating set of old medical equipment that Liz had purchased for use as her doctor character at Knight Realms. The kit featured small bottles, bowls, and a terrifyingly large syringe. Brendan mimed bleeding each of us as part of his process of healing. Chip lay on the bed, eyes staring up at the ceiling, dead. After everyone else was healed, Brendan remained in the room along with me, although I was out-of-game because I wanted to see what was about to occur. Brendan set a cloth and a bowl on top of Chip's chest and began chanting in a strange language. Just as he Kali-Ma'd out Chip's heart, using a handy heart prop, an injured detective Jerome picked the lock on the door and fell into the room. Lucky for Brendan, a reanimated but now heart-less Chip was up and evil.

The whole scene, running from Gene's demon and being made evil, was a highlight for Chip, whose experience seemed to echo my own feelings—excitement, fear, and hilarity—about the first big battle I faced at Knight Realms.

I died almost instantly, and as I lay there on the stairs being dead, I could hear the carnage throughout the house—in the form of demons counting, people shouting their actions ("One! Two! Three—Evade! Four! . . ."), people role-playing their injuries, the noises coming from the kitchen, the dining room, outside, the battle splitting into branches—all I could do was hear it, and I was surprised at how totally exciting it was, and how the combat procedures of the game, regulated though they are, created a simulation of chaos, exactly like a battle but in very slow motion. And then I was carried up to the Doctor's room, and lay there in triage until he operated on me, took out my heart, and turned me evil. And still as I lay on the bed in his room I could hear battles outside, characters good and bad trying to get inside. It was terribly exciting. It showed how completely this game, when acted out and taken seriously by a large group of people, can turn into an experience very realistically heart-pounding.

Daniel, a web designer from Boston who played a cryptozoologist connected to Chip's character, thought that the big brawl helped unify Team Good. He remembered, "Everyone was on the brink of death; there were undead chasing us from every direction." After he helped drag the dead upstairs, "the wounded characters bounded together to regroup and confront it [Gene]. It was a compelling, almost epic moment because at that point everyone was working together to fight the same thing—we had the nun's paladin wielding the holy sword we'd acquired earlier and a slew of characters gunning it out on the stairs uncertain as to whether we'd survive. And we did, because we were awesome."

The players' highlights weren't all action oriented. Aatish, a physicist who played an undercover member of the Knights Templar, really got into the role-play. Later, he explained, "The moment when I woke up in the doctor's office and was staring at the ceiling, having just been chloroformed was a real in-character moment for me. The doctor played his character so well that I really found my sense of out-of-game reality sort of melt away and became increasingly convinced by the reality of what was happening in-game. I started getting stressed out by my conflicting allegiances, which I think is hilarious. That incredible moment of suspension of the disbelief was definitely the high point of my experience."

I missed what was, perhaps, the most memorable scene of the game. Both the evil and good rituals required a statue from another place, through a portal to another dimension. Gene had decided that the players would get the statue from a being who is part of the Cthulhu oeuvre, a demony creature named Nyarlathotep, essentially a stand-in for the devil. He decided that the NPCs would portray the seven deadly sins when the players entered and asked my permission to run a scene that had what could kindly be called "mature" themes. He warned everyone going on this mission out-of-game before they went down the stairs into the basement. No one will ever forget the sight. Two male NPCs unwillingly coupled on the floor, leaving a stream of fake blood below them. One of Gene's NPCs force-fed him cookies, beer, and cream puffs, personifying gluttony. Three months later, Gene said the thought of sugar cookies still made him sick. For the characters, the commitment of the NPCs to terrifying them raised the level of the game. The detective bartered away his skill at lock picking—to such an extent that he was unable to use doors at all afterward—in exchange for the statue the team so needed, and everyone returned to the house, their sanity levels a little lower after the numerous checks performed in the portal.

Events quickly unspooled after the portal group returned. The mystic and the nun powered up the statue, with Sarah, who played the mystic, breaking out some chants she knew from yoga. One of the businessmen bartered away his hand in exchange for a ritual implement needed for the good ritual. The mobster, turned evil by the doctor, had to shoot one of his prostitutes in order to get an implement that Team Evil needed for its ritual. She survived, and he blamed her injuries on the zombies that happened to attack at that moment. When the doctor attempted to revive her and remove her heart, something went awry, and she was able to remember what had happened to her and tell the others. As Liz "killed" her boyfriend in retaliation for his corpse-animating ways, a series of fish-demons stormed the house, killing Team Evil in mid-ritual and disrupting Team Good's subsequent attempt to bar Cthulhu from this world. Jeramy described the carnage as Cthulhu created a swirling vortex that destroyed much of the house, killing those inside. The final round of sanity checks, as Cthulhu began emerging from the center of the ritual circle made in the backyard, left nearly every character insane. At the last minute, Dieter the mobster, hewing to his backstory as a devout Catholic, broke through the evil doctor's hold on his soul and gave up the statue. An angered Cthulhu ate him, but with the statue in hand, the remaining good characters were able to close the vortex.

With that, the game ended, and we all headed into the living room for debriefing. We went around in a circle, talking about what had happened to each of us during the game. George thought it was funny that while Cthulhu was sucking everyone into his tentacly mouth, the big game hunter walked into the vortex to retrieve her gun but failed to retrieve George's unconscious body. The shady businesswoman was delighted to have sold her whaling company to the dilettante, the mystic liked being the unofficial leader of Team Good, the precog artist liked drawing the "visions" the GMs gave her, and the nun liked retrieving the skull of St. Catherine she'd been sent to locate, even though her character died. As we went around the room, it was plain that almost everyone had had a good time. Jeramy said it was the most smoothly run game he'd seen. Even the NPCs seemed to have enjoyed donning latex prosthetics and scaring the bejeezus out of the players. I was so relieved it was over that I almost threw up.

We spent the rest of the evening getting to know each other out-of-character and kvetching over all the things that had happened in-game.

My inbox filled up with post-game questionnaires in the following weeks, and a number of common experiences emerged. I felt nervous to read the questionnaires, since I had encouraged the players to write scathing criticisms, but as it turned out most people enjoyed the game, and their writing articulated a number of key truths about the hobby, impressions that reinforced my own. For starters, most everyone felt surprised that larp was so fun. Though he had never larped before, Chip immediately connected larp with childhood pretend, echoing a typical explanation of the hobby, that it is cops and robbers for adults. He wrote:

I was surprised, really, by how absorbing the experience was; it was like playing make-believe when I was a child, and having no sense of passing time. I expected it to be more awkward, that we'd spend a lot of time giggling at ourselves and that we'd eventually fall out-of-character completely and the whole thing would descend into chaos. But no: within minutes I felt transported, simply by putting on the trappings—the clothes, the mannerisms, the motivations—of someone I was not, and it was surprisingly easy to fall into that role and be there for an extended time. Time passed very swiftly and I hardly noticed that the sun had set. I think it had to do not only with playing a role, but playing that role with some goal in mind, a motivation—the game element of it. It was a quest, full of intrigue, danger, shotguns, whispered asides, hidden nooks, tight stairwells, people you couldn't trust—it was surprisingly absorbing and one of the most fun weekends I've had in a long time. It was also utterly exhausting—I was surprised by that.

As a new larper, I'd had trouble really getting into character and out of my awkward self, so I'd tried to help my players by providing longer, interlocked backstories, costuming tips, and realistic props, and by bringing in role-play veterans to model game behavior. Still, before the game I'd been anxious that my rookies wouldn't play through the awkwardness and into their characters, something I was rarely able to do even after a couple of years on the scene. As it turned out, in many ways, my efforts paid off. As John, a physicist who played a wealthy businessman put it, "I thought things would be a little more awkward, but when everyone around you is doing their best, then it puts pressure on you to keep up your own character as well. Acting in-character was another thing that I thought might feel sort of weird, but it was surprisingly natural."

Not everyone found it so simple to get into character. Several players definitely felt self-conscious, like Jenn, Jeramy's girlfriend and our precognitive artist, who cleverly figured out how to keep that awkwardness in-game. She wrote, "As the game went on, I noticed I wasn't the only one who was having trouble not laughing sometimes . . .

but that could easily be passed off in-character as insanity eking through." For many players, the role-playing breakthrough came when they realized they didn't have to perform the character as if it were Shakespeare but could relax and let some of their own personality come through. August, a physicist who played the mob boss, explained, "Rather rapidly, the character just devolved into me being me. Once I started yelling, telling jokes, and directly engaged in all affairs, I was simply acting in the way I would if I were put in that situation (and happened to have a criminal history). A fifty-year-old, brutal, German, mob boss would *never* be that loud and engaged in a room with strangers."

My cousin Phoebe and Daniel the web designer, both tabletop role-players, found that playing in a larp changed their geek-on-geek prejudices about the hobby. Daniel wrote, "Like many other role-players (and probably the rest of the world at large) I'd always secretly looked down my nose at the activity. . . . But I also think I secretly felt that I was going to love it." Phoebe came from a similar place. She wrote, "Having previously developed a pretty negative opinion of larping and larpers through my self-perceived placement in the geek hierarchy, I was most surprised by how much fun I had. . . . It really did feel like a natural next step in gaming for me, combining my beloved tabletop with my hobby of costuming. Larping was exactly what I expected it to be: people in costumes running around killing things and solving mysteries almost completely in real time. I guess I've moved to a lower level in the geek power rankings now."

Not everyone loved the game—one of the players, a mathematician, said that the game caused her to realize that "Larp is not for me. . . . I couldn't get into my character at all; I didn't know what she should be doing. And since everybody else was really into it, I felt strange. . . . For me, at least, a lot of things just felt like 'milling around.'" I hadn't avoided dull cocktail party syndrome completely.

The larp also evoked feelings in the players that lingered after the game ended. Sarah, for example, who played the mystic and unofficial leader of Team Good, felt betrayed by Daniel, who had been turned evil toward the end of the game. As she put it, "I felt so much closer to everyone after [the game]! I'd never met Daniel, but talked to him

Friday and then we ended up on the same 'team' in game. When I found out after it was over that he'd been turned to the dark side right at the end, I felt totally betrayed and the game was over already!" To me, the fact that Sarah couldn't shake the feeling of betrayal meant the game had been successful in forcing her to invest emotionally in her character.

Although the game had ended, several players weren't ready to let it go. The return to normal life from this metaphoric vacation was difficult for August, who felt "a jumble of emotions days afterward that took some time to weed through," adding that the event had been "a whole day of being bawdy, violent, aggressive, powerful, well-dressed, and deeply engaged in life and death situations. The following day I had to go back to worrying about pleasing a poten-tial advisor." Vijay, a mathematician who played the detective, had to leave early the next morning to get to an event with his advisor and wished he had more time to spend with the other players out-of-game. His early departure left him with "this strange empty feeling," because "I had spent a lot of time with many really cool people the previous day, but I didn't know their names or anything about them and didn't even say goodbye to most of them. I would have at least liked an extra day to hang out with them in real life!" In other words: larp can create a yearning for out-of-game social contact.

Nearly everyone felt the game had brought them closer to their fellow players. After the game, Daniel felt like he'd known some play-ers for a long time and that he "could strike up a conversation with them without fear because, after all, we faced the hideous unknown together," and said that the game worked as an icebreaker. Jenn found it easier to socialize in-character, because "I didn't have to worry about being awkward or making a good impression," but after the game was over, she felt that it was "a common experience we could all relate to." Chip said simply, "I loved my fellow gamers. We were an amazing group of people." John felt that the experience "was somehow more intimate than, say, going camping for the weekend."

So what was the verdict? Of the fifteen new larpers who tried Cthulhu Live, thirteen said they'd try larp again, given similar cir-cumstances and a similar group of people. Several people expressed concerns about larping regularly, worrying that the game might take on an inappropriate level of importance in their lives, since it was so absorbing.

The lingering effects of the game were more substantial than I expected. The game drew people together and bonded them, serving as the core topic of conversation for the rest of the evening. Afterward, Team Good met up for drinks in Boston a couple times. A month after the game, when George and I went to a gathering where many of the physicist and mathematician gamers were present, we talked about the game for nearly two hours, boring those who hadn't been there.

It is hard to explain the bonds that a larp can set into place. As one of the Cthulhu players put it, "No one else will get it when you talk about it later" because larp is a strictly "you had to be there" kind of event. Although I hadn't really played this game, afterward I felt a deep fondness for everyone who had contributed to the game and helped me run it. I had needed the larp community's help, and they had turned up with latex wounds, fake blood, boffers, and imaginations ready to help me give the experience of larping to people none of them had met before. There is no way I could have put on a larp without them. The players had faced death together and come out on the other side, a bond between them that won't be easily forgotten. Brendan, Jeramy, Gene, Liz, and I had faced a possible real-life disaster together, and they had come through for me, like friends do, filling in for my ineptitudes. We had been a true team, with each person's best qualities shining through. Mine were planning and organization, theirs were skills at improv, plotting, and aesthetics. Larp itself created the bond among us, and one that has proven enduring. Cthulhu may have destroyed the house, killed most of the characters, and driven the rest insane, but this vortex of horror had only confirmed the bonds of friendship and mutual interest within the GM team.

A Week in Denmark

A few months after Cthulhu fhtagn-ed in Cape May, I hopped a plane to Copenhagen to attend Knudepunkt, a yearly gaming convention focused on arty larp that rotates its way around Denmark, Sweden (Knutpunkt), Finland (Solmukohta), and Norway (Knutepunkt), changing its name according to the local language. Literally, Knudepunkt translates to "nodal point" or "knot point" though it means something like "hub" or "junction." Lucky for me, at the actual convention everyone speaks English.

When I left New Jersey, I wasn't feeling particularly adventurous. In fact, after a couple years studying the stateside larp scene, I felt jaded, doubtful that I'd learn anything new abroad. And yet here I was, humoring myself, curious about the famous Nordic avant-garde scene. I'd heard all sorts of rumors about Scandinavian larp, that the gamers were crazy hard-core, ran games that lasted for an entire week, built working medieval villages, and shunned those who wore machine-made moccasins or elasticized underpants. I'd heard that larp wasn't stigmatized abroad, that shockingly, larpers managed to get government funding for games. And I'd heard that the games themselves weren't even fun, that this scene was so avant-garde that, for example, getting some people together to act out the final hours before an alcoholic's death wasn't unheard of. It turned out that the rumors had some truth to them. After spending some time reading up on the Nordic scene I concluded that to high-art larpers, my Cthulhu Live game might be considered cute. If my game were a fluffy bunny, arty Nordic larp would be the secret policeman executing your first-born—but for artistic reasons. Discovering the Nordic scene felt like reading James Joyce or Gertrude Stein after spending a lifetime on fairy tales. The arty Nordic games can be seriously high-concept. If stateside larp is *Lord of the Rings*, *Nancy Drew*, and *Star Wars*, then Nordic larp is *Mrs. Dalloway*, *120 Days in Sodom* (I am not kidding; some Nordic gamers once ran a game based on this), and *Schindler's List*. The Nordic scene is proof that fun is not a necessary or essential component of larp, proof that the hobby can sustain high-art aspirations.*

I spent nine days in Denmark learning about Nordic larp culture. Before Knudepunkt officially started, I participated in A Week in Denmark, six days of organized games, touristing, and parties that convention organizers ran to acclimate out-of-towners to local gaming culture. My Nordic larp adventure began with a six-hour tango lesson I attended mere hours after my jet-lagged self touched down in

---

* Although the arty larp scene of Knutepunkt is robust, visible, and international, it represents only a small component of the larger Nordic larp culture, which is a fragmented collection of smaller groups doing mostly medieval boffer and vampire games, though these genre games typically feature fewer rules than their American counterparts. There is no monolithic pan-Nordic scene per se; rather, there are many small, local scenes that may communicate domestically, but rarely across borders. In the past few years, some arty larp academics have claimed the name "Nordic larp" for their style of game, dubbing the genre games "mainstream larp." For the sake of brevity, in the next two chapters, I'm using "Nordic larp" interchangeably with "artsy Knutepunkt-style larp that brings together practitioners from Sweden, Denmark, Finland, and Norway."

Copenhagen. I had signed up for a game called In Fair Verona, which required its players to attend a workshop before the game in typical Nordic fashion. In Verona, characters used dance, not boffers or card pulls, to interact with one another, and so at the workshop, we learned how to tango and used it to develop characters.[1]

About twenty of us, half women and half men, met with GMs Tue Beck Saarie and Jesper Bruun in an oblong dance studio. They warmed us up with some silly games and then taught us the moves. At first, we moved in couples, walking side-by-side, and from there we graduated to dance steps performed in a variety of embraces, swapping partners with each song. As we learned the steps, Tue and Jesper talked to us about how physicality could convey character personality. We practiced dancing lightly and heavily, as if we were slump-shouldered introverts and extroverts cruising for a new date. The studio dance floor was partitioned with masking tape, creating a five-foot-wide aisle on either side of the studio's long sides, aisles which were, in turn, partitioned into a number of smaller "rooms," representing the game's setting, a street in New York City's Little Italy ghetto of the 1920s. We practiced dancing up and down the length of the studio and also inside the small, masking-tape rooms.

With the dance moves somewhat under our control, we moved into character creation, a process that involved neither a thousand-page-long rule book nor any set of statistics. Each player had brought one or two period-appropriate props from home, which were laid out on a table. I had brought a lacy black scarf, but there were also hats with black netting, a rosary, a gun, a top hat that could be compressed to flatness, an exotic necklace, and a wooden fan, among many other items. Each of us selected a prop from the table as inspiration. The character description, Tue and Jesper told us, didn't have to be a history but could be a list of key words or a drawing of how we thought the character might look. We repeated the procedure with a second prop. Next, we paired up a couple times, talking about the characters and swapping away one of our sheets until everyone had a role they were happy with. I ended up with a matchmaker I'd written based on a tiny glass bottle of perfume I'd snagged from the table. It looked like a love potion to me. As a professional observer, I find it difficult to invest myself into the moment, and since the theme of In Fair Verona was love, I thought that casting myself as a matchmaker would give me plenty of reason to interact with others during the game.

Next, our GMs poured many slips of paper onto the ground and told us each to take one. The slips had character dilemmas written on them, coupled with two outcomes, a positive outcome—what would happen if your character overcame the dilemma—and a negative outcome—what would happen if your character failed to change. We split into groups to discuss how to integrate these dilemmas into the characters we'd written and then repeated the procedure with a second slip of paper, choosing the dilemma that fit best. My character's flaw was that she thought her view of the world was correct and preached about it to others. If she overcame this flaw, she'd be open to new relationships, but if she didn't, she'd become irrelevant.

Next, we developed the social milieu of the street through dancing. We paired up at random for dances representing positive, negative, and oppositional relationships. As we danced, we talked to our partners, sussing out the details. My positive relation was with another American, playing a watchmaker who wanted to join the Mafia. We agreed that he was my godson and that I would try to dissuade him. I had a negative relationship with an out-of-work artist, a former client of mine who had failed to marry the woman I'd set him up with, bringing my matchmaking ability and taste into question. The local Catholic priest and I had an oppositional relationship—I thought he was uptight, and he thought I promoted lasciviousness, but at the end of the day we shared a common goal: to marry off the single folk.

With that, our pregame workshop ended, and after a raucous dinner at the community house, the base of operations for A Week in Denmark, I went to sleep in a basement room along with perhaps twenty other foreigners—Swedes, Frenchmen, Germans, Israelis, Czechs, and Finns. It was the only full night of sleep I got all week.

The following morning, In Fair Verona reconvened for the second part of the workshop. After warming up with some tango, we made a status line with bum characters at one end and the highly educated rich at the other. You could negotiate with your neighbors to move up or down. As a businesswoman, my matchmaker fell somewhere in the middle. We danced with partners who were near to us on the status line to gain two more relationships. Finally, we divided ourselves into groups according to status. Tue and Jesper gave us masking tape and instructed us to create hangouts for our characters. A dockworker, a writer, a café owner, and I decided our haunt would be a café. Around us, we saw other rooms being made. The tony end of town held a church/school, a flower shop, and some private space, where characters could go to be alone. The other end of the room, the poorer side of town, included a speakeasy with a shady back room, an alley, and a place under a bridge, complete with a tiny masking-tape octagon that represented a fire in a trash barrel. On Tue and Jesper's advice, we also included a sleazy motel room at that end of town. We all knew what dancing in there would mean.

With that, my first pregame workshop ended, and we broke for lunch. The pregame workshop is a typical Nordic practice and allows the players to get comfortable with one another. Sometimes the workshops include lessons on the philosophy of the game world, including feminist philosophy or the politics of a historical era. Sometimes workshops include lessons in physical game mechanics. And GMs often use workshops to help players develop character concepts and webs of relationships. The inclusion of workshops in Nordic games represents a key difference in attitude between American and Nordic organizers. Most American larps follow a CEO-style model with someone like Knight Realms' James C. Kimball at the helm, imagining the game universe, creating rules for it, and fleshing out its history and culture. American GMs typically present a fully formed reality with concrete, planned plot obstacles for players, whose characters generally enter the game without an elaborate network of ties to the in-game community. The players arrive ready to be entertained, ready to go on a quest, and prepared to grab some part of the main plot for themselves, prepared to steal a moment in the limelight. The Nordic style of workshopping seems socialist in comparison. Through workshopping, players help create the world of the game by forging relationships among themselves and, in Verona, quite literally by inventing the shops along the in-game street. Similarly, the responsibility for the in-game action sits more firmly on the players than it does in American larp. Nordic GMs rarely create plots for the players to pursue or solve; rather, they set up the scenario and step back—it is up to the players to create their own fun and to embark on their own emotional journeys.

The In Fair Verona workshop accomplished several objectives: it taught us the core game mechanic, the tango; it developed relationships among us as characters and as people so no one had to feel like the new kid in the lunch room; it offered each character a possible emotional arc, a character goal to reach or reject, and in doing so, the workshop dispersed what might be thought of as the traditional larp plot (no invite-only mods here); and finally, the workshop invested us in the world we created together and set our expectations of what might happen during the game. In short, the workshop helped avoid some of the pitfalls of more conventional, stateside larp by giving us full, round characters who would arrive at the game already enmeshed in the community.

During the lunch break we got into costume, supplementing what we'd brought with spare items from the props table. Meanwhile, Tue and Jesper set up the dance studio, covering the windows with cloth so that the room's only light emanated from the theatrical lamps they'd set up, spotlighting certain rooms and allowing others to remain shadowed. The sleazy motel room got lit with a red light, the better to indicate its symbolic, in-game purpose.

The game's actual rules were incredibly simple. Since these characters worked out their emotions through dance, to refuse a dance, even with someone your character hated, was forbidden. We would play out three acts, each of which lasted a preset number of songs. The GMs would light candles during the last few dances of each act to let us know the end was nigh. Sometime during the first act, we had to dance with our negative relation, a move that should catapult our characters into their predetermined crises. During the second act, we would explore our character dilemmas, and in the third act we'd drift toward our positive or negative outcomes. Anyone who felt unsure about where their character was going could request a dance with Tue. The theme of the game was love, so we should be actively seeking love, Tue and Jesper told us, and most of us should find it during the course of the game.

Over the three acts, my matchmaker danced with almost everyone, from the writer to the funeral director to the priest to the bum. My most fun dance was with the male busybody, who wanted to make his old girlfriend (his negative relation) jealous. We danced as she followed us and glared. My character gave love advice. She persuaded the teacher to apologize to his protégé, the shoeshine girl, for striking her in anger. She tried to set up her godson with the flower seller. She told the gambler he should ask out the fast woman who hung around the bar, and the two of them married, confirming my character's worldview.

As the game progressed, my character became ever more convinced of her judgment and taste and thus failed to change her ways, drifting toward the negative outcome on my character sheet. Increasingly, she felt left out as the rest of the characters paired up, for who could match the matchmaker? Several times over a widow, she knew that she had missed her chance at love tonight and forever. She ended the game depressed and alone, the young, lascivious priest-in-training attempting to strong-arm her into the motel room with him.

I can't help but wonder if my American prejudices about larp motivated my character's depression at the end of In Fair Verona. In general, games that explicitly model sex and love aren't played in the states— I've certainly never encountered one—although US larps aren't completely without romance. Knight Realms, for example, has a handful of coupled characters, most of them also couples in real life. FishDevil's Deadlands campaign does model sex with an unsexy mechanic; prostitutes ask their johns over to a quiet corner and have them draw a card—the higher the card, the better the romp was. Perhaps Americans don't play love because there aren't a lot of representative or satisfying mechanics—such as tango—bouncing around the scene. Maybe Americans don't play love because it seems emotionally dangerous. As Finnish game researcher Jaakko Stenros put it, love may feel more dangerous to play than violence because love is a common human emotion—few people in the developed world will ever stab something with a sword, but most of us will fall in love. Violence seems more fantastical and may therefore feel easier to leave behind at the end of a game. Furthermore, violence is a physical act, while love is an emotional one, and physical boundaries seem easier to maintain than emotional ones. Larp violence isn't permanent. If I "die" from a boffer strike, at the end of the game I can still ride home with the friend who struck me down. I might be mad, but it's the emotions that persist, not the physical violence. But if I really try to fall in love with another character during game, how do I turn off that emotion, and what happens if I can't or don't want to? Many Nordic larpers told me stories of relationships, including marriages, that ended after intense games that had love or relationships as a through-thread. Furthermore, they seemed to view the mild post-larp crush as a natural byproduct of the game, and one that players can deal with. Perhaps since I'd come from a gaming culture bereft of love plots, I felt nervous about the unwritten rules and couldn't locate the social boundaries when it came to playing love. I worried about conflating my emotions with my character's, and so instead, both of us opted for emotional distance.

Even so, I had a great time at the game. I learned a real life skill, how to tango, and even without the larp trappings that would have been fun. The Nordic way clearly had advantages—my character felt round and developed before the game started, and as a result I'd been able to really feel her feelings during the game. Even better, I didn't have to worry about memorizing rules or looking stupid while trying to recall how a skill off my character sheet worked. As a mechanic, the inability to refuse a dance and the interaction inherent in dancing tango meant I couldn't retreat into myself and stand uninvolved on the edges of the game. I'd really invested in my character, and when the game ended, I felt legitimately drained and depressed, emotions that dissipated in the hours afterward, as all of us returned to the community house for a traditional Danish Christmas dinner—a way of sampling Danish cuisine—with the rest of the A Week crew. After the requisite toasting ended, Tue and Jesper cued up some tango, and everyone from the game danced for another while. It felt like we could have tangoed forever.

One Danish scenester I interviewed called Nordic arty games "an extreme social sport," and the day after the tango larp, Valentine's

Day, I got a sense of what he meant. In honor of the love-based holiday, the A Week folks organized a host of love games for us, and I played in one, a freeform game called Doubt.

Defining the word *freeform* (or indeed many terms used on the Nordic scene) is a little like starting a land war in Asia: you're destined to fail. For starters, there's a translation problem—the Knudepunkters are collectively translating terms with local sensibilities from four languages into their common language, English. The terms might translate into the same English word—"immersion," "character," "larp"—but carry different local nuance. According to Stenros, the Knudepunkters spent the first few years of conventions attempting to figure out these differences in language. Knudepunkters also take an unholy joy in debating technical terms, and larpwrights frequently create games intended to push the boundaries of any definition that's been agreed upon. On top of this, Nordic larpers come from a culture that disdains rule books and character sheets, along with their clear parameters. After a week of asking scenesters to explain it to me, as near as I can figure, freeform is a large, catch-all term that denotes games with both larp and tabletop aspects. Finnish larpwright Juhana Pettersson told me to imagine a continuum with elaborate, fully immersive, high-production medieval games at one end of the spectrum and traditional D&D at the other end. Freeform would be the stuff in the middle, he said, games that combine some larp techniques—like acting out the stuff your character does—with some tabletop techniques—like fast-forwarding through the boring two-mile hike your character takes to get to the dungeon.

The freeform game I was about to play, Doubt (2007), belonged to a particular school of freeform gaming—it was a jeepform game.[2] The jeepers (catchphrase: "We go by jeep.") formed in Sweden in 2001 in reaction to the perceived staleness of the freeform scene. They have a website, www.jeepen.org, that lists the artistic tenets they endeavor to follow, along with PDFs of some of their games and bios of the inducted jeepers. Jeepform games tend to be small—usually for three to five players. Sometimes there is a game master, and sometimes not. Typically the games have few rules and realistic premises. As jeeper Frederik Berg Østergaard explained, the jeepers believe that "the drama in everyday life is equally as interesting as playing vampires on spaceships. I mean, I know how to play out a relationship drama or the sad clown in a circus but not so much about playing a three-thousand-year-old vampire on Titus." Jeepform games also make frequent use of "meta-techniques," game elements that deliberately break the flow or reality of the narrative in order to advance or deepen the story. The meta-technique of monologuing, for example, allows GMs to stop time inside the game so that a character may talk about his or her feelings. Jeepform games often allow multiple players to portray the same character as a way of heightening tension and enhancing the emotional meaning of the game. Although Fredrik Axelzon and Tobias Wrigstad wrote Doubt, neither of them would be GMing the game, which is typical of jeepform games and other short games on the scene.

I embarked on my jeepform adventure along with four other people in a small, white room outfitted with some basic furniture—a coffee table, a worktable, several upright chairs, and a couple bean-bag chairs. Our GM, a slight Swedish woman named Ida Nilsson, had unusual hair: the left half of her head was shaved close to the scalp, but on the right side her honey-brown hair fell almost to her chin. She had thin, pixie-like facial features perpetually set in a serious and intense expression. My three fellow players included a pair of female friends in their twenties, one with cropped red hair and a hoop nose ring who looked as though she belonged in art school. The other woman wore a large bohemian scarf around her throat and had a smile that was both easy and nervous. A tall, theatrical man in a dark turtleneck completed our quartet.

Ida explained the premise of Doubt to us. The game dealt with relationships and temptation through two main characters, Tom and Julie, successful actors who were currently performing a play about Peter, a stockbroker, and Nicole, a successful fashion designer. Over the course of the game, we would play scenes in real life—between Tom and Julie—and scenes from the play—between Peter and Nicole. In real life and in the play, members of both couples would be romantically tempted.

Ida explained that this game was meant to induce bleed. "Bleed" is a technical term used on the Nordic scene to describe what happens when a player's emotions and a character's emotions get mixed up. If I show up at Knight Realms feeling angry and Portia picks a fight with someone, that is "bleed-in," since my personal emotions are affecting my character actions. Conversely, if someone insults the *Travance Chronicle* and I feel mad after the game is over, that is "bleed-out," since Portia's emotions are leaving the game and staying with me in real life. Most larps, intentionally or not, involve some level of bleed, but certain jeepform games, such as Doubt, actively play off these feelings. Related to bleed is the idea of playing "close to home," one of the jeep ideals. To play close to home means to put yourself and your real emotions on the line during a game to induce maximum bleed. Doubt intentionally features paper-thin characters—if all a player knows about Tom is that he's an actor, then during the game he or she will have to improvise a fleshed-out character, ideally one drawn from real life. The idea is that when players put their own emotions on the line, the game has the potential to lead to self-discovery and catharsis.

Doubt has a highly structured format divided into a number of scenes set in real life and in the play. The larpwrights laid out a long list of scenes in the game materials, a few from real life—for example, Tom and Julie returning home after having a great show—and then a bunch from the play, for example, the time when Peter watches Nicole's fashion show with Maud, her assistant. Together, the five of us were supposed to splice eight additional scenes from real life into the set list. In order to create the new scenes, we matched up people and places from prewritten lists. The people included generic figures such as the ex, the barmaid, and the double-date couple, while the places included locations such as at the song coach's, the restaurant, and the wonderful apartment. A half hour later, we had our scenes set and spliced.

Ida also explained that we would be using monologues. If she pointed at one of us and said, "Monologue," we would give a soliloquy on our character's feelings at that moment in time, though in-game no one else would hear it. Monologues had the capacity to create a positive sort of metagaming; if one character expressed feelings about her infertility during a monologue, for example, other players could then use that knowledge to help raise a scene's emotional stakes later by, for example, bringing up children in conversation.

The rules of the game, outside of its structure, were simple. Tom and Julie could only be tempted by members of the opposite sex, and at most, only one of them could succumb. One-night stands were not permitted—there needed to be at least a two-scene buildup before succumbing to temptation. We could only use people and places from the lists to create our new scenes. Time must proceed in a linear fashion—no flashbacks. Finally, we could go to Paris once. Whatever happened in Paris did not affect the game permanently—if Julie and Tom broke up in Paris, for example, they would be together in the next scene.

We talked about how much physical contact each of us were comfortable with and sang "head and shoulders, knees and toes" to warm up. Ida paired up the woman with the scarf and the man in one improvised scene and the red-haired woman and I in another scene and then cast us. The man and smiling woman would play Tom and Julie, while the redhead and I would play Peter and Nicole, respectively. We all stood in a circle and gave a short personal monologue on the meaning of love and relationships. With the pregame activities complete, we were ready to begin.

Ida served as the director of our impromptu play. She announced the setting and characters in each scene while the four of us arranged the room's furniture to set the stage. To represent Tom and Julie's apartment, for example, we put two chairs next to each other, mimicking a couch, with the coffee table in front. During scenes that involved Tom and/or Julie, the redheaded woman and I played any other necessary parts—the double date couple, the barmaid, Tom's parents. During Peter and Nicole's scenes, the other players returned the favor. Sometimes, Ida egged us on, whispering incitements in our ears, telling us to hold our scene partners to the wall, to really try to seduce them, to ignore their weak excuses. Sometimes, if we weren't ratcheting up the tension, she'd ask us to go back a few lines and begin again. Most of all, she listened for the rhythms of the scenes, saying "cut" to end them on lines of emotion. She also cut scenes in which we began to ham it up. For example, when Tom asked me, his father's new trophy wife, where I was from, I paused dramatically and then said, "Belgium." We dissolved into giggles. Ida cut the scene, and we moved on. As the game progressed, Ida delivered a few monologues drawn from her own life on the nature of love, jealousy, and flirtation.

I found it easy to become Nicole, in part because her job as a fashion designer felt similar to my own by dint of its artiness. More important, I didn't have to become an abstract character or measure myself against some pre-written sheet, didn't have to imagine myself into a world of magic while trying to act "naturally." When in doubt, all I had to do was to say what I really thought. In scenes focusing on Tom and Julie, I enjoyed stretching my creative writing muscles, trying to imagine ways to help raise the tension between them. As the game progressed, our characters deepened. We discovered that Tom was more famous than Julie, who felt neglected and overshadowed. He felt she didn't understand or respect him enough. He flirted outrageously with the barmaid. By the end of the game, during a talk on their couch, Tom told Julie that he thought her view of love was immature. At the end of the game, they stayed together, but only barely so. During the play scenes, the conflict between Peter and Nicole escalated. Nicole wanted to get married, but Peter demurred, continually putting off serious discussion. Nicole felt he never made time for her, didn't care enough to develop shared activities, and at one point, she broke up with him. During the final scene, they reconciled, as Peter proposed and she accepted, with reservation and dread.

After the game ended, we sat in a circle for the debriefing, a common and important element of Nordic gaming. A debrief serves as the buffer between the game and the return to real life, offering players a chance to kvetch about what happened in-game and the opportunity to discuss anything that was or could have been problematic. Debriefs can help build community among the players and provide a forum for organizer feedback. In general, more intense games require longer debriefs.

Our little debrief lasted about forty-five minutes. Ida asked me and the woman who played Julia how it felt to play the same character, and she asked the red-haired woman and the man the same thing. She asked the players of Tom and Julia what it had been like to watch the play end as it did, to know the two of them were playing that hard scene every day. Ida asked what of ourselves we put into the game. We revealed a little of our true selves as we talked. The red-haired woman said she'd been with someone who was always putting off their serious talks until later and that she'd tried to personify that through Peter. Her friend admitted that when Tom called her "immature" during their final scene, it had felt like a blow to the stomach. The turtlenecked man admitted that the game had resonated with him but didn't elaborate—he was a game designer who believed that playing for bleed was a bad idea but had wanted to try it before he levied criticism. As for me, I had a revelation after a scene in which Nicole showed Peter some fashion drawings, to his apparent disinterest. I realized that on some level it bothers me that my husband doesn't read my work, although we talk about it frequently. In general, I think this is a good thing, since it means his love for me isn't contingent on whether I'm a good writer—he'll love me even if my writing is terrible. Nevertheless, I discovered during Doubt that there's something in me that's a little sad that he's not my first reader.

With the debriefing, the game came to an official close. From start to finish, it lasted about five-and-a-half hours, and in that time I'd had to renegotiate my ideas about what larp could be.* I loved the personal nature of the storyline, which is typical of arty larp. The characters hadn't participated in an epic campaign against evil; rather, as flawed people, they struggled against the forces of society and themselves in the pursuit of happiness. The narrow scope of the game and the bleed it intentionally produced had given me a completely different experience than Cthulhu or Knight Realms had. This wasn't a vacation from reality; it was a journey into my own psyche. At the end of the game I felt the same pleasant quietness, the same awe that I feel after reading a work of literary fiction, a final quiet moment of medi-

---

* Although I considered this game a larp, primarily since it required the players to physically act out the story, in the Nordic countries jeeps are considered tabletop games, a fact of terminology that caused me several days of confusion.

tation, one that always feels like a poignant exhale to me, a moment containing the pathos and nuance of everything that came before. The game hadn't been playful or comic, and I wouldn't exactly call it "fun," but it felt meaningful and profound and stuck with me over the next few days.

The rest of A Week in Denmark was a blur of parties and planned events for me, though a few moments stood out. For starters, I saw evidence that larp has crossed over to the mainstream in Denmark. Random bartenders unaffiliated with the convention knew what live role-playing was, for example. And one night, we partied at Rollespil-sakademiet, the Role-Playing Factory, which is, amazingly enough, a professional larp group that runs games for Denmark's many child larpers. I went on a tour of the Copenhagen City Hall led by a local representative, a larper elected with the help of the Role-Playing Factory. I also met teachers from Østerskov Efterskole, a Danish school for ninth and tenth graders that bases its lessons around role-play. Most notably, I attended the Nordic Larp Talks, a set of short, polished lectures from luminaries on the scene and modeled after the TED lecture series on innovation and technology. [2]

At the nightly parties, people swapped stories about larp in different countries, talked aesthetics, and answered my many questions about the Nordic scene. Apparently, it is possible to get public funding of a few hundred euros or more for larps. I learned about techniques like "fateplay," in which players receive slips of paper emblazoned with their character's future, for example, "You will fall in love with a man wearing a tall hat." [3] I learned about safe words, a Nordic way of modulating psychological well-being during heavy and emotionally potent games. Players had code words they could use to regulate the intensity of scenes, to ask their scene partners to go harder, slow down, or stop entirely. I learned that "hard-core" means different things to American and Nordic larpers. Sure, any hard-core gamer stays in-character as much as possible, but this means more in the nitty-gritty world of Nordic gaming. While gung-ho American larpers might sleep outside in February, hard-core Nordic gamers go further in the service of their characters. I heard and read stories about medieval larpers hunting down, butchering, and eating real sheep and games in which players had actual sex in-character. Then, of course, there are the hyperslummers from *System Danmarc* (2005), a game that simulated a dystopian future slum with a highly organized caste system. The organizers built a slum out of shipping containers in the middle of Copenhagen. Some of the three-hundred-plus players chose to play hyperslummers, the lowest caste, and the game organizers brought in former drug addicts to share their experiences with them. According to organizer Peter Munthe-Kass's account, published in *Nordic Larp*, a coffee-table book documenting fifteen years of Nordic games, "During the game these players slept on the street or in makeshift sheds and were beaten and humiliated by other players. Some hyperslummers were even urinated on while sleeping."[4] Now that's hard-core.

Between the games, the outings, and all the fascinating cocktail conversation, I barely slept during A Week in Denmark. And so when we were bussed an hour out of Copenhagen, to Helsinge, for the actual convention, I hadn't even gotten over my jet lag and was starting to feel a bit loopy.

Knudepunkt Blew
My Mind

The Knudepunkters weren't the conventioneers I was used to. If these people spent their evenings playing D&D and watching *Battlestar Galactica*, like gamers in the States, then they seemingly spent their mornings reading Foucault and Chomsky before heading off to part-time bartending jobs while supported by the famous Scandinavian social safety net or to gigs in academia and the arts. They were still geeks, but geeks of a different breed—art geeks. I had never seen so many artistic haircuts gathered in one place—fantastic combinations of blue, purple, and red dye and dreadlocks peppered among heads shaved bald and long, death metal singer–style hair. The crowd dropped words like *indexical* and *ludology* into casual conversation while referencing *Star Trek* episodes and wore non-ironic elf ears with 1940s swing dress to costume parties.

This scene had a visible gender-queer presence, unlike the larp scene I studied in the States, which tended to smile on bisexual women but not lesbians and certainly not on gay male larpers, who statistically must exist in greater numbers than I encountered. In contrast, Knudepunkt had a visible gay and trans population, one that didn't seem to warrant any special comment from its peers.

The three-hundred-odd Knudepunkters were the only guests at the small, Spartan hotel hosting the convention, and fliers pasted up on doors throughout the building announced the clique-busting empty chair rule: any group sitting and talking needed to include an empty chair in their circle, signifying that anyone could come and join them.

My Knudepunkt began in the bar. I bought myself a beer, perched on a deserted couch, and was settling in for a bout of people-watching when a large contingent of Finns, swathed in black, swooped in with their drinks and started talking to me. Among them were Maria and Juhana Pettersson. Maria had deep purple hair gathered into a ponytail, wore glasses with heavy, plastic frames, and had a slight smile perpetually hovering in the corners of her lips. Her husband, a noted larpwright, had shaved his head bald and had a face permanently set on "neutral." They were both making my favorite fashion statement: head-to-toe black. Within minutes of our meeting, we were discussing a game Juhana had helped write and run called *Portaikko* (2010), which means "staircase," in which players experienced the loneliness of an obscure sexual fetishist. The first player to swing by the art gallery where the game ran had been an eighty-year-old woman, and Juhana had had to explain her sexual attraction toward fences and walls to her. Yet, he said, the woman got it and enjoyed the game.

Over the course of that evening I met Israelis, Italians, Frenchmen, Czechs, Brits, and Germans, all here to talk larp theory. Joined by their collective envy of the vibrant Nordic scene, they discussed their desires to create something similar at home. From the Scandinavians, I learned about some of the year's buzziest larps, such as Delirium (2010) and Mad About the Boy (2010). The former dealt with romance in a mental institution and ran for fifty hours, plus two weekend-long pregame workshops and a day of debriefing.[1] The organizers used a variety of tactics to make their players feel crazed. For example, they had players sign up for the game in male/female pairs, formed when one person invited a partner to play the game. Whoever had done the inviting was placed in the male ward of the in-game asylum while the invitee joined the female ward, regardless of player gender. The game featured non-linear time, so, for example, the ward's patients cleaned up after a party early on in the game but played the scene of the party later in the weekend. The intense game split up some real-life couples and created new ones. Ida, my jeep GM, for example, left the game with a new boyfriend.

Mad About the Boy was inspired by the comic *Y, the Last Man* by Brian K. Vaughn and Pia Guerra. The game had a simple premise: all the men on earth died a few years back, and now the government was running a pilot program to artificially inseminate women with sperm from sperm banks. The game's characters portrayed families—each composed of three women—applying to be part of this program. Halfway through the game, the last man shows up, naked and beaten, and the women have to decide what to do with him. The game ran twice, once with an all-female cast of players, except for the last man, and once with mixed-gender players all portraying women, excluding the last man.[2]

Everyone seemed to be in the bar, catching up with old friends, flirting, talking about games they'd been to or games they wanted to run, bandying about terms I didn't yet know the meaning of, like "pervasive" and "360° illusion," and amiably arguing about terms like "character" and "immersion." I ran into Juhana and Maria again on the stairs outside the bar, now realizing that Juhana had created a couple games I knew about from reading past Knutebooks—the books of larp theory that the convention organizers put out each year. In one of Juhana's games, characters tried to allocate the inheritance of a dead relative, expressing their hidden emotions by breaking cheap plastic coffee cups on the ground. Another game had featured characters with terminal cancer and involved players rolling around in flour in their underwear for a couple hours.

It was late, and then it was later. I decided to check my e-mail and go to bed, but Ida bounced up to me as I stood at the communal computer in the hotel lobby. "Want to come to an after-party?" she said.

Ida and I and perhaps four dude jeepers crowded into a small hotel room. The jeepers could have been some emo rock band, sporting, in varying combinations, plastic glasses, graphic T-shirts, sweater vests, blazers, tousled hair, and deliberate stubble. We took turns drinking concoctions out of plastic cups and sitting on one of the room's two double beds, and when one of them filled up with people, bouncing across to the other, as if in a game of musical beds. Apparently, Ida and two of the guys were trying out a new game someone in the room was working on, and their voices rose and fell in joy and pain as they cajoled and persuaded each other. I couldn't understand what they were saying—it was late, and they'd lapsed into Swedish—but it sounded intense. Whoever wasn't currently in the scene sat next to me on the bed, sarcastically describing what was happening on the other side of the room, only I wasn't sure whether I was being told about the game or the actual relationships among the players. At that late hour, it didn't seem to matter much. The game went in and out, and in between the scenes, we sat around and laughed. Finally, I headed to sleep.

Three hours later, I dragged myself out of bed, threw on some clothing, and desperately tossed cups of coffee down the hatch. I couldn't miss the "First-Timers' Guide to Knudepunkt Theory," a session designed to help everyone understand the cocktail conversation. As our speakers flipped through their PowerPoint, we got a crash course in Knudepunkt history. I knew a little from my pre-trip research and from all the mingling I'd done during A Week in Denmark. I'd watched video of journalist and larper Johanna Koljonen in the first Nordic Larp Talks, who noted that larp arose out of tabletop games in the Nordic countries, much as it had in the United States.[3] However, larp was easier to organize in Scandinavia because in Finland, Sweden, and Norway the public has the "freedom to roam" or "everyman's right": the right to sunbathe, picnic, swim, gather mushrooms or berries, and camp on public or private land, so long as the land isn't permanently damaged and people stay a respectful distance away from others' dwellings. That, combined with the lack of cultural litigiousness, made it easy to organize a larp in the woods, which contributed to the strong larp culture in Nordic countries. By 1994, summer medieval games in Scandinavia were drawing more than a thousand participants, and soon thereafter Erlend Eidsem Hansen, Hanne Grasmo, and Margrethe Raaum organized the first Knutepunkt in Norway in 1997, with the aim of building community among larp organizers across the region.

From the panel, I learned about the intellectual development of the scene. Between 1999 and 2004, members of the community wrote a great many larp manifestos. The two most famous of these were the Dogma 99 manifesto and the Turku manifesto. The Dogma 99ers patterned their declaration on the Dogma 95 film manifesto, written by Danish filmmakers Lars von Trier and Thomas Vinterberg in 1995. The Dogma 99 manifesto envisioned larp as a transparent venture, one focused on great, self-sufficient stories. [4] Their manifesto forbids many of the features prevalent in stateside larp: secrecy, organizer interference in the game once it has started, main plots (as opposed to plots for all characters), game mechanics, larps based on tabletop games, and a number of other elements. In contrast, the Turku manifesto, a Finnish school of design, emphasized immersing in a character over a story. [5] In this view, the true point of larp is to become one's character, simulating that character's internal thoughts and view of the world to the exclusion of all else—solving plots, creating dramatic situations that might be fun for other players, and so on.

The speakers defined a few more helpful terms for us, including "360° illusion" or "360° ideal," a design aesthetic focusing on set and costuming, creating the reality of the game as physically and completely as possible. Larpers into the 360° ideal care whether your underwear is period appropriate. I'd read about a couple 360° games in the recently released *Nordic Larp*, a book that was part of the new Nordic trend toward documenting the ethereal nature of larps. One such game, *1942—Noen å stole på?* (Someone to Trust?), explored life under the Nazi occupation of Norway. The players had done hundreds of pages of historical reading before the game and played characters based, in many cases, on actual people who lived during that period. At pregame workshops, players had their photos taken in costume to create period-appropriate identification papers, such as passports. Characters were either members of the local community, which was divided into family units, or part of a nearby German garrison, which contained Eastern European POWs, soldiers, and members of the Red Cross. During five days of game play the characters lived a simple, everyday life. Fishermen spent their days on boats catching fish, seamstresses sewed, housewives shopped for groceries, and everyone cowered during midnight air alarms. The community viewed the Germans, and those perceived to be collaborating with them, with suspicion. The game itself wasn't about resisting the occupation, although some characters belonged to the resistance. Rather, it was about understanding the mentality of people participating in and living under Nazi rule.[6] Many Nordic larps seem to be about trying out a certain mindset or exploring an emotion rather than saving a town from orcs or finding enough loot to buy a sweet magic item.

Finally, the speakers explained "pervasive" games to us, games played in real world locations. For example, a scavenger hunt is a pervasive—players go out into the real world and potentially interact with people who aren't a part of the game. Larp can be pervasive, though it often isn't. For example, the vampire games that police detective "Brian" played in a go-go club were pervasive, as the real-world club, full of real-world non-larping people, provided the game backdrop.

Impromptu chats in the hallways and panels filled the rest of my day, and by 5:00 PM I felt utterly exhausted from lack of sleep and lack of privacy. As a writer, I generally spend ten to twelve hours a day by myself in a coffee shop or at home, writing. Since arriving in Denmark, I hadn't had a second to myself—I'd been sleeping in a basement room with thirty other people, or now, in a hotel room with a roommate. We took all our meals communally, and every evening called for me to put on my extrovert hat and converse with the locals.

I'm not sure I felt this at the time, but in retrospect, I think my trip to Knudepunkt could be deemed an elaborate larp built for one, a larp conducted in public without the knowledge of those around me, a pervasive game. Like all games, it had a couple rules, ones I imposed on myself for the duration of the visit, my cardinal rules of travel (1–3) and reportage (4–6).

1. *Be flexible.* If you think something will be OK, it probably will.
2. *Talk quietly.* Do not add to the stereotype of loud Americans.
3. *Be polite.* Learn how to say *please, thank you,* and *excuse me* in the local language.
4. *Rule of yes.* Say yes as much as possible, because it leads to adventures. Like jeep parties. The corollary to this rule is that you must be a good sport. Don't just say yes; behave as if you mean it.
5. *Rule of neutrality.* Don't judge people with unusual habits or opinions.
6. *Rule of humanity.* Treat people as people; everyone has a story worth hearing.

The circumstances of the game took a toll on my psyche—I was alone in a foreign land, sleep-deprived, out of my element, without a home base, and surrounded by people who were used to slipping in and out of different roles. In short, as a person I had no context for myself, no one there to remind me of who I was by treating me in a certain way.

That Friday evening, I wanted to take a nap but was afraid to do so, lest my alarm-clock-less self fall asleep permanently. With so many events running in tandem, I feared I'd miss something—already the previous evening I'd missed the launch of *Playground Magazine*, a new publication on larp and gaming.[7] At the same time, I required some sort of rest—my ability to think and speak diminished sharply as the day wore on. Instead of sleeping, I hit the sauna, an important part of Knudepunkt for many participants, and one that was more restful than I expected.

After a solitary hour or two and a shower, I felt more like my old self again. I had regained the ability to form a coherent sentence, so when I ran into Ida and her boyfriend we struck up a conversation. The sauna might have restored my faculties of speech, but perhaps unfortunately, it also seemed to have removed my internal filter, so I spoke voluminously about any subject lobbed my way, including the strange things I'd noticed in Denmark. I'd never traveled abroad on my own before, and I'd kept my observations to myself over the last week, only daring to voice them in small dribbles to the three other Americans present. For example, I'd noticed that the overall level of education was higher on the arty larp scene than it was on the larp scene I'd followed in the States, due, perhaps, to the value that Nordic culture seemed to put on both education and art. I speculated that the scene's exposure to academia was part of what made its artiness possible, if the number of people writing larp theory and dropping words like *diegetic* was any measure. In film theory, *diegetic* refers to elements within the frame of a film. When a noir hero watches a jazz band play, that music is diegetic—the audience hears it, and so do the characters in the scene. In contrast, the techno music blaring as our samurai heroine kicks some girl-gang butt is non-diegetic—the music doesn't exist for her; it's dubbed in by the sound designers to set a mood for the audience. After subjecting poor Ida and her boyfriend to my logorrhea for a couple hours, we retreated down to the bar, and soon it was midnight, and time for a mysterious mini-party-game I'd received an invitation for earlier in the day, part of what Stenros called Knudepunkt's tradition of "one-hour parties, secret parties, 'secret' parties, and short weird theme parties."

Perhaps fifty or sixty people filed into one of the convention rooms, which was ringed with tables that had people—including the purple-haired Maria—standing on them, dressed in black, hands frozen in claws, fake blood dripping from the corners of their mouths. Several people passed out plastic cups of port wine, and our host announced the rules. We were allowed only three bites, "so make them count," he said. We had until the music ended—about six minutes—to make them. We milled around the room, flirtatiously eyeing one another, pouncing to bite strangers and acquaintances on the neck, laughing and talking, until the track ended. Then it was time for an after-party. I went with the jeepers again, who continued to party like rock stars, late into the night.

When I woke the next morning after a hearty two hours of sleep, I felt funny. Not funny ha-ha, more funny Kafka. I couldn't remember who I was. Oh sure, I knew I was Lizzie Stark, writer-wife-daughter-friend-pickle enthusiast of the monochromatic fashion sense. I was

Lizzie Stark, dammit, knower of song-lyrics, lit mag editor, and as my husband had titled me, "finder-of-things and ruler of Australia." But none of these things seemed to have any meaning. Maybe these ideas I had about who I was weren't as important as I thought they were, and maybe I didn't need to be any of these things. But if so, how could I still be me? More than that, if these identities were something I could put on or take off at will, if all identity was fluid, how could anyone have an identity at all? My mind went around and around on these questions. I'd lost myself somehow, amid the sleeplessness and identity play of Knudepunkt. I dragged myself to lunch and back in this peculiar mental space. My internal filter was still clicked off— courteous questions from people in the hallways, like "How are things?" provoked quixotic responses I couldn't control, like, "There are no good things or bad things, only things." I couldn't lie, not even for the sake of politeness, and I couldn't muster enough personality to prefer, say, coffee to tea. I was definitely in the middle of some sort of existential quandary. At the lobby computer I read some old e-mails to help remind me of myself, and although I still felt bizarre, outside of myself and outside of everything, I attended a couple panels, most notably one on *Ars Amandi*, a method of simulating love and sex in which Emma Wieslander, a Swedish larper and creator of the mechanic, spoke about it and some of the larps that used it.

Emma had a slight build, sported a frosted fauxhawk, and radiated a certain gravitas. In her essay "Rules of Engagement," from the 2004 Knutebook *Beyond Role and Play*, she made the case that sex and violence both deserve their own game mechanics, because rules "are all about portraying physical situations that one doesn't want the player to experience the same way the character does and vice versa."[8] Larpers use boffers because no one wants to be stabbed for real. During her impromptu Knudepunkt talk, she suggested that violence and sex represent the two extremes of human emotion, and that in the past, larps were more likely to tell violent stories than relationship stories, in part due to a lack of mechanics for representing romance and sex.

In her essay, Wieslander laid out the methods that contemporary Nordic games employed to simulate romance. Some games used a wysiwyg (what you see is what you get, pronounced "wizzy wig") method, allowing players to dry hump each other or, at the hard-core end of the spectrum, to have actual sex in-character. Players with romantically linked characters are encouraged to talk about physical limits before the game begins. The wysiwyg technique adds to the realism of the game, but it crosses a personal line for many people, particularly those involved in relationships with someone else out-of-game. This method seems pretty risky to me, but then the United States has a more litigious culture than Scandinavia, and in fact, my informal poll of stateside game organizers revealed either explicit or implied "no-touching" rules, designed to prevent creeps from being creepy, across the board. In some Nordic games, players simply talk through a sex scene, deciding what happened, although this method breaks the immersion of the game by introducing chatter, and it can give players the giggles during what might otherwise be a serious moment. There are also symbolic ways of representing sex: one player gives another a shoulder massage, people feed each other fruit, or perhaps an impromptu dance scene occurs—hey, it worked for Jane Austen. And finally, there is *Ars Amandi*.[9]

Wieslander came up with the method for the influential 2003 larp *Mellan himmel och hav* (Between Heaven and Sea), a game that explored gender as a social construct. *Ars Amandi* provides boundaries for touching and being touched in a larp. Players may use permitted body parts—hands, arms, and neck—to touch others in the permitted zones—on the arms, shoulders, or neck. Full *Ars Amandi* permits touch on the neck below the ears, on the upper portion of the back, around the shoulder blades, and on the upper chest, around the clavicle but above the breasts. This mechanic is highly adaptable—if full *Ars Amandi* seems too intimate, organizers can always restrict the region of touch to the elbows and below, or even to the hands. I briefly tried out the full version with some other noobs right after Wieslander's talk and found it both versatile and capable of conveying emotional nuance. Players can touch each other lightly or firmly and may use rhythmic breathing to amp up or dial down the tension. They may look each other in the eyes, drastically increasing the intimacy, if desired. This technique may be used to simulate sex symbolically—two vampires feel each others' arms and declare it represents the act of sex between their characters—or it may be used diegetically, as it was in *Mellan himmel och hav*, where within the game world the arms and shoulders, not the genitals, were the primary erogenous zones of the human body.

The world of *Mellan himmel och hav* was inspired by the short stories of fantasy writer Ursula LeGuin and played with gender. This world did not have men and women, but morning people and evening people. Evening people wore red and yellow, concerned themselves with philosophy and decision-making, and served as the objects of sexual gaze. Morning people wore blue and green, served as the sexual initiators, and were responsible for practical arrangements and implementing the decisions of the evening people, according Stenros, who participated in the game and wrote about it in *Nordic Larp*. In-game, marriage was not between two people, but among four—two morning and two evening people, who mated for life. An upcoming wedding in the community provided the occasion for the game play. During pregame workshops, players helped cocreate the world and learned about feminist theory. Like Mad About the Boy, *Mellan himmel och hav* had political and feminist aims and explored what it would mean to destabilize prevailing views of gender and monogamy. These larps are part of a movement of political larp on the Nordic scene that includes *System Danmarc* (2005), the slum of future dystopian Copenhagen, which was designed to bring home a message about present-day homelessness to its players.[10]

Learning about political games made me consider whether any of the larps I'd witnessed in the States had political leanings. James C. Kimball, a staunch conservative, runs Knight Realms, and although though he doesn't seem to have intentionally endowed his game with a political agenda, the game reflects his conservatism in a roundabout way. As a for-profit game, Knight Realms relies on things returning to normal between events, so the evil players can never take over the town, for example. The players' inability to permanently affect the world of the game in a major way fits with a conservative view of reality: that there is one natural, right, good way of being and that, inevitably, we will return to it between upsets.

Wieslander's explanation of the way rules function in Nordic games, that they "are all about portraying physical situations that one doesn't want the player to experience and vice versa," also suggests how different the Nordic and American larp scenes are. Broadly speaking, Nordic games, even boffer games, introduce rules sparingly, and most have rules thin enough to carry around in one's bra— typically no longer than a paragraph. Oftentimes, these games lack character sheets, instead offering short character histories. In contrast, American games tend to hew to the tabletop style, with hundreds of pages of rules, sometimes published over multiple books. The rules system of a game affects the experience of the players. In Nordic games with minimal rules, the players, not a randomized mechanic, decide what happens in any given scene, which encourages players to work together to create a meaningful outcome. The elaborate, numerically oriented character sheets typical of many American games emphasize leveling up to achieve the next skill advance and imply competition among PCs or with NPCs. Furthermore, elaborate rules create power gamers and rules lawyers—players who understand the numerics of the rules are likely to build powerful characters faster and more effectively—and imply the necessity of GMs, who are needed to settle the inevitable rules debates. Both methods have their advantages. The rules-light nature of Nordic games keeps the illusion of the game world intact—if Portia wants to persuade Billiam of something, she doesn't call a skill, she talks to him. And if he wants to rob her, he must sneak into her room without being seen. It's natural and easy to remember. The rules-heavy American sensibility, however, equalizes the players—even if I'm on crutches, my character can call a skill allowing her to be fleet-footed, the same as any track-star player could.

After the *Ars Amandi* panel, the academic portion of my Knudepunkt was over, and only the party remained. I hit the sauna again, in lieu of a nap, and gussied myself up for the evening's costume party. Tonight I'd try to play the role of myself, in the traditional stark costuming of a black dress and red lipstick. Other people were far more inventive. There was a woman with wild blond hair wearing orange eyelashes and dressed as a flame, a man in a pink cravat dressed as a bunny. I saw shirtless male angels, characters from *A Clockwork Orange*, people in 1950s party dresses, elves from sundry historical periods, pirates, satyrs, princesses, do-wop singers, demons, witches, and vampires. Earlier in the day, there had been a mass swing-dance lesson, and couples on the dance floor displayed what they'd learned. Everywhere I turned I saw people with their arms around one another, showing off tattoos, buying each other drinks, curling the corners of their Salvador Dali–esque moustaches, kissing each other on the lips with a friendly, easy intimacy, and most of all, talking. The next morning, I'd witness a mournful counterpoint to this in the hotel lobby, grown men and women hugging one another, weeping openly, whispering meaningful, deep words in one another's ears, and kissing goodbye both romantically and platonically, promising to write, to Facebook, to see one another next year or next month at another gaming convention.

Although it took me a couple weeks to stop waiting for Godot, to finish riding the existential wave that overtook me in Denmark, eventually I returned to "normal." And yet I feel forever changed by my experience there. The Nordic scene is proof that larp can be more than escapist entertainment; as a medium it has high-art potential. If I went to Denmark unsure of whether I'd ever game again, I returned as an aspiring larp evangelist, unable to stop talking about my experience for some weeks, to my husband's consternation. Knudepunkt evoked in me the yearning to return to that terrifying and fascinating place where there were no boundaries or rules, where there was no self, where identity itself seemed impossible. I felt as though I had peeked over the precipice of human existence, and in that one moment I was terrifyingly, truly alive.

Epilogue

I came into this book with a simple idea about larp, that people used it to compensate for something lacking in their everyday lives. What I discovered was a rich, complex hobby, just beginning to enter mainstream imagination in the United States. As it turns out, larp is anything but simple—oftentimes it requires the best efforts of numerous people laboring in concert. People larp for many different reasons. Some people want to escape from the world, while others enjoy solving puzzles, crunching numbers, experiencing extreme emotions, or dressing creatively. For some people larp is a vacation, and for others it's a way of exploring their most secret selves. Some larps are tiny, run with as few as two or three players in their street clothes, while others are huge, requiring full sets and entertaining hundreds of participants. Larp can convey a political message, evoke strong emotions, or simply engross its participants in their shared fantasy. In short, larp is a medium, much like theater or movies or novels, and just as film has *Lord of the Rings*, *Annie Hall*, and *Gettysburg*, so too does larp have its Knight Realms, its Doubt, and its *1942—Noen å stole på?*

Larp in the United States is beginning to diversify. Edu-larp, short for educational larp, is a hot topic on the Nordic scene right now and has started to crop up in the United States in the form of literary summer camps for kids. A July 16, 2010, *New York Times* article by Sharon Otterman looked at Camp Half-Blood, a summer camp run in Decatur, Georgia; Austin, Texas; and Brooklyn, New York. The sold-out camp, based on Rick Riordan's best-selling *Percy Jackson and the Olympians* book series, arms kids with foam swords, teaches them about Greek mythology, and encourages them to keep reading.

The theater scene may also improve larp's crossover appeal; several plays that break the fourth wall, offering dispersed action, and in some cases, multiple narratives have cropped up recently in New York City under the guise of participatory theater. Most notably, there is *Sleep No More*, an amazing theatrical installation put on by the British-based company Punchdrunk in New York City, where I saw it in early 2011. The wildly popular show, which also ran in Brookline, Massachusetts, had its New York run extended at least three times and garnered rave reviews from the *New York Times*, *Vanity Fair*, *Vice*, and many other publications. Audience members were decked out in white masks and unleashed into a six-story set to explore their surroundings and silently follow the actors and scenes of their choice for a couple hours. The production riffed on *Macbeth* and felt like a larp for voyeurs, since for the most part, the masked audience watched the unfolding, wordless scenes without interfering—the audience, though players in some important sense, couldn't affect the course of events. And like a larp the action was dispersed, with different scenes occurring at the same time. I missed, for example, the witches' rave that one of my friends loved, because I wasn't in the right place at the right time.

Arty larp is also making forays into the US scene. On the West Coast, larpers have begun gathering each year at Wyrd Con, a

Knutepunkt-like convention that offers both games and talks on larp theory, while on the East Coast, Intercons, conventions focused on small prewritten larps, continue to thrive. I suspect that if the US arty larp scene grows, it will legitimize larp as an art form, give it some cultural capital, and in doing so, diminish the social stigma around all forms of the hobby. After all, the idea of game design as an art is beginning to gain mainstream traction—in May 2011, the National Endowment for the Arts expanded its guidelines, making digital games eligible for funding, in essence, legitimizing them as an art form.[1] More strangely, it appears that the US government has already funded larp . . . in Norway. According to Ole Peder Giæver of *Playground Magazine*, the US embassy in Oslo gave a local larp group nearly $5,500 for the Cold War larp A Doomsday Eve.[2] Perhaps, like their Nordic fellow-hobbyists, US larpers will someday be able to apply to their own government for grant money.

As for me, I learned a great many things about myself through larp in the course of reporting this book. I'm a self-conscious, nosy, organized, vain, unspontaneous sort of person who loves words, art, and performance. As a player, I prefer role-play and plot discovery to hack-n-slash. While I quite enjoyed my long stint in an escapist campaign game, I think that my natural proclivities lean more toward the Nordic-style games; I felt less self-conscious imagining myself into emotional dramas than I did imagining myself into some magical fantasy world. Plus, I suck at remembering rules.

Most importantly, during this book I learned to embrace my own weird. With so many exotic costumes and haircuts on display, with so much nerdy talk about the subtleties of Dungeons & Dragons rules or the ins and outs of *Doctor Who* plots, I felt no need to hide the fixations that make me unique, from pickles to *Xena* to Dorothy Parker.

Will I keep larping? Maybe. Putting on or playing in a larp takes up a stupid amount of time and energy, although with the right playmates, it can be exhilarating. Despite my walk on the larpy side, I have other deep commitments, like, say, a drive to write books, that might prevent the return of Portia, Ophelia, or Madame Blavatsky. And yet, the game is hard to relinquish. Portia wants to get her new altar, Madame Blavatsky requires reanimation, and I can almost see

myself rolling around in six inches of flour while discussing the terminal ovarian cancer that will kill me next month, working out conflicts in 1980s NYC through break dancing (or in contemporary NYC
through krumping), or enmeshed in some sort of future gender dystopia in which gangs of women roam the streets. New York–based
artist Brody Condon already ran an artsy game in 2010 called Level
Five in two US-based art galleries in conjunction with Danish and
Swedish larpwrights.[3] If only someone would invite me to a nearby
game like that. American larpers: could you get on that, please?

Acknowledgments

I am deeply grateful to the US and Nordic communities of larpers, to whom I owe the deepest debt a writer can owe. A great many gamers, GMs, and game designers generously shared their time with me, although only a handful appear in this book. To everyone who sat down with me for fifteen minutes or multiple hours, thank you—I learned something new from every conversation.

My immersive research would have been impossible without the cooperation of James C. Kimball of Knight Realms, and Avonelle Wing, Kate Beaman-Martinez, and Vincent Salzillo of Double Exposure.

Several gamers went above and beyond to help me in the course of my research. Special thanks to my guides to the world of larp: Geoffrey Schaller, for his all-around kindness, for many introductions, and for generously answering every question I lobbed his way over more than three years; and Gene Stern, who endured numerous interviews, explained rules, arranged rides to Knight Realms for me, and so much more. I am also grateful to Brendan O'Hara, Liz, and Jeramy Merritt for putting me up at conventions and helping me run the Cthulhu larp in Chapter 11.

Any larper will tell you that the best thing about larp is the people. Thanks to the Knight Realms and Avatar communities, which made me feel welcome, especially Jason Michaeli, Frank Martinez, Renny Stern, George Pereira, Ian Penny, and the rest of the FishDevil team, along with Carol Stanley, Terri DePrima, Molly Mandlin, Charlie Spiegel, Michael Smith, and the court of Drega'Mire.

The following people greatly assisted me in reporting several chapters: Anthony Lodato transcribed hours of taped interviews and conversations; Scott Trudell hipped me to Elizabethan pageantry; Major Cory Angell arranged my visit to Fort Indiantown Gap; Associate Professor Mark Rom of Georgetown reviewed my account of Knight Realms's economics; the members of the LARP Academia listserv alerted me to Atzor, the Nordic scene, and military larp; and Tobias Demediuk Bindslet helped me navigate the Nordic scene and reviewed my Nordic chapters. I'm also grateful to the crowd that attended a Vampire game with me at DREAMATION 2010 and the vast, transatlantic group of gamers who answered my many technical queries via Facebook. Jaakko Stenros and Markus Montola, editors of the incomparable *Nordic Larp*, provided useful feedback on an early version of the manuscript and patiently answered many queries. Sarah Miles first told me of larp's existence.

My father's comments and copyedits were almost as valuable as the love and encouragement that he and my mother offered. My husband, George Locke, provided unwavering support. The *Fringe* armada helped me find the time. Urban Waite and Chip Cheek read drafts, helped me battle the challenges of solitude, and cheered me on from afar. Thank you.

Thank you to my agent, Jane Dystel, my editor, Cynthia Sherry, and all the other people at Chicago Review Press—especially Michelle

Schoob and Mary Kravenas—who worked so hard to make this book a reality.

Samuel Freedman, who runs the book seminar at the Columbia journalism school, was the first one to believe I could write this volume, and I owe a special debt of thanks to him and to all the other tough writing instructors I've been lucky enough to study with over the years, particularly Pamela Painter, but also Sally Alexander, Joeseph Hurka, DeWitt Henry, Margot Livesey, and Sanford Padwe. To paraphrase a Flannery O'Connor story, I wish you were there to shoot me every day of my life.

Glossary

ACRONYMS

BADD	Bothered About Dungeons & Dragons
CACTF	Combined Arms Collective Training Facility
D&D	Dungeons & Dragons
DM	dungeon master
EOD	explosive ordnance disposal
FOIG	Find out in-game
GM	game master
IC	in-character
IG	in-game
KR	Knight Realms
larp	live action role-play
NPC	nonplayer character
OOC	out-of-character
OOG	out-of-game

PC   player character
PvP   player versus player combat
RP   role-play
RPG   role-playing game
RPGA Role-playing Game Association
SCA   Society for Creative Anachronism
ST   storyteller
TPK   total-party kill

TERMS

bleed: What happens when the emotions of a character and a player are conflated. *Bleed in* occurs when a player's mood affects a character's mood—if my bad day makes my character irritable in-game, for example. *Bleed out* occurs when a character's mood affects a player's mood—if my character falls in love and I develop a real-life crush on her boyfriend. Larps generally produce some level of bleed, whether unintentionally or by design.

boffer: A weapon made out of PVC pipe or kite rod (hollow fiberglass tubing), covered with pipe insulation foam and then swathed in various shades of duct tape, so as to imitate a sword or other weapon. Boffers are safe for live combat. Their more realistic brethren are latex weapons, which are molded or cast using foam and then coated with latex.

buff: A beneficial spell that one player casts on another. A buff might increase a target's total health points, allow them to swing for more damage, or provide another benefit.

campaign: An episodic game run over a series of sessions, where each session offers the next installment of the adventure. Campaigns can last for a specified amount of time, say eight sessions spread over two months, or they can be open-ended, continuing for years. (See also: one-shot)

canon: The official narrative of a larp or RPG as determined by the GM. It distinguishes what is shared fantasy from what a player might make up. This term also applies to TV show fandom and distinguishes between the official contiguous narrative and fan fiction. For example, "The scene in which Lord Apollo destroyed the world was not canon."

card pull: A mechanic used during role-playing games that employ cards as a randomizer instead of dice. Player characters draw one or more cards from small decks created and stacked according to level in order to determine whether their actions—such as opening a locked door or striking an opponent—succeed.

character card: Each player carries one of these for the duration of a tabletop game or larp. The sheets list a character's base statistics and skill set, and many games use them to keep track of health points, mental points, and bank funds during play.

con: An abbreviation of *convention*. For example, "I'll see you at the con."

Con Suite: The public room at Double Exposure conventions that contains snacks, soda, and seating.

cosplay: Costume play, a subculture related to both larp and reenactment, in which participants dress up as figures from popular culture, particularly anime, with a high premium on replicating the original outfit exactly.

Cthulhu fhtagn: A Lovecraftian phrase meaning "Cthulhu waits," or possibly "Cthulhu waits, dreaming."

d_: A means of specifying dies with different numbers of sides used in tabletop games. A d20 is a die with twenty sides, while a d6 has six. Sometimes, a number precedes the d. A player who rolls 2d8 damage would roll two d8 dice to determine the amount of damage her character inflicts on the enemy.

Double Exposure, Inc.: Company that puts on the gaming conventions DREAMATION and DEXCON each year in New Jersey.

elven princess: A damsel-in-distress type character who is very nearly useless and almost always a goody-two-shoes. Also known as a Mary Sue. Gamers revile her.

farb: Reenactment term used to describe casual reenactors with careless regard for historical accuracy. Farbs don't care whether the topstitching on their Revolutionary War uniform was done by hand. (See also: stitch counter)

fatbeards: They're fat, they have beards, and they're into all known forms of geekery. This self-labeled contingent has a presence at fandom, comic, and gaming conventions.

freaking the mundies: A game that larpers play, in which they wear funny outfits and behave strangely in public for the sole purpose of attracting strange gazes from that sad species, norms. (See also: norms)

game master: The impartial referee who administers the rules and settles disputes in a tabletop role-playing game or in a larp. GMs also organize games, coming up with plot, treasure, and monsters. In Dungeons & Dragons, the GM is referred to as a Dungeon Master or DM. In many games, GMs responsible for creating plot are called Storytellers or STs. In Cthulhu Live, GMs are called Keepers.

gank: This term is often used loosely, meaning to kill or be killed, as in, "I ganked that goblin," or "I got ganked by phase spiders on the way to bed." At Knight Realms, the "gank shift" is the late-night NPC shift during which bands of monsters circle the camp and get ganked by the PCs. The term's more technical meaning applies to PvP, or player-versus-player combat, as in, "Team Evil ganked me last night."

garb: Costuming, especially reproduction costuming, in larp or reenactment communities.

hack-n-slash: A style of gameplay that emphasizes combat.

homebrew: The house rules used during a tabletop role-playing game that are not included in an official rule book. For example, some GMs will allow their players to count a 19 as if it is a 20 when rolled on a d20.

in-game/out-of-game: The distinction between IG and OOG is the line between what is happening in the imaginary and real worlds; it's the difference between what you know and what your character knows. Imagine a car driving through the camp during a Knight Realms game, for example. Cars don't exist in 1209 Travance, so the car is OOG, and players must either pretend that it doesn't exist or that it is something else that fits into the game world, say, a strange caravan of gnomish design. Character cards are OOG items, since a person doesn't carry around a list of their own attributes. Players who are walking to their NPC shift wear white headbands or place fists atop their heads to signify that they are out-of-game; these markers make a player physically "disappear" from the game world. IG players who see that herd of OOG NPCs must not react to them, for in Travance, they do not presently exist. Occasionally players might refer to OOG NPCs as "wind," to acknowledge their presence while allowing the game world to remain unaffected. In some games, in-character (IC) and out-of-character (OOC) are the preferred terms for this. The Scandinavians use the term "off-game."

initiative: In a tabletop game or a larp with turn-based combat, each player rolls or draws initiative at the beginning of a fight. The numbers determine the order in which each player and NPC may take his or her action.

Keeper: Name for a GM in the Call of Cthulhu and Cthulhu Live gaming systems.

logistics: The place where sign-up occurs in a larp. Often a gathering place for GMs or NPCs.

level up: When a character achieves enough experience points to go from one level to another. At Knight Realms, a character levels up after every 10 build he or she spends. In many tabletop games, a character receives points for fighting certain kinds of monsters and overcoming specific challenges. Accumulate enough points, as dictated by the rules, and that character moves up a level. Move up a level, and a character may be able to learn new skills or spells, wield special items, or increase his or her base statistics. Levels are important in many role-playing games, in part because they serve as measures of experience, allowing GMs to match plot obstacles to characters' abilities, preventing mass death.

lowbie: A low-level character. When used self-referentially, it is not pejorative, but when used by upper-level players, it sometimes is.

mage: A magic-user.

meta-gaming: The practice of using out-of-game feelings or knowledge to affect something inside the game. For example, learning which character is a necromancer from a friend on the ride to the game and then persecuting that character or finding the all-powerful jewel because one saw an out-of-game (and therefore "invisible") GM hide it.

min-maxer: A player who employs an extreme version of power gaming to create a powerful character. Min-maxers work the system of a game, placing the bare minimum number of points in skills that are neutral or undesirable and placing lots of points in skills or stats that maximize desirable traits. A min-maxer might create a "glass cannon" character—one with lots of awesome offenses but next to no defense. (See also: power gamer, munchkin)

mod: Short for "module" and used in Knight Realms and in some other games. A mod is the basic unit of adventure. It's a discrete encounter that takes place over the course of a campaign. A mod can be as small as two rogues trying to rob a cabin and fighting its inhabitants or as large as a battle pitting the whole town against an army of dark elves. Sometimes, players at Knight Realms will playfully hold "bacon mod," during which several pounds of bacon are cooked and fed to whoever wanders by.

moulage: Makeup and latex prosthetics used to simulate wounds.

munchkin: A player who seeks to amass power and items at all costs, even at the expense of his or her party in a role-playing game. Considered pejorative. (See also: power gamer, min-maxer)

mundania: The real world, according to some reenactors and gamers.

newbie/noob: Fresh meat in the world of gaming. Noob or newbie may also refer to a gamer of any experience level who is behaving in an annoying way. Generally considered pejorative.

nonplayer character: Almost always referred to as NPCs, these characters are the scenery for a larp or tabletop game. NPCs are the monsters, the local barkeep, the strange man with the magic shop, the random policeman. They play any necessary role that is not filled by a PC, or player character. *To NPC* means to play an NPC role, an action that generally requires an NPC to wear some kind of costume and often to carry a character card similar to but generally less detailed than the ones that player characters carry. (See also: player character)

norms: Dear reader, have you ever worn a strange costume in public on a day other than Halloween? If you answered "no," then this word describes you. Norms are normal people who are non-gamers. They are sometimes called "mundies" or "mundanes."

off-game: The Nordic way of saying out-of-game. (See also: in-game/out-of-game)

one-shot: A self-contained game intended to be run only once, usually over the course of four to eight hours. (See also: campaign)

period correct: Used in reenactment to indicate whether a piece of costuming, prop, or method of performing a task is historically accurate.

pervasive game: A game that uses the real world as a backdrop, involving possible interaction with people or places that aren't an immediate part of the game world. A scavenger hunt is an example of a pervasive game, since during play participants may encounter or interact with people who aren't playing the game. Some larps are pervasive.

player character: A player character, or PC, is the hero of a tabletop RPG or a larp. PCs go through the plots that the GM has laid out for them, solving puzzles and leveling up, often collaborating with their fellow PCs as part of a "party" that works together.

power gamer: A player who tries to make his or her character as powerful as possible within the confines of the rules. (See also: munchkin, min-maxer)

player versus player: Combat that occurs between players, as opposed to between players and NPCs. PvP, as it is almost always called, is a hot topic among gamers. Many games ban it, because it can cause ill will between players that extends beyond the realm of the game and into real life. The term is sometimes used more generically, to describe any major conflict with lasting impact, not just actual combat, that occurs between players.

Ren Faire: Shorthand for "Renaissance Faire."

rolling up: In Dungeons & Dragons, players literally "roll up" their characters by tossing predetermined sets of dice in order to generate a list of numbers that will become their characters' basic statistics. The verbiage has carried over to many role-playing games, including ones that don't use dice. To roll up a character simply means to create a character's core statistics according to the game's rules.

rules lawyer: A player who argues rules technicalities with a GM, sometimes to advance his or her own character, sometimes for the sake of argument, sometimes to prove a point. Rules lawyers typically forsake the spirit of the rule in favor of the wording of a rule and are often, but not always, well-versed in the rules of a game. The term is considered pejorative.

soak: An effect of some armor and weapons in Knight Realms and other games. Equipment that has a soak diminishes the amount of damage the user takes from a given hit. Wear a breastplate with a soak of five, and if a goblin hits you for fifteen damage, you only take ten points of damage—the armor soaks away five points.

Society for Creative Anachronism: A group dedicated to reenacting medieval life, with chapters all across the United States and all over the world. Historical accuracy is very important to the SCA.

steampunk: A genre similar to cyberpunk, but instead of taking fans into the dystopian future, steampunk imagines a world, usually a Victorian- or Edwardian-era one, in which steam power beat out electricity. The symbol of the steampunk subculture is brass goggles or a bare watch gear.

stitch counter/stitch Nazi: These hard-core reenactors are obsessed with the minute historical accuracy of costumes and props. (See also: farb)

Storyteller: Another name for a GM. While the term can generically refer to any GM, in some games the title Storyteller implies that a GM is responsible for some aspect of the game's plot, as opposed to logistics, decor, or rules mechanics.

stupid o'clock: The hour at which sleep-deprived gamers begin acting ridiculously. Sometimes coincides with beer o'clock, when at a venue that permits alcohol.

support class: Describes characters who are not frontline fighters but who benefit other characters, serving a support function. Examples are bards (who typically buff others), healers, and alchemists (who provide beneficial potions). Sometimes, support-class characters in a larp are demeaned by fighters as "girlfriend-class" or "scenery."

sword jockey: A boffer larp player who doesn't care about immersion or building a realistic character, only about killing monsters with his sword; someone who enjoys the sport of boffer fighting. Also known as a "stick jockey."

tabletop RPG: A pen-and-paper role-playing game, usually played with a variety of dice. Tabletop games, in contrast to larps, take place around a table, with players describing their characters' actions to the group rather than acting them out. Dungeons & Dragons is the most famous tabletop RPG.

tacticals: Improvised battles that historical reenactors fight in private; fights that don't mimic a specific historical battle and do not have a predetermined victor.

Travance: Fictional town in which Knight Realms takes place.

total party kill (TPK): Refers to an adventure in which the entire party dies as the result of player stupidity, dumb luck, or a GM who made the monsters too difficult.

war gaming: A type of strategy game played on a terrain map, or miniature terrain, with small figurines, each of which represents a unit.

Whedon, Joss: Our new overlord (*Buffy, Firefly, Dollhouse*). He deposed George Lucas (*Star Wars*), who deposed Gene Roddenberry (*Star Trek*), who deposed J. R. R. Tolkien (*Lord of the Rings*). May have to cage-fight J. J. Abrams (*Lost, Fringe*) in order to maintain supremacy.

Notes

CHAPTER 3: QUEEN ELIZABETH, LARPER

1. Brian Morton, "Larps and Their Cousins Through the Ages," *Lifelike*. Jesper Donnis, Morten Gade, and Line Thorup, eds. (Copenhagen: Projektgruppen KP07, Landsforeningen for Levende Rollespil, 2007), 244–259.
2. Cornelia Emilia Baehrens, *The Origin of the Masque*, (Groningen, Netherlands: Drukkerij Dijkhuizen & Van Zanten, 1929); see also Suzanne Westfall, "'A Commonty a Christmas gambold or a tumbling trick': Household Theater," from *A New History of Early English Drama*, John D. Cox and David Scott Kastan, eds. (New York: Columbia University Press, 1997) 39–58.
3. Ibid., 14.
4. George Gascoigne, *The Princely Pleasures at Kenilworth Castle (Gascoigne's Princely Pleasures: with the masque, intended to have been*

presented before Queen Elizabeth at Kenilworth Castle in 1575: with an introductory memoir and notes) (London: J.H. Burn, 1821), 87, note to page 8. Historian Alan Haynes contends that the amount was much less, about £1,700 for the seventeen days, stating, "The notion that he poured out many thousands of pounds is absurd." Still, that is more than enough for Dudley to have visited the theater more than 56,000 times. Alan Haynes, *The White Bear: Robert Dudley, the Elizabethan Earl of Leicester* (London: Peter Owen, 1987), 119–120.

5. www.measuringworth.com/ppoweruk, Accessed Nov. 2011.

6. Jeffrey L. Forgeng, *Daily Life in Elizabethan England*, (Santa Barbara, CA: Greenwood Press, 2010), 102–104.

7. Westfall, 43.

8. Gascoigne, 80, note to page 5.

9. Ibid., 7; see also David Bergeron, *English Civic Pageantry: 1558–1642*, (London: W & J Mackay, 1971), 31; see also *Robert Langham: A Letter*, (Leiden, Netherlands: EJ Brill, 1983), 39–40.

10. Langham, 45.

11. Gascoigne, 24.

12. Bergeron, 34.

13. According to Alan Haynes in *The White Bear: Robert Dudley, the Elizabethan Earl of Leicester* (London: Peter Owen, 1987), the cancellation was "unexpected and unexplained," though Sarah Gristwood blames it on the rain in *Elizabeth and Leicester* (New York: Viking, 2007).

14. E. K. Chambers, *The Elizabethan Stage*, vol. 1, (Oxford: Clarendon Press, 1923), 123; see also Bergeron, 58.

15. Bergeron, 64.

16. *Lady of May* details from Bergeron, 36. *Neptune's Triumph* info from Lauren Shohet, "The Masque in/as Print," *The Book of the Play: Playwrights, Stationers, and Readers in Early Modern England*, Martha Straznicky, ed. (Amherst: University of Massachusetts Press, 2006), 177.

17. Ian Anstruther, *The Knight and the Umbrella: An Account of the Eglinton Tournament of 1839*, (London: Geoffrey Bles, 1963), 147.

18. Anstruther, 124.

19. *Life*, March 3, 1941, 102. Accessed June 2011 via GoogleBooks. http://books.google.com/books?id=IUoEAAAAMBAJ&pg=PA2 &dq=life+march+3+1941&hl=en&ei=6YniTOriNsWqlAf0zfDaA w&sa=X&oi=book_result&ct=result&resnum=1&ved=0CCoQ6 AEwAA#v=onepage&q=life%20march%203%201941&f=false.

20. Daniel Mackay, *The Fantasy Role-Playing Game*, (Jefferson, NC: McFarland, 2001). The last sentence in this paragraph is a paraphrase of what MacKay says on page 13.

21. Ibid., 13. See also J. R. Hammond, *An H. G. Wells Chronology* (New York: St. Martin's, 1999), 67.

22. Lawrence Schick, *Heroic Worlds: A History and Guide to Role-Playing Games*, (New York: Prometheus Books, 1991), 17.

23. Mackay, 14–15; see also Schick, 18.

24. www.sca.org/officers/chatelain/sca-intro.html, Accessed Nov. 2011.

CHAPTER 6: CLOSETED GAMERS
AND THE SATANIC PANIC

1. William Dear, *The Dungeon Master: The Disappearance of James Dallas Egbert III*, (Boston: Houghton Mifflin, 1984), 18.

2. Ibid., 280–281.

3. Lisa Levitt Ryckman, "Murder and Suicide Among Teens Caught Up in Dark World of Satanism," February 13, 1988, Associated Press.

4. Gary Alan Fine and Jeffrey Victor, "Satanic Tourism: Adolescent Dabblers and Identity Work," *Phi Delta Kappan*, September 1, 1994.

5. Mary Elizabeth (Tipper) Gore, *Raising PG Kids in an X-Rated Society*, (Nashville, TN: Abingdon Press, 1987), 118.

6. Daniel Martin and Gary Alan Fine, "Satanic Cults, Satanic Play: Is 'Dungeons & Dragons' a Breeding Ground for the Devil?," *The Satanism Scare*, James T. Richardson, Joel Best, and David G. Bromley, eds. (New York: Aldine De Gruyter, 1991), 109.

CHAPTER 9: LARP AS TRAINING TOOL

1. Stephen Balzac, "Reality from Fantasy: Using Predictive Scenarios to Explore Ethical Dilemmas" from Schrier, Karen, and David Gibson, eds. *Ethics and Game Design: Teaching Values Through Play* (IGI Global, 2010), 291–310.

CHAPTER 12: A WEEK IN DENMARK

1. www.danceaffair.com.
2. Doubt (2007) by Fredrik Axelzon and Tobias Wrigstad is available for download at http://jeepen.org/games, Accessed Nov. 2011.
3. www.nordiclarptalks.org, Accessed Nov. 2011.
4. http://fate.laiv.org/in_fate.htm, Accessed Nov. 2011.
5. Peter Munthe-Kaas, "*System Danmarc*," *Nordic Larp*, Markus Montola and Jaakko Stenros, eds. (Stockholm: Fëa Livia, 2010), 214.

CHAPTER 13: KNUDEPUNKT BLEW MY MIND

1. Bjarke Pedersen, "Delirium," *Nordic Larp*, 288–297.
2. Tor Kjetil Edland, Trine Lise Lindahl, and Margerete Raaum, "Mad About the Boy," *Do Larp: Documentary Writings from KP2011*, (Copenhagen: Rollespilsakademiet, 2011), 92–107.
3. http://nordiclarptalks.org/post/576668918/introduction-to-nordic-larp, Accessed Nov. 2011.
4. Dogma 99 manifesto is available here: http://fate.laiv.org/dogme99/en/dogma99_en.htm, Accessed Nov. 2011.
5. Turku manifesto by Mike Pohjola is available here: www2.uiah.fi/~mpohjola/turku/manifesto.html, Accessed Nov. 2011.
6. Eirik Fatland, "*1942 – Noen å stole på*," *Nordic Larp*, 90–99.
7. http://playgroundmagazine.net, Accessed Nov. 2011.
8. Emma Wieslander, "Rules of Engagement," *Beyond Role and Play: Tools, Toys and Theory for Harnessing the Imagination*, Markus Montola and Jaakko Stenros, eds. (Helsinki: Ropecon ry, 2004), 181–186.

9. Ibid., 183.

10. Jaakko Stenros, *"Mellan himmel och hav,"* Nordic Larp, 158–167.

EPILOGUE

1. www.techspot.com/news/43696-the-us-legally-recognizes-video-games-as-an-art-form.html and http://arts.gov/grants/apply/AIM-presentation.html, Accessed Nov. 2011.

2. http://playgroundroleplayingmagazine.wordpress.com/2011/05/01/u-s-funds-doomsday-scenario, Accessed Nov. 2011.

3. Jaakko Stenros, "Nordic Larp: Theatre, Art, and Game," *Nordic Larp*, 312, caption.

Resources

FURTHER READING

Bowman, Sarah Lynne. *The Functions of Role-Playing Games: How Participants Create Community, Solve Problems, and Explore Identity.* Jefferson, NC: McFarland, 2010.

Brown, Stuart, with Christopher Vaughn. *Play: How It Shapes the Brain, Opens the Imagination, and Invigorates the Soul.* New York: Avery, 2009.

Caillois, Roger. *Man, Play and Games.* Tr. Meyer Barash. Chicago: University of Illinois Press, 1958.

Fine, Gary Alan. *Shared Fantasy: Role Playing Games as Social Worlds.* Chicago: University of Chicago Press, 1983.

Gilsdorf, Ethan. *Fantasy Freaks and Gaming Geeks: An Epic Quest for Reality Among Role Players, Online Gamers, and Other Dwellers of Imaginary Realms.* Guilford, CT: Lyons Press, 2009.

Horwitz, Tony. *Confederates in the Attic: Dispatches from the Unfinished Civil War.* New York: Vintage, 1999.

Huizinga, Johan. *Homo Ludens.* Oxon, UK: Routledge, 1949.

Mackay, Daniel. *The Fantasy Role-Playing Game: A New Performing Art* Jefferson, NC: McFarland, 2001.

Montola, Markus, and Jaakko Stenros. *Nordic Larp.* Stockholm: Fëa Livia, 2010.

KNUTEBOOKS

Andresen, Lars, Charles Bo Nielsen, Luisa Carbonelli, Jesper Heebøll-Christensen, eds. *Do Larp: Documentary Writings from KP2011.* Copenhagen: Rollespils Akademiet, 2011. http://rollespilsakademiet.dk/kpbooks.

Bøckman, Petter, and Ragnhild Hutchinson, eds. *Dissecting Larp: Collected Papers for Knutepunkt 2005.* Oslo: Knutepunkt 2005, 2005. http://knutepunkt.laiv.org/kp05.

Donnis, Jesper, and Morten Gade Line Thorup, eds. *Lifelike.* Copenhagen: Projektgruppen KP07, Landsforeningen for Levende Rollespil, 2007. www.liveforum.dk/kp07book.

Fritzon, Thorbiörn, and Tobias Wrigstad, eds. *Role, Play, Art: Collected Experiences of Role-Playing.* Stockholm: Föreningen Knutpunkt, 2006. www.jeepen.org/kpbook.

Henriksen, Thomas Duus, Christian Bierlich, Kasper Friis Hansen, and Valdemar Kølle, eds. *Think Larp: Academic Writings from Kp2011.* Copenhagen: Rollespils Akademiet, 2011. www.rollespilsakademiet.dk/kpbooks.

Holter, Matthijs, Eirik Fatland, and Even Tømte, eds. *Larp, the Universe and Everything.* Oslo: Knutepunkt 2009. http://knutepunkt.laiv.org/2009/book.

Gade, Morten, Line Thorup, and Mikkel Sander, eds. *As Larp Grows Up: Theory and Methods in Larp.* Copenhagen: Projektgruppen KP03, 2003. www.liveforum.dk/kp03_book.

Larsson, Elge, ed. *Playing Reality: Articles on Live Action Role-Playing.* Stockholm: Interacting Arts, 2010. www.knutpunkt.se/book.

Montola, Markus, and Jaakko Stenros, eds. *Beyond Role and Play: Tools, Toys and Theory for Harnessing The Imagination.* Helsinki: Ropecon ry, 2004. www.ropecon.fi/brap.

————. *Playground Worlds: Creating and Evaluating Experiences of Role-Playing Games*. Helsinki: Ropecon ry, 2008. http://2008
.solmukohta.org/index.php/Book/Book.

Raasted, Claus, ed. *Talk Larp: Provocative Writings from KP2011*. Copenhagen: Rollespils Akademiet, 2011. www.rollespilsakademiet.dk/kpbooks.

US-BASED LARP GROUPS

Camp Half-Blood—http://web.mac.com/camphalfblood/
Camphalf-blood.com
Dagorhir—www.dagorhir.com
Dystopia Rising—www.dystopiarising.com
Knight Realms—www.knightrealms.com
LAIRE—www.laire.com
NERO—www.nerolarp.com
One World By Night—http://oneworldbynight.org

CONVENTIONS

Double Exposure (runs DEXCON and DREAMATION)—
www.dexposure.com
Fastaval—www.fastaval.dk
Intercon—http://intercon.larpaweb.net
Lunacon—www.lunacon.org
Wyrd Con—www.wyrdcon.com
Solmukohta—www.solmukohta.org

OTHER RESOURCES

Dance Affair—www.danceaffair.org
Fëa Livia—www.fealivia.se
The Forge Forums—www.indie-rpgs.com/forge

International Journal of Role-Play—http://journalofroleplaying.org
Jeep or Vi Åker Jeep (We Go by Jeep)—http://jeepen.org
LARP Alliance—www.larpalliance.net
LARPA—www.larpaweb.net
Nordic Larp—http://nordiclarp.wordpress.com
Nordic Larp Talks—http://nordiclarptalks.org
RPG.net—www.rpg.net
RPGA—www.wizards.com/rpga
Shade's LARP List—www.larplist.com/list.php

ADDITIONAL RESEARCH SOURCES CONSULTED

Anglo, Sydney. *Spectacle, Pageantry, and Early Tudor Policy*. Oxford: Clarendon Press, 1997.

Baker, Simon, and Hillary Hinds, eds. *The Routledge Anthology of Renaissance Drama*. London: Routledge, 2003.

Bergeron, David M. *Practicing Renaissance Scholarship*. Pittsburgh: Duquesne University Press, 2000.

Fine, Gary Alan. *Shared Fantasy: Role-Playing Games as Social Worlds*. Chicago: University of Chicago Press, 1983.

Haynes, Alan. *The White Bear: Robert Dudley, the Elizabethan Earl of Leicester*. London: Peter Owen, 1987.

Hollander, John. *An Entertainment for Elizabeth: English Literary Renaissance Monographs, vol. 1*. Storrs, CT: University of Connecticut, 1972.

Kipling, Gordon. "Wonderfull Spectacles: Theater and Civic Culture." From *A New History of Early English Drama*. John D. Cox and David Scott Kastan, eds. New York: Columbia University Press, 1997. 153–171.

Palmer, Daryl W. *Hospitable Performances: Dramatic Genre and Cultural Practices in Early Modern England*. West Lafayette, IN: Purdue University Press, 1992.

Parry, Graham. "Entertainments at Court." From *A New History of Early English Drama*. 195–211.

Reay, Barry. *Popular Cultures in England 1550–1750*. New York: Addison Wesley Longman, 1998.

Schechner, Richard. *Performance Studies: An Introduction*. London: Routledge, 2002.

Shaw, Catherine. "'Some Vanity of Mine Art': The Masque in English Renaissance Drama," from *Jacobean Drama Studies*, James Hogs, ed. Austria: Institut Für Anglistik un Amerikanistik Universität Salzburg, 1979.

Victor, Jeffrey S. *Satanic Panic: The Creation of a Contemporary Legend*. Chicago: Open Court, 1993.

Weimann, Robert. *Shakespeare and the Popular Tradition in the Theater: Studies in the Social Dimension of Dramatic Form and Function*. Baltimore: Johns Hopkins University Press, 1978.

Index